WITHDRAWN 302 345

Small Screens

Studies in Communication and Society

Series editors: Ralph Negrine and Anders Hansen
University of Leicester

Also published in this series:

TV News, Urban Conflict and the Inner City
Simon Cottle

The Economy, Media and Public Knowledge
Edited by Neil T. Gavin

Spinning into Control: News Values and Source Strategies
Edited by Jerry Palmer

Dazzled by Disney? The Global Disney Audiences Project
Edited by Janet Wasko, Mark Phillips and Eileen R. Meehan

Small Screens

Television for Children

Edited by
David Buckingham

Leicester University Press
London and New York

Leicester University Press
A Continuum imprint
The Tower Building, 11 York Road, London SE1 7NX
370 Lexington Avenue, New York, NY 10017–6503

First published 2002

British Library Cataloguing-in-Publication Data

A catalogue record for this book is available from the British Library.

ISBN 0–8264–5943–9 (hardback)
    0–8264–5944–7 (paperback)

Library of Congress Cataloging-in-Publication Data

Small screens : television for children/edited by David Buckingham.
    p. cm. — (Studies in communication and society)
    Includes bibliographical references and index.
    ISBN 0–8264–5943–9 — ISBN 0-8264–5944–7 (pbk.)
    1. Television programs for children. 2. Television and children. I.
Buckingham, David, 1954– II. Studies in communication and society
(Leicester, England)

PN1992.8.C46 S63 2002
791.45′6—dc21   2001038928

Typeset by YHT Ltd, London
Printed and bound in Great Britain by MPGBooksLtd,Bodmin,Cornwall

Contents

Contents

About the contributors

Helen Bromley is a freelance consultant who works throughout the UK delivering in-service training on the teaching of literacy. She has a particular interest in popular culture, and the opportunities it offers children to develop insights into more traditional literacy practices. She has published several articles on this subject, including 'There's no such thing as Never Land', in Mary Hilton's *Potent Fictions* (Routledge, 1996).

David Buckingham is Professor of Education at the Institute of Education, University of London, and Director of the Centre for the Study of Children, Youth and Media. He has directed several major research projects on young people's relationships with the media, and has lectured in more than twenty countries worldwide. He is the author of numerous books and articles, including *Children Talking Television* (Falmer, 1993), *Moving Images* (Manchester University Press, 1996) and *After the Death of Childhood* (Polity, 2000).

Hannah Davies has been a Research Officer at the University of London Institute of Education and the University of North London. She is the co-author with David Buckingham, Ken Jones and Peter Kelley of *Children's Television in Britain: History, Discourse and Policy* (British Film Institute, 1999). She is currently working as a freelance consultant, specializing in children's creative uses of information and communication technologies.

Máire Messenger Davies is a Senior Lecturer in the School of Journalism, Media and Cultural Studies at Cardiff University. A former journalist, her PhD was in psychology, studying TV and audiences. Her books include *Television is Good for Your Kids* (Hilary Shipman, 1989), *Fake, Fact and Fantasy: Children's Interpretation of TV Reality* (Lawrence Erlbaum, 1997) and *'Dear BBC': Children, Television Storytelling and the Public Sphere* (Cambridge University Press, 2001).

Merris Griffiths is a Lecturer in the Department of Education, University of Wales, Aberystwyth. Her research interests focus on children and television, and the ways in which the mass media contribute to processes of (gender) identity formation in early childhood.

Ken Jones is Senior Lecturer in the Education Department at Keele University. He has written widely on culture, policy and education, most recently (with David Buckingham) on shifts in education and cultural policy under New Labour. His books include *Right Turn: The Conservative Revolution in Education* (Hutchinson, 1989) and *Schooling in Britain since 1944* (Polity, forthcoming). He is co-editor of the journal *Education and Social Justice*.

Karen Lury teaches in the Department of Theatre, Film and Television Studies at the University of Glasgow. Her most recent publication is *British Youth Television: Cynicism and Enchantment* (Oxford University Press, 2001). She is also an editor of the international film and television studies journal *Screen*.

Helen Nixon is a Senior Lecturer in the Centre for Studies in Literacy, Policy and Learning Cultures in the School of Education at the University of South Australia in Adelaide. She has lectured in English literature, media and cultural studies, English curriculum studies and literacy education. Her research interests include popular culture and education, and the connections between information and communications technologies and changing sociocultural constructions of literacy and educational disadvantage.

Julian Sefton-Green is the Head of Media Arts and Education at WAC Performing Arts and Media College in London, where he directs a range of digital media activities for young people and co-ordinates training for media artists and teachers. His books include *Cultural Studies Goes to School* (with David Buckingham,

About the contributors

Taylor and Francis, 1994), *Digital Diversions* (UCL Press, 1998), *Creativity, Young People and New Technologies* (Routledge, 1999) and *Evaluating Creativity* (Routledge, 2000).

Paul Wells is Professor of Media and Cultural Studies and Head of the Media Portfolio at the University of Teesside. He has published and broadcast widely on aspects of popular culture, including *Understanding Animation* (Routledge, 1998), *Animation and America* (Edinburgh University Press, 2002), and *Animation: Genre and Authorship* (Wallflower Press, 2002).

CHAPTER 1

Introduction

The Child and the Screen

DAVID BUCKINGHAM

Once upon a time . . .

In 1998, at a time of rapidly accelerating change in British broadcasting, the BBC began screening a series of short promotional films. Perhaps the most memorable of these was 'Perfect Day', which featured an astonishing cast list of media stars singing the Lou Reed song – all implicitly endorsing and proclaiming the achievements of the Corporation. While other films focused on news and sports, one of the earliest was concerned with children's programmes. It is worth examining this film in some detail, particularly for what it has to say about the history of children's television – and, by extension, about the changing nature of childhood.

The film features a white boy of around eight years of age, dressed in a grey uniform that most British viewers would associate with a private (or so-called preparatory) school. It follows his progress through a series of animated studio sets and sequences that represent a more or less chronological history of BBC children's programmes. The journey begins (in black and white) in the garden featured in the *Watch with Mother* programme *Bill and Ben*, first produced in the early 1950s; and it takes us through the village of *Chigley* and the gardens of *The Magic Roundabout* and *The Herbs* (from the 1970s), on to the studios of *Blue Peter* and *Newsround* and the dramatic landscapes of *The Chronicles of Narnia* and *The Borrowers*. On his way, the boy interacts with the characters, and they seem to respond to him: he hails a ride in Noddy's car, delivers a parcel to Bagpuss for Postman Pat, enters Mr Benn's shop and emerges from the Tardis into a scene from *Doctor Who*. Other well-known characters and programmes also make brief appearances, often accompanied by snatches of the appropriate songs and theme tunes: Andy Pandy and Teddy, the Woodentops, Morph, Pingu, Dennis the Menace, Crystal Tips and Alistair, *Camberwick Green*, *Trumpton*, *Play School* and *The Really Wild Show*. The computer graphics very effectively create the illusion that the boy is walking through each of these fictional worlds: this is clearly not an inexpensive three minutes of television.

As he proceeds on his journey, the boy delivers a commentary:

> Once upon a time, on a small island where it often rained, there was a broadcasting corporation which realised that small people – like me – were different from big people ... and so they decided to make programmes for small people as well ... programmes that small people would learn from without even knowing it ... But small people soon became big people too ... and magically produced small people of their own ... So the corporation decided to make even more programmes, this time for a new generation of small people ... The corporation continues to entertain and educate small people ... with an enormous variety of programmes ... But they can only continue to make small people's programmes thanks to the unique way the corporation is paid for by the big people ...

As the film concludes, the boy appears in the screen of a Teletubby's stomach, and finally resurfaces in an editing suite. He presses a button and we cut to a clip of the presenter Zoë Ball, from the Saturday morning magazine show *Live and Kicking*. She says, 'Well, didn't we turn out to be a nation of well-rounded individuals!' The irony of her comment is marked by her facial expression that follows it; and perhaps by the boy's 'cheeky' look to camera with which the film closes.

Some months after the BBC's film began to be screened, the commercial children's channel Nickelodeon UK broadcast its satirical response. It offers a rather different account of the history of children's television, and of the nature of contemporary childhood. The one-minute film begins in a 1950s-style living room, also in black and white. A man of around 30, dressed in an ill-fitting child's school uniform, is sitting on the carpet watching an antique television. 'Once upon a time,' he begins, 'there was only a few TV channels. They hardly played any kids' programmes. And when they did, they weren't up to much.' At this point, the television is screening what looks like a parody of an old Open University programme. This is followed by a cookery programme, with the presenter saying 'here's one I prepared earlier' (one of the often-satirized catch phrases of the BBC's *Blue Peter*), and finally a sequence featuring a puppet made from a sock. 'Then came satellite and cable – with it, Nickelodeon. And that's when things really took off.' To a rock music soundtrack, the man/boy is then cast off into space, passing the Nickelodeon satellite, and is beamed down into a two-dimensional garden taken from the set of a cartoon. 'Suddenly there was a whole channel stuffed full of kids' programmes ... like wicked cartoons ... brilliant live shows ... and fantastic comedy.' Following a brief encounter with Sabrina (the Teenage Witch) – which echoes a similar encounter in the BBC film with the White Witch of *Narnia* – he too finishes up in an editing suite. 'And the best bit,' he says, 'is it's all paid for by the big people. And you little people don't have to pay anything!' We cut to a Nickelodeon puppet – who asks 'Now is that cool, or what?' – and the film concludes with a similar (although rather more knowing) 'cheeky' look to camera. The final caption reads: 'Nickelodeon – paid for by grown-ups, made just for kids.'

The contrast between these two promotional films encapsulates many of the debates that currently surround children's television, not just in Britain but in many countries around the world. To some extent, these debates are a reflection of the changing political economy of broadcasting. On the one hand, we have the tradition of public service (represented here by the BBC), increasingly struggling to sustain its legitimacy – and, in this instance, the 'unique way it is paid for', which is in effect through a form of compulsory taxation. On the other, we have the new cable/satellite channels, funded through subscription and advertising – a growing number of which are directed towards children. Like Nickelodeon, all such channels in the UK are partly or wholly US-owned, and they are investing very little in domestic production. Yet they are gradually taking a growing share of the child audience – a fact which implicitly calls into question the future of the licence fee.[1] While the BBC is of course a major player in the wider global marketplace, in the UK it must emphasize its role as a *national* public broadcaster – an emphasis that is apparent in the film's initial reference to the 'small island where it often rained', and (however ironically) in Zoë Ball's closing remark. In recent years, children's television has become one of the key points of tension in this ongoing debate about the future of public broadcasting, and its historic role of producing 'well-rounded individuals'. Indeed, for some lobbyists, children's television has taken on a symbolic importance that seems curiously detached from any interest in what real children actually want to watch.[2]

Significantly, however, the BBC has to direct its claims towards parents – who, of course, are the ones paying the licence fee – rather than to children themselves. This is apparent in some of the language used in the film (not least its 'cute' talk about 'small people' and 'big people'), and in its invoking of education ('programmes that small people would learn from without even knowing it'). However, it is most evident in its appeal to adults' nostalgia for the television of their own childhoods. The large majority of the programmes featured here would not be recognized by contemporary children; and indeed, several of them might only be familiar to their grandparents.

In its appeal to history, the BBC is effectively 'inventing a tradition', in the manner of the contemporary heritage industry[3] – and in this respect, it echoes the approach of some academic authors, who have likewise celebrated a 'great tradition' in children's television, which they believe to be threatened by the forces of commercialism.[4] And yet, as Máire Davies has pointed out, this film is in fact a highly selective version of the BBC's own traditions. It neglects what she refers to as the 'public service broadcasting radicalism' that is also part of that history. Thus, programmes with urban or contemporary settings – such as *Jonny Briggs* or *Byker Grove* – are missing; and it is particularly surprising to see no mention of one of the BBC's longest-running children's programmes, *Grange Hill*, noted for its storylines on controversial social issues. Furthermore, as Davies asks: 'Where are the wild animations, the pop videos, the sassy American and Australian imports, the psychedelic graphics and the rock-chick presenters, currently found all over the children's schedules?'[5] As Davies suggests, the film offers a fundamentally unthreatening, sentimental view of childhood that seems designed to reassure 'policy-makers and opinion-formers who don't watch much television' about the need to retain the licence fee – although it will almost certainly be rather less than convincing for the majority of contemporary parents. In this respect, it seems not just nostalgic, but positively reactionary:

> The use of a little boy in a 1950s-style prep-school uniform, rather than a girl (even less, a black girl), seems primarily intended to reassure the chaps who run things that the ethos of their own educations, where boys were groomed to be public spokespersons, and girls and 'persons of colour' were behind the scenes, continues securely unchallenged in the hands of Auntie Beeb.[6]

Unlike the BBC film – which was frequently screened between adult programmes – the Nickelodeon film was unlikely to have been seen by many adults. As such, its appeal seems to be more explicitly directed towards children themselves. This is again apparent in its language (both its simplicity, and its use of slang terms like 'wicked' and 'cool'); in its music, which is significantly more contemporary than the BBC's vaguely 'magical' soundtrack; and in its selection of extracts, such as the scene from *Sabrina, The Teenage Witch* and a particularly anarchic clip from a teen entertainment show. Notably, the Nickelodeon film mentions just three genres of programming: cartoons, live shows and comedy. While these are (and have always been) among the most popular genres with children – and indeed represent the vast bulk of Nickelodeon's output – it is notable that none of them is explicitly mentioned or featured in the BBC film.[7] In the world of Nickelodeon, children are not 'small people' (except perhaps ironically); they are 'kids'. The film's use of an adult dressed as a child clearly satirizes the BBC's nostalgic construction of childhood, and its appeal to what Máire Davies calls 'the well-scrubbed infants of the middle-classes'. Meanwhile, the BBC's notion that children's television might have an educational function – however stealthy ('without them even knowing') or even ironically proclaimed (as in Zoë Ball's closing remark) – seems quite impossible to sustain here.

Of course, Nickelodeon's film offers an equally partial and self-serving representation of the history of children's television – one in which nothing of note took place until its own arrival. Its construction of childhood is also, in its own way, equally sentimental and patronizing: in this universe, 'kids' are compulsorily anarchic, 'wacky' and 'cool' – although the distinction between 'kids' and 'youth' is significantly blurred.[8] Meanwhile, its analysis of the economics of commercial television – 'paid for by grown ups, made just for kids' – is simultaneously specious and almost breathtakingly blunt. Nevertheless, the Nickelodeon trailer – and the brand identity it represents – also embodies a view of childhood that is both more refreshingly contemporary and less diligently conformist than the BBC's. Given the choice, it is not difficult to understand its appeal for children themselves.

Imagining the child audience

Promotional discourse of the kind I have considered here is often very revealing of the broader relationships between media industries, texts and audiences. In this case, we can clearly trace the relationships between the changing political economy of broadcasting and the changing construction (or targeting) of a specific audience; and the ways in which particular textual or generic forms are used in doing so. In this instance, however, what is most striking is how this audience – namely, children – is always, however implicitly, defined in relation to another – namely, adults.

Like children's literature, children's television is not produced *by* children, but *for* them. Elsewhere, I have drawn on Jacqueline Rose's classic study of *Peter Pan* in attempting to account for the fundamental dilemma that lies at the heart of children's television. As Rose argues, children's fiction rests 'on an acknowledged difference between writer and addressee. Children's fiction sets up the child as an outsider to its own process, and then aims, unashamedly, to take the child in.'[9] In this sense, the texts which adults produce for children represent adult constructions, both of childhood and (by implication) of adulthood itself. They are one of the means by which 'we' attempt to regulate our relationships with 'them' – and perhaps also our relationships with those 'childlike' aspects of our own identities. As such, children's television should perhaps be read, not so much as a reflection of children's interests or fantasies or desires, but of adults'. As well as asking what children want or need from the text, we need to analyse what it is that adults, through the text, want or demand of the child.[10]

These issues have been taken up by several recent accounts of children's media. For instance, Tim Morris's book, *You're Only Young Twice*, develops similar arguments in respect of children's fiction – both 'classic' and contemporary – and children's films. From *Black Beauty* and *Lassie* through to *Goosebumps* and *Jumanji*, Morris traces the ways in which texts for children inevitably involve 'negotiations of cultural power' between adults and children – in many instances, achieved through violence. Like Rose, Morris argues that this process reflects fundamental anxieties and tensions on the part of adults, not least about the uneasy achievement of adulthood itself. The crucial problem here is to do with sustaining the boundary between adults' and children's identities – a problem Morris argues is repeatedly dramatized in contemporary Hollywood movies such as *Big* and *Hook*. Here, the figure of the child is necessary in order to define the adult: it becomes 'the mechanism whereby every adult body can be assured of a status in the social order'.[11] Childhood and adulthood can be blurred temporarily – not least in order that we can regain a connection with our 'inner child' – but they must be immediately and forcefully separated. Nevertheless, the success of this ideological work is not straightforward or guaranteed. Although they are produced by adults, texts for children do not inevitably take the adult 'side'. As Morris points out, such texts can also 'act as an advocate for the child in the face of oppression'; and they can serve as a focus for adults' own responses to their lived experiences as children, which may be far from innocent or idyllic.[12]

Similar tensions and negotiations are manifested in other areas of children's culture – even where critics might be ill-disposed to find them. The contemporary 'family' films of Walt Disney or Steven Spielberg, for example, offer both adults and children powerful and seductive stories about the relative meanings of childhood and adulthood. As in a good deal of nineteenth-century literature, the figure of the child here is at once a symbol of hope and a means of exposing adult guilt and hypocrisy. Such films often define the meaning of childhood by projecting its future loss: both for adults and for children, they mobilize anxieties about the pain of mutual separation, while offering reassuring fantasies about how it can be overcome.[13]

Cultural texts addressed to children are thus often contradictory. They frequently say much more about adults' and children's fantasy investments in the *idea* of childhood than they do about the realities of children's lives; and they are often imbued with nostalgia for a past Golden Age of freedom and play. However, nostalgia does not merely represent a kind of helpless longing for what we have lost: it can also serve as a vehicle for social critique. In this respect, it would be false to dismiss such representations as merely illusory. Their power depends upon the fact that they also convey a certain truth: they must speak in intelligible ways, both to children's lived experiences and to adult memories, of pain and powerlessness and violence, not just of lives 'free of care'.

As Patricia Holland argues, these representations of childhood are part of a continuous effort on the part of adults to gain control over childhood and its implications – not only over actual children, but also over our own childhoods, which we are constantly mourning and constantly reinventing. Such imagery, she argues,

> displays the social and psychic effort that goes into negotiating the difficult distinction between adult and child, to keep childhood separate from an adulthood that can never be fully achieved. Attempts are made to establish dual and opposing categories and hold them firm in a dichotomy set against the actual continuity of growth and development. There is an active struggle to maintain childhood – if not actual children – as pure and uncontaminated.[14]

As Holland emphasizes, then, these cultural constructions of childhood serve functions not merely for children, but also for adults. The idea of childhood serves as a repository for qualities which adults regard both as precious and as problematic – qualities which they cannot tolerate as part of themselves; yet it can also a serve as a dream world into which we can retreat from the pressures and responsibilities of maturity. Such representations, Holland argues, reflect 'the desire to use childhood to secure the status of adulthood – often at the expense of children themselves'.[15]

Nostalgia and irony: a postmodern response?

This process may sometimes appear to take the form of nostalgia – although in the contemporary media, it is also frequently suffused with irony. At least in the UK, there is now a growing enthusiasm for recycling children's television programmes from previous decades. Shows like *Thunderbirds* have enjoyed a substantial cult audience for several years; and at the time of writing, video compilations of some of the more bizarre and surrealistic children's series of the 1970s (*Captain Pugwash*, *Bagpuss*, *The Moomins*) are selling well. Fan websites for many of these programmes have recently emerged; and even somewhat unlikely programmes like ITV's *Rainbow* (also from the 1970s and 1980s) are becoming key reference points among the *cognoscenti*. This approach is also informing new production. Over the past few years, Hollywood has produced several feature film versions of old children's TV shows such as *The Flintstones*, *The Brady Bunch* and (most recently) *Scooby Doo*; while the BBC has recently begun screening a new series of *Bill and Ben*, last produced almost 40 years ago. Perhaps most interestingly, this new enthusiasm is by no means confined to adults who can remember these programmes from their first broadcast: it also seems to be growing among children and teenagers who are far too young to recall the antics of Zippy, Bungle and George – let alone the appeals of Shaggy and Scooby or Little Weed.

To some extent, this phenomenon could be seen to reflect a more general sense of irony which increasingly suffuses contemporary popular culture. Thus, in Britain and the United States at least, 'retro TV' has become increasingly popular in the last decade. As channels proliferate, and the need to recycle old material intensifies, irony has become a valuable marketing device for schedulers. What used to be disparaged as mere 'repeats' are now re-packaged with knowing commentaries and 'period' graphics on channels like Nick at Nite in the US and Channel 4 in Britain. Meanwhile, programmes like *Mystery Science Theatre 3000* effectively do the 'work' of ironic viewing for you. Children's television is almost inevitably a prime target for this combination of irony and nostalgia. Adults can now enjoy *The Wombles* or *Captain Pugwash*, reminiscing with the safety of hindsight; while their children may be taking it 'at face value', first time around. What is more, they can watch these things together, in a way that is much less likely to happen with *Pokémon* or some of the more impenetrable (for adults) contemporary animation shows. This adult nostalgia may be regressive – a hankering for a simpler time, in which men were men and women knew their place. Yet there is also a sense of superiority to the past, and indeed to our *own* past: a disbelief that we could ever have taken such fake and corny material seriously.

Interestingly, however, this kind of response is also characteristic of the reception of some contemporary programmes. For example, one might point to the instant irony with which the BBC's *Teletubbies* was first received, particularly among teenagers and young adults. Among other things, the cult celebrity of the programme led to a proliferation of 'unofficial' websites and pirated merchandise that was regarded with considerable alarm by its producers. Yet *Teletubbies* seems almost designed to evoke such a response. On the one hand, it embodies a kind of innocence that adults will typically describe as 'cute' or 'sweet'. And yet there is also a kind of knowingness here. The Teletubbies' fantasies often have a mildly anarchic, absurdist quality that is enhanced by the deadpan delivery of the adult narrator. In terms of its *mise en scène*, the programme has a strongly surreal or hyper-real quality, which the style magazine *The Face* has not been alone in describing as 'psychedelic' and 'hallucinatory'.[16]

Ultimately, it could be argued that the intensity of our reactions to these programmes reflects the depth and the ambivalence of adult investments in childhood – both in our own childhoods, and in the *idea* of childhood itself. From one perspective, the success of programmes such as *Teletubbies* with young people and adults could be seen as a form of regression or infantilization – or at least, as further evidence of the blurring of boundaries between children and adults. Yet it could also be interpreted as a necessary process of recovering 'childlike' pleasures – in silly noises and games, in anarchy and absurdity – for which irony provides a convenient alibi. On the other hand, it could also be argued that 'childishness' – like 'youth' before it – is becoming a kind of symbolic commodity, that is marketable to consumers whose biological status places them well beyond the obvious target audience. It is not simply children who are buying the idea of childhood, but adults too; and they are doing so, not merely on children's behalf, but also for their own purposes. Indeed, this 'subversive' celebration of 'childish things' – or at least the self-conscious mockery of adult norms of respectability, restraint and 'good taste' – has also become increasingly apparent in 'adult' television in recent years. The child-like anarchy and game-playing of Chris Evans's *Big Breakfast* and *TFI Friday* and the crossover success of children's hosts like Zoë Ball point to the growing appeal (and indeed the commodification) of 'child-ishness' as a kind of style accessory. Childhood, it would seem, isn't just for children any more.[17]

An overview of the book

The central focus of this book, then, is on the 'texts' of children's television. As such, it only provides part of the picture. As I have implied, media analysis should be concerned with the interactions between media institutions, texts and audiences. Nevertheless, different aspects of the process need to be addressed more closely at different times. While there has been an enormous amount of research on children as an audience, critical discussion of media texts that are specifically designed for them has been severely lacking. While children's literature is now a relatively legitimate topic for academic work, children's media is not. Like its pre-decessor, *In Front of the Children*,[18] this book represents a further attempt to fill this gap.

Some contributors here focus on a single text, chosen for its symptomatic relevance to wider debates about childhood and children's culture. Helen Nixon's piece on *South Park*, for example, raises broader questions about what *counts* as a 'chil-dren's programme', and what the controversy surrounding this show tells us about contemporary views of childhood. As she indicates, *South Park* frequently provides incisive commentary on the very concerns that surround children's enthusiasm for such 'disapproved' texts. Likewise, my own analysis of *Teletubbies* sees it in terms of broader shifts in the economics of children's tele-vision, and the changing ways in which children are addressed. Here again, the heated debates that surrounded the programme reflect much broader concerns – in this case, to do with the changing relationships between 'education' and 'entertainment'. Ken Jones's and Hannah Davies's analysis of *Grange Hill* also sets the programme in a wider context, both of the development of children's television and of the changing politics of education. Here too, the controversy that surrounded this programme in its early years reveals a good deal about popular assumptions about the 'place' of childhood.

Other contributions provide a more broad-ranging analysis of particular genres or media forms. Paul Wells offers a comprehensive historical account of one of the most consistently reviled genres of children's television, namely cartoons. Through two comparative case studies, of *The Flintstones* and *The Simpsons*, and of *Tom and Jerry* and *Ren and Stimpy*, he traces how the forms of animation have changed, offering space both for subversive pleasures and for social criticism. Likewise, Máire Davies's piece on costume drama makes a powerful case for retrieving such programmes from the general critical disdain that characterizes discussions of 'heritage culture'. As she argues, such programmes can offer powerful points of connection for modern audiences, and provide the basis for a critique of contemporary conditions. By contrast, Merris Griffiths's analysis of children's toy advertisements suggests that they largely reinforce established gender stereotypes, not only in their overt themes but (less obviously) in their use of technical and formal features.

Three further pieces range more broadly, using textual analysis to address more general questions about children's viewing. Karen Lury's piece is concerned with the new forms of scheduling that are developing on children's 'niche' channels, and their implications for children's changing sense of time and place. As she suggests, the new economic imperatives of television may have unforeseen consequences in terms of the everyday experience of viewing. Julian Sefton-Green looks at the textual form of children's TV-related websites – an issue which, amid all the hype about the 'digital generation', has been rarely addressed. His analysis suggests several new questions for investigation, not least in relation to the notion of 'interactivity'. Finally, in the closing chapter, Helen Bromley analyses a range of children's programmes and films in terms of broader debates about narrative and literacy. Her contribution is certainly the most 'personal' in the book, and makes particularly interesting reading in the light of the general nostalgia for children's television I have discussed in this introduction.

This book has been produced at a moment of significant transition in children's television. For some – not least in the media industries – this is a moment of great commercial opportunity. For others, it is one of insecurity and anxiety. We seem to be poised on the brink of far-reaching change, in which the continuing existence of dedicated children's television appears to be hanging in the balance. In the global, commercial media markets that are now emerging, how will television for children manage to survive, let alone to flourish? In my view at least, such high anxiety is far from justified; but it does raise an even more fundamental question. Is television for children *necessary* in the first place – and if so, why?

All the contributors to this book would probably agree that it is; but they would also acknowledge that the reasons why cannot be fixed for all time. Like any other social group, children undoubtedly have a right to programming that is designed for them, and that reflects their experiences and concerns. But such programming is unlikely to survive if it fails to keep step with the changing realities of children's lives. Ultimately, children's television must speak to 'children', and not merely to adults.

Notes

1. For a detailed account of the political economy of children's television in the UK, see David Buckingham, Hannah Davies, Ken Jones and Peter Kelley, *Children's Television in Britain: History, Discourse and Policy* (London: British Film Institute, 1999), particularly Chapter 2. For international perspectives, see the special issue of *Media International Australia/Culture and Policy* (eds Wendy Keys and David Buckingham), no. 93, 1999.
2. See Buckingham *et al.*, *Children's Television*, Chapter 2.
3. For a discussion, see John Corner and Sylvia Harvey's collection *Enterprise and Heritage: Crosscurrents in National Culture* (London: Routledge, 1991). Some of these points are taken up in Máire Davies's chapter in this volume.
4. See, particularly, Jay Blumler, *The Future of Children's Television in Britain* (London: Broadcasting Standards Council, 1992); and for a critique, Buckingham *et al.*, *Children's Television*.
5. Máire Davies, 'Revisionist small people', *Times Higher Education Supplement*, 8 January 1998.
6. *Ibid*.
7. Of course, there is some 'animation' in the BBC film (*Postman Pat*, for example), but no 'cartoons'.
8. For an analysis of contrasting constructions of childhood in the discourse of contemporary television producers, see Buckingham *et al.*, *Children's Television*, Chapter 6.
9. Jacqueline Rose, *The Case of Peter Pan: Or the Impossibility of Children's Fiction* (London: Macmillan, 1984), p. 2.
10. These themes are developed in my article 'On the impossibility of children's television: the case of Timmy Mallett', in Cary Bazalgette

and David Buckingham (eds), *In Front of the Children: Screen Entertainment and Young Audiences* (London: British Film Institute, 1995), pp. 47–61.

11. Tim Morris, *You're Only Young Twice: Children's Literature and Film* (Urbana, IL: University of Illinois, 2000), p. 142.

12. *Ibid.*, pp. 9–10.

13. See David Forgacs, 'Disney animation and the business of childhood', *Screen* 33 (4), 361–74, 1992.

14. Patricia Holland, *What is a Child? Popular Images of Childhood* (London: Virago, 1992), pp. 12–14.

15. *Ibid.*, p. 14.

16. Although this may not be quite so new after all: indeed, the most obvious similarity is to *The Magic Roundabout*, the 1960s children's programme beloved by hippies for its implicit references to drug culture.

17. For further discussion, see Hannah Davies, David Buckingham and Peter Kelley, 'In the worst possible taste: children, television and cultural value', *European Journal of Cultural Studies* 3 (1), 5–25, 2000.

18. Edited by Cary Bazalgette and David Buckingham (London: British Film Institute, 1995). A useful bibliography of previous work on children and media, compiled by Karen Orr Vered, can be found in Marsha Kinder's edited collection *Kids' Media Culture* (Durham, NC: Duke University Press, 2000).

CHAPTER 2

A Time and Place for Everything

Children's Channels

KAREN LURY

> To be sure, children's lives are largely scheduled *for* them rather than *by* them.[1]

The continuing expansion and popularity of niche television channels for children, made available through cable, satellite or digital modes of transmission, has provoked considerable interest and – as ever with children's television – concern. In this chapter I will look at some of the provision available on British television. Firstly, I will discuss how the channels differ in terms of their schedules and presentation – if not always in their content – from the kinds of children's television available through terrestrial networks. In particular, I focus on the importance of the 'branding' of channels within this changing dynamic. Secondly, I suggest that there seem to be two distinct ways in which channels are negotiating the spread of media culture. On the one hand, certain channels celebrate and encourage the erosion of temporal and aesthetic boundaries between children's 'television culture' and adult or teen viewing pleasure. On the other hand, channels may deliberately position themselves as being exclusively 'for' children, and define their audience along increasingly narrow age ranges. In conclusion, I argue that the scheduling practices of niche channels are beginning to erode the traditional way in which time is structured by the television schedule and its relationship to the domestic routines of the child viewer. My claim is that the way in which children experience and learn about the world is becoming increasingly detached from temporality and literary models of comprehension. Instead there is an engagement with spatial and visual modes of cognition. I justify this by thinking through the ways in which the proliferation of programmes and channels has radically altered the way in which channels transmit and organize their schedules. In turn this is seen to have necessarily affected how viewers use and understand television in relation to memory and identity. Finally, in a short analysis of Nickelodeon's *Blue's Clues*, I reveal how strategies that emphasize the visual and spatial characteristics of the text also appear to be successful within the programmes themselves.

The context

The tradition of British children's television has been dominated by the public service model provided by the BBC, characterized by an emphasis on education, access and variety within an entertaining package or 'mini-schedule'. Today, the terrestrial version of BBC children's television (CBBC) continues to address a wide range of different age groups with a wide selection of programmes – from the *Tweenies* (aimed at pre-schoolers) to imported cartoons such as *Casper* and the *Rugrats*, as well as domestic drama aimed at the pre-teen and teen audience such as *Byker Grove*. Children's television is distinguished in this context by its attempt to embrace a range of age groups, a diversity of formats and genres, and by the 'developmental' structure of a schedule that follows a perceptible age sequence as the afternoon (broadly from 3.25 p.m. to 5.35 p.m.) or (more recently) the morning (from 7 a.m. to 9 a.m.) progresses. Frankly, the shape and content of these schedules differ little from those I experienced as a child 25 years ago.[2]

The new 'niche' children's channels break this mould, largely as a result of economic imperatives, but also as a response to the way in which television is increasingly used by families and children. Whilst many children continue, as I did, to come home from school and watch an hour or two of television to wind down, the fact that children's television is now available early in the morning, and later in the evening, means that children are no longer confined to viewing at specific periods during the day. Of course, this increase in availability is clearly tied in to the apparent erosion of the traditional family meal time – with the family eating together around a table, and thus away from the television screen. It is also affected by the increase in the number of television sets per household, which may even include a set in the child's bedroom.[3] Though such changes are not universal, they do suggest why, and how, children are increasingly watching at different times of the day. For example, one of the surprises of the BBC's shift to showing children's television in the morning (on BBC2) was that traditional stalwart of children's tea-time viewing – *Blue Peter* – was actually gaining higher ratings in its repeat slot in the new breakfast schedule.

In addition, the new children's channels are also an important part of the way that children's television and thus the programmes and characters it proffers are now firmly established as part of a wider popular culture. 'Children's' programmes may never have been formally restricted to the child audience, but it is clear that niche channels have been part of the process by which certain programmes openly attract late teen and adult audiences. Thus, the most popular characters are increasingly available to diverse audiences, in a variety of media forms and associated paraphernalia. This includes films (on video and in the cinema), magazines, comics, websites and a variety of merchandising from T-shirts to keyrings. Children's television culture is unquestionably bound into a popular culture that is oriented through and by consumption. This is not to say that children's programming did not previously attract older audiences, or 'leak' into other media or merchandising. Rather it is that this previously covert audience and market has become more visible, unabashed and acknowledged in its liking and consumption of characters and programmes. This can be seen in many of the programmes' 'knowing' or dual address, and through the kinds of merchandising available. And it is not just the goods themselves, but where they may be purchased: for example, clothing featuring the *Powerpuff Girls* (a 'cartoon cartoon' from Cartoon Network) is on display and available in adult clothing shops and Woolworths and other toy stores.

Excessive repetition

I will return to the way in which the channels, programmes and characters appeal to and exploit different audiences; but at this point, I want to examine certain characteristics of the niche channel in more detail. Perhaps the most obvious of these is repetition. Firstly, there is repetition at the level of form. For example, Cartoon Network, and its recent spin-off, Boomerang, are channels that only show animation. Boomerang unselfconsciously demonstrates that repetition is the name of the game, for here the quality of the boomerang implies not just the repetition of form, but also the coming around again of certain characters and cartoons. Boomerang's schedule is dominated by Hanna–Barbera cartoons from the 1960s and 1970s ('classic cartoons'); the channel therefore repeats repeats. In these channels there is no variety of form and no live action unless it is within the advertising.[4]

While channels such as Nickleodeon and Trouble do schedule programmes that exhibit a greater variety of form, many of the programmes tend to rely heavily on similar formats. Sitcoms about the American high school and the trials and tribulations of the teenager predominate. Even programmes that superficially contain quite diverse characteristics – twins (*Sister, Sister*), witchcraft (*Sabrina the Teenage Witch*), international students (*USA High*), superheroes (*Mighty Morphin' Power Rangers*) or predominantly black rather than white characters (*Hangin' with Mr. Cooper, The Fresh Prince of Bel Air, Moesha*) – are all geographically grounded in the (televisually) familiar world of the American high school and a broadly middle-class domestic environment. This geography nearly always features schools with wide corridors, lined with personal lockers for the crucial meetings between and after class; the teenage bedroom for soul searching and telephone conversations; living rooms with a large central couch (and often a television) for the 'family' grouping; and generally, an expansive dining kitchen in which the various moral dilemmas and confrontations reach their dénouement.

One of the few British programmes to succeed in Trouble's schedule is *Hollyoaks*, a teen drama, which uncannily also takes place in various clean and brightly coloured school and café environments. Despite its sometimes controversial subject-matter, the programme is primarily distinguished from other British teen drama by its glossy production sheen, the prettiness of its main actors and the way in which its narrative is broken up into acts, with a story-line hook or 'teaser' carefully situated before each commercial break and after the end credits. Whilst embracing the look and feel of the teenage story-lines in the Australian soap *Neighbours*, the programme also deliberately mimics the pace and feel of many of the American programmes listed above.

A second aspect of repetition is the fact that the niche children's schedule is no longer constructed as a 'developmental' sequence. Instead, programmes are often stripped on the hour or half-hour. On Trouble, for example, *Saved by the Bell: The New Class* can be seen on weekdays at 8.00 a.m., 2.30 p.m. and 6.00 p.m. (often the same episode). Many of the channels also provide a '+ 1' channel. This means that (for example) the same programmes screened by Fox Kids are shown on a neighbouring channel 'Fox Kids +1' one hour after the initial transmission. All the major satellite networks – Disney, Cartoon Network and Nickelodeon – offer this facility for at least one of their channels. Such channels aren't exactly 'repeats'; but this is true only because there isn't really a clear sense of an 'original' moment or transmission date for the programmes being shown. Presumably the 'original' schedule is the one that is 'published' – electronically or in the different listing guides. Yet however this facility is understood, in practice it means that the viewer can easily and immediately 'repeat' their viewing experience whenever they wish.

Theme-ing

There is also a common practice of 'theme-ing' channels at certain times and at certain periods. Mornings, evening, weekends, or in some instances entire weeks, can be occupied by one programme. Cartoon Network, for example, has transmitted a *Scooby Doo* week – every programme from 7 a.m. until 9 p.m. was a *Scooby Doo Show* in all its possible variants – from the earliest shows made and transmitted in the late 1960s to spin-offs, including characters such as Scooby Dum and Scrappy, as well as more recent productions, such as *Scooby Doo on Zombie Island*, which revisits the gang in the 1990s. Bank Holidays are also often marked by festivals such as a *Tom and Jerry* marathon, in which

Tom and Jerry cartoons from their earliest incarnations (when Tom was Jasper) are shown again and again throughout the day. Similarly, Disney offers an 'Out of this World Weekend' as an event that can be 'shared by the family'. Basically, an 'other world' – effectively a science-fiction theme – is constructed to incorporate different Disney properties: thus a screening of the live action film *Men in Black* can be linked to a relatively new animated series stemming from the *Toy Story* franchise – *Buzz Lightyear of Star Command.*

Theme-ing and excessive repetition mean that individual episodes from particular series are generally shown with no respect to chronology, or to their own production history. Each of the channels transmits a proliferation of old and new programmes, with episodes sealed into 30 or 60 minute chunks.[5] The regular viewer could see the same episode of *Dexter's Laboratory* or *Playdays* several times over a period of weeks. If there are new episodes of a particular show, their rarity is such that they are especially privileged, and they are promoted exhaustively before they are transmitted. Disney, for example, promotes 'new episodes' with a trailer showing a computer-generated exclamation mark bouncing around the screen; clearly, this is meant to express excitement – although I can't help reading it as surprise. As for the few programmes that do rely upon chronology (such as *Dragon Ball Z*) these are exceptional in their apparently 'one and only' appearance in heavily advertised time-slots. And unsurprisingly their one-off status is only apparent: the week's episodes are in fact repeated in a mammoth omnibus session each weekend.

This ceaseless repetition and chronological abandon can make for some amusing viewing for the adult viewer across the spread of children's channels. Presenters such as Dave Benson Philips age and get younger, fatter and thinner in one day as he appears in *Playdays, Playhouse Disney* or on terrestrial television in *Get Your Own Back*. Older programmes such as *Pigeon Street* and *Mr Benn* nestle next to the *Tweenies*. Vintage *Bugs Bunny* cartoons appear next to the *Powerpuff Girls*. In this context, mistakes can happen and seemingly cause little disruption: for example, whilst watching Cartoon Network with my four-year-old daughter I realized she was only a little disconcerted when halves of two different episodes of *Scooby Doo* were shown in one half-hour slot.

This kind of mistake can happen because the number of

channels and the huge amount of air time that needs to be filled means that the appetite for programming is all but insatiable. With a limited number of episodes, programmes will be repeated far more frequently and quickly than was previously the case on terrestrial television. Theme-ing of course works to justify and repackage this need for repetition: by addressing the viewer as connoisseur or fan, theme-ing distracts the viewer from the fact that this 'new package' contains old episodes.

Many of the channels' schedules also largely ignore the established 'chronology' of the conventional broadcasting day established by the terrestrial channels. Whilst most channels do show programmes aimed at older children later in the day, or show programmes aimed at pre-schoolers early in the morning, what distinguishes the channels is how their schedules are relatively elastic; and they are fixed week by week, rather than seasonally. On BBC Choice the mini-schedule simply loops in three-hour segments throughout the day. However, I am not making an implicit value judgement here. The existing culture of the VCR and the popularity of sell through video has already made evident the desire of children, particularly young children, for repeat viewing of their favourite programmes.[6] Repetition and a hazy chronology are not necessarily 'bad' or boring for the child viewer: it simply implies a different kind of viewing practice than that of the child viewer twenty years ago.

Branding

The problem for the channels is this very plenitude and the increased opportunity to view. How do the channels secure their audience if there is so much choice and if the child can catch the same programmes at different times on different channels, or even on the same channel? The strategy of the channels is to define their identity as a brand, and through this, effectively to establish them as a *place*. As with other satellite channels, all the children's channels run with a fixed logo in the corner of the screen: Nickleodeon's orange splodge, Disney's Mickey Mouse ears and Cartoon Network's black and white boxes act as a constant reminder to the viewer as to where they are. Branding makes the space of transmission, the channel, into a *place* you can go to. As Toon Disney claims, this means that you can 'Find all your favourite cartoons in one toontastic *place.*' Finding your way is aided by new remote controls which allow for 'favourite' channels and for 'home' channels to be established, and the logo in the screen is a visual reminder to the viewer that a programmed number, or the favourites' button, gives access to a particular place.

In addition to the logos, each channel establishes its identity through idents or promotional trailers, mini-sequences that celebrate the programming and attitude of the channel. Nick Jr., for example, eschews the live presenter and is hosted by 'Face', a cartoon face, consisting of a simply drawn mouth and eyes, which speaks to the audience directly, chatting inconsequentially or introducing particular programmes. In addition, it has short sequences showing a close-up of a child who simply says, 'Just for me.' Nick Jr. is therefore a 'personality' and a place; whilst it literally has a 'face', it is also 'owned' and inhabited by the child viewer – it is 'just' for them. Three things are crucial here, and I will return to them in my discussion of *Blue's Clues.* Firstly, there is an interesting mix of two-dimensional images (the animated face, the graphics) and three-dimensional ones (the live action child playing with others or alone). Secondly, there is the significant presence of the child's voice at crucial points in the channel's 'discourse'. Lastly, it is also important to note the way in which the image – and more often than not this means a 'face' – is seen in close-up.

In contrast to this, on Cartoon Network, letters spelling 'Cartoon Network' bounce and fart into place and fake advertisements for Wazco products tease the viewer. Similarly, spurious histories of different cartoon characters may amuse the younger part of the audience whilst hinting to older viewers that the channel has an ironic take on its output. Cartoon Network thus presents itself as an illusory archive or virtual art gallery. In one ident the channel's morning schedule is presented as if the programmes were paintings, so that each show is represented as a framed picture, and they are seen hanging across the screen, side by side. Each programme is therefore apparently 'exhibited' at a certain time of day.

Appropriately for an archive/museum/gallery, the channel also celebrates the mix of old and new programmes that I've already outlined. In a short series of teasers, entitled 'Tooned 4 life', one features a spurious connection between Johnny Bravo (a recent

Cartoon Network production) and the Warner Bros. skunk character Pepé le Pew. The question is, are they in fact the same?[7] Comparisons are easily made through the illustrations: both have quiffs, funny walks and a marked lack of success with the opposite sex. Such sequences make what could seem an incongruous mix of different shows appear as a deliberate and 'cool' programming policy.

Again, working within the context of the channel as museum/gallery, many of Cartoon Network's exhibits employ inter-textual references to encourage viewers to see them in a new light. Trailers for the *Scooby Doo* week, for example, featured Scooby Doo in a precarious rock climb identical to the one undertaken by Tom Cruise's character in *MI: 2* – which, not coincidentally, was also being heavily promoted at the time. The release of a new film (originating from the television programme) of *Charlie's Angels* was also used to reaffirm the parody at the heart of the *Powerpuff Girls*.[8]

The cartoons produced by Cartoon Network – such as *Johnny Bravo* – have episodes that also celebrate this inter-textuality. In one episode of *Johnny Bravo*, he acquires a nanny in the shape of Donny Osmond; while in another, he meets up with the Scooby Doo gang. While both episodes are comprehensible on their own terms, they incorporate many in-jokes that only the experienced – and perhaps the adult or older teen – viewer are likely to understand. Donny Osmond, for example, must have little or no extra-textual meaning for the child viewer. In the episode featuring Scooby Doo, the way in which each adventure generally involved a particular sub-division of the group – Velma, Shaggy and Scooby Doo in one group, Daphne and Freddie as another – is made problematic, even exposed, by Johnny's overt sexuality. Since Daphne is clearly the kind of 'hot mama' Johnny conventionally lusts after, he is unhappy about his placing with Shaggy and Scooby. He wants to be with Daphne and openly mistrusts Freddie's motives. Sexual or intimate relationships between the characters were never present in the original series, but 'fans' or experienced viewers may well have speculated about (or invested in) their existence. Johnny's disruption of the traditional format for the *Scooby Doo Show* is clearly designed to signal to older viewers that the text can be read ironically.

In a similar fashion Cartoon Network also has a trailer which involves the 'gang' waiting impatiently by the mystery machine.

Finally it is revealed that they are waiting for Velma and that she won't leave her house until she has found both her orange socks. This is a rather laboured reference to the fact that throughout the earliest series Velma's outfit – orange pullover, brown pleated skirt and knee high orange socks – never changed. Thus the limitations of Hanna–Barbera's 'reduced animation' format – which limits each character to one 'outfit' – is held up to ridicule. At the same time, however, it is also in some way being celebrated. Velma's socks are a part of the series' iconic history. This combination of ridicule and celebration is, of course, a version of a camp sensibility and one designed to appeal to Cartoon Network's adult/teen viewers.[9]

Branding enables each channel to develop an appearance of depth and fixity in what might otherwise appear as a fluctuating and ephemeral media landscape. If successful, the channel can also benefit by following the business practice of the Disney corporation and branch out into other kinds of media. Cartoon Network, for example, has already established a comic and a website (see Julian Sefton-Green's chapter in this volume); and it has also organized 'live' tours of cartoon characters to different cities in the UK enabling it to promote and sell both the channel and its products. As many of the channels have been successful in establishing a strong brand identity, most are now actually better understood as 'families' of channels. Nickelodeon is the branding family for Nick Now, Nick Replay (its '+ 1' channel) and Nick Jr. (aimed at pre-school viewers). Disney has the Disney Channel, a '+ 1' channel, Toon Disney (classic cartoons from the Disney archive) and Playhouse Disney (a series of programmes and activities literally 'housed' and thus themed for the pre-school audience).

The success of this strategy has already influenced terrestrial broadcasters. Both ITV and BBC now identify their children's schedules as 'mini-brands' within their respective networks and both display their logo at the corner of the screen during their scheduled hours. 'T4', the identifying brand for the 'children's/ youth schedule' on Channel 4, also effectively 'zones' its Sunday morning programmes for young viewers. This strategy, pioneered on terrestrial television by T4's producer Andi Peters – an ex-presenter of children's television on the BBC – packages old and new programmes together in a way that is identical to the practices of satellite and digital channels. In essence, Channel 4 continues to screen similar programmes to those it did five years ago; the audience, however, has been increased, secured and made identifiable to themselves – and, of course, to advertisers – through this 'packaging'. In effect, the programmes are 'wrapped', linked and given a new status through the hip and ironic attitude of T4's presenters and idents. As a response to T4's success, the BBC in turn has employed an established brand – its long-running popular music programme *Top of the Pops* – to create a spin-off programme *TOTP Plus* which is designed to attract the same audience.[10] Branding is therefore primarily concerned with visibility: it is a defensive strategy used with increasing frequency as the traditionally linear schedule is placed under pressure.[11]

From when to where – the problem of time

That channels and schedules have become brands is therefore symptomatic of a changing media landscape, but it also suggests that the temporal positioning of programmes – *when* something is 'on' – is increasingly being displaced by spatial concerns – *where* something is 'on'. As we leave the four channel era behind, channels are no longer 'given' but 'chosen'.[12] Unlike previous generations, the current child audience is and will continue to be unable to understand the television schedule solely as a temporal procession of 'events' – 'if it's Saturday, *Doctor Who* is on at 5.20 pm'. A cursory examination of published schedules for satellite channels makes this obvious: whilst the claim is still to show the evening's viewing 'at a glance', it is clearly no longer feasible to comprehend the schedule in this way. Whilst certain programmes may sometimes have the status of events – '*Dragon Ball Z* is on at 5.00 pm' – this is mitigated by the fact that it is *on* Cartoon Network and it is on every weekday and repeated at the weekends. For contemporary child viewers the question is not so much 'when is *Pokémon* on?' but rather 'where can I find it?' If brands make channels places, they therefore reinforce this spatial dimension, and encourage a way of negotiating the media landscape that privileges spatial and visual cognitive abilities over those characterized by time and linearity.

One way of conceptualizing this shift might be through reference to pelmanism, the practice of memory and mind training developed in the nineteenth century which gave rise to a series of related games: one version is known as 'old maid', whilst other, less complex versions are simply called 'pairs'. In the games the child is confronted with a number of playing cards randomly placed face down. The cards are either in 'pairs' or 'families' of different kinds (usually occupations or animals).[13] The task is to collect all the pairs or families of matching cards together. The catch is that this can only be done by turning one card up at a time. If the card is not immediately matched it is returned face down to in its original place. The player therefore has to rely on luck, a combination of trial and error, and a visual, spatially organized process of memorization to match the cards up as quickly as possible.

What I am suggesting, therefore, is that the recent proliferation of channels and programmes requires the child viewer to develop this skill or to play this game: the schedule in its entirety is no longer a book, but a map, and the child orientates themselves spatially rather than temporally. This is not because time doesn't matter anymore; rather that time itself has become the problem. Indeed, one of the most obvious aspects of a multi-channel environment is that whilst the number of programmes and channels have expanded, the time available to view remains pretty much the same as it was before. As Peter Larsen explains:

> The screen is a 'place' in de Certeau's sense of the word, we said; two things cannot be in the same place *at the same time*. The problem the viewers talk about and which the construction of the imaginary space is meant to solve is precisely this: the problem of time, the flow of time ... We know that at any given time there is an abundance of programmes 'out there', programmes that could be there on the screen instead of the one we are watching at the moment.[14]

Thus the kind of spatial memory developed through pelmanism – or playing similar games – could be a useful tactic in a media-saturated environment that might otherwise seem overwhelming. Understanding the iconic significance of the 'brand family' may create a short cut for the viewer, producing an easier pattern of channels to remember and sift through. As Larsen suggests, in relation to the adult audience in his study, such practices allow the television viewer 'to grasp and to remember complicated and confusing phenomena, to perform the routines of everyday life in a practical, sensible way'.[15]

Caution: children at play

This vision of the child viewer at 'play', or even being 'sensible' with their time, is seductive and should be treated with caution. It carries with it the notion that it is the child not the scheduler who can control the outcome of the game, and that it is the child who is responsible for their interaction with the new media environment. The apparent usurping of the rigidly time-determined 'production line' schedules of the terrestrial channels might also be seen to free the child from the dictates of outdated, paternalistic or patronizing adult schedulers who presume to understand what the child wants to view and when he or she wants to see it. Indeed, Nickelodeon is currently encouraging viewers to 'ring in' over the weekend to apparently construct their own schedule. On one Sunday afternoon, between 1.00 and 7.00 p.m., for example, *Sabrina the Teenage Witch* and *Kenan and Kel* were 'head to head' – meaning that the show that received the most telephone requests or website 'hits' was shown.[16] Similarly, on *Nick News*, the promise is that you should 'watch it because you're on it': children are invited to write or mail in to become reporters for the show.[17]

The fact is, of course, is that it is not only children who are 'players' here – the schedulers and thus the channels are also playing, and with more at stake. In the multi-channel environment the scheduler is playing with very few significant attractions (valuable 'cards' or high-rating programmes); he or she is therefore required to tease, cajole and even dupe the audience into watching their channel. The 're-packaging' achieved through branding and theme-ing and switching – tweaking the schedules – works to seduce and confuse the audience, so that the game seemingly allows them to be the active agent, the keen observer who can win out in this new media context. In fact, the scheduler holds the cards and arguably dupes the viewer into seeing novelty when there is none, or perceiving plenitude when ultimately the 'choice' is not necessarily greater than before, but simply structured differently.

Karen Lury

Time, habit and duration

Of course, at any one specific time during the day the choice of programmes is far wider than it would have been before. Over a longer period of time, however – once episodes and formats have become familiar – it becomes clear that it is the same well-thumbed cards which are being presented again and again. Television in this context is increasingly functional – it fills a particular time slot. It could be argued that it is not so much a question of 'wanting' particular programmes but searching out a programme that 'will do' for the time available. It might seem that the individual qualities and attributes of different programmes become less important in this context. Similarly, the purchase that individual programmes might have on memories and identities is potentially distorted by the kind of deliberate saturation evident in the strategy of the 'head to head' or 'marathon'. Previously, for example on terrestrial television, 11 episodes of a series would have been nearly three months of viewing, once a week; three months when the child would, like Sabrina and her friends, mature, make and lose friends, or encounter special events like birthdays and Christmas.

Paddy Scannell has vividly described this 'durational' aspect or long-term effect of the 'time' of television on the viewer:

> The contents of radio and television, like the content of daily life, change from day to day; but their structures remain unchanging and unchanged. That is where the *longue durée*, the unheard music of slow time, shows up in radio and television. It unobtrusively structures their existential role in supporting the routine structures of our daily lives through the course of the lifetime of each and every one of us.[18]

Significantly, he further comments that this '*longue durée*' works across and between generations of viewers; and like me, remembers *Doctor Who* as a memorable television 'event' in this context. He suggests that *Doctor Who* is a programme that could be seen as articulating a 'structure of notations', an 'embryo involvement structure' that can capture audiences across time, because it is 'outside human time':

> This shows up very clearly in long-running drama series and serials. *Doctor Who* was watched as much by adults as by children.

I myself remember watching it at home in the early sixties and 20 years later I sat with my two young sons who watched it cushion in hand. Watching it with my children was a small act of sharing something with them – something which no longer had (for me) the spell it had for them (for whom the 'Daleks' et al. were real and scary). But watching it and talking about it was a shared experience across their generation and mine. In such ways programme structures are devices for regeneration, for bringing tomorrow's generation into today's generation and, in due course, handing over and handing on to them. Thus, again, broadcasting's phenomenal now is always a past-becoming-future.[19]

What Scannell is implying, therefore, is that programmes – especially long-running programmes such as *Doctor Who* – form part of what he calls the 'dailiness' of media, the ability to look to the future whilst incorporating the past in a continuing sense of ongoing-ness, of 'timeliness'. In this instance specific programmes can link generations of viewers, not because they share the exact same experience but because the previous viewing experience is made resonant through regeneration, the continuing growth and change of a familiar programme.

In terms of structure, *Doctor Who* is not very different from the kinds of programmes that occupy the new satellite and digital channels. What has changed, however, is the way in which programmes like *Doctor Who* became so embedded in different domestic routines. My feeling is that *Doctor Who*'s timeliness is also to do with the fact that each four-part story would be transmitted over four Saturdays (a month of the child viewer's lifetime) at a particular time, with very few programmes available as an alternative. The programme has a special place in people's memories and experience because it was a weekly, rather than daily or even hourly 'event', it was shown in order (it was a serial within a series format) and the internal history of the programme was carefully maintained.

Now, whilst *Sabrina* is a show that is equally 'involving' in terms of its essential 'structure', the fact that 11 episodes, ranging not just across one programming 'season' but over a period of years, can all be viewed in one afternoon means that the phenomenological link between viewer and programme will be of a very different order. In this context, the sense of chronology, the anticipation as to 'what will happen next' as well as the sense of characters' histories mirroring individuals' lives simply cannot be maintained when many of these programmes are transmitted by cable or satellite channels.

Of course, certain viewers could and probably do choose to construct routines or viewing 'habits' in relation to the scheduling of particular programmes even when they could see the same programme at other times. *Dragon Ball Z* is currently such an 'event', although I think this is partly because the 'epic' structure of this particular programme obliges interested viewers – and schedulers – to remain tied to a more traditional sense of chronology.

Nonetheless, in relation to the majority of teen dramas/comedies, and the vast number of cartoons and different animations transmitted, it would seem that their self-contained structure means that programmes can and are shown out of sequence much more freely than before.[20] In many instances, although programmes are listed in printed and electronic schedules, it is not clear what the actual story-line will be of the episode shown at any specific time. A description for *Kenan and Kel* on Nickelodeon, for example, is reduced to 'US teen drama about two boys who are forever hatching schemes which get them into trouble' or even 'US teen drama about two teenage boys'. The series' reduction to its generic essence suggests that the programme may act as a kind of 'utility' that can be guaranteed to crudely assuage a relatively unfocused need for distraction, which may or may not be shared with others. These kinds of programmes therefore act as 'texts' that are easily read and enjoyed without any great sense of commitment from the viewer. In effect, it doesn't really matter where you are in the narrative of the programme. Thus the phenomenological and pleasurable aspects are, for some viewers, about filling time rather than any sense of 'timeliness' or regeneration.

This is clearly not the kind of viewing practice that the channels themselves would wish to promote. Their strategy of branding, theme-ing and tweaking suggests that they wish to encourage an alternative to this by persuading the viewer that they are acting as a connoisseur or 'fan'. By contextualizing the programmes as if they were objects with unique properties ('just for me'), or as objects that are there to be consumed through viewing 'orgies' (in marathon sessions, in chunks, over and over again), the channels recast the programmes as objects to be *collected*. The collection, as Susan Stewart has noted, has its own particular relationship to the past, and thus to temporality:

> The collection does not displace attention to the past; rather, the past is at the service of the collection . . . the past lends authenticity to the collection. The collection seeks a form of self-enclosure which is possible because of its ahistoricism. The collection replaces history with *classification*, with order beyond the realm of temporality. In the collection, time is not something to be restored to an origin; rather, all time is made simultaneous or synchronous within the collection's world.[21]

Rather than an articulation of a 'past-becoming-future', the new schedules' 'phenomenal now' (in Paddy Scannell's terms) has become an 'all-at-once' availability, offering repetition rather than regeneration. Once again, the channels' scheduling operations can be understood to be spatial rather than temporal: 'the collection replaces origin with classification, thereby making temporality a spatial and material phenomenon.' It may be that only the 'all-at-once-ness' of spatial relationships can contain the proliferation of programmes in the new media environment. Certainly, in relation to the programmes themselves, it seems that, as Stewart also notes, 'the spatial whole of the collection supersedes the individual narratives that "lie behind it" '.[22]

The programme that most obviously follows this model is, of course, *Pokémon*. The *Pokémon* catch-phrase 'Gotta catch 'em all' and its series of collectable, portable monsters whose individual biographies are subsumed within a greater meta-narrative fit superbly well into this new media context. It is no surprise that the programme should have been so successful within a multi-channel environment. The aspiration of the central human characters is mastery; and to achieve this, they must travel, consume and memorize each monster they encounter. I hesitate to emphasize the point, but the characters' ambitions and actions are not so different from those of the child in contemporary popular culture. Whilst it has been noted before that children are now 'learning to consume' from television, my point is that they are also learning about their world in ways that emphasize visual and spatial cognitive abilities. To further justify this claim, I want to conclude by examining how one programme articulates – in a very different way – this new emphasis on spatiality and visuality as a way in which the child can be engaged, and in this instance, simply begin to 'learn'.

Blue's Clues

Blue's Clues is a 30-minute programme aimed at pre-school children; and the British version produced by Nickelodeon UK follows the original American format very closely. In each episode, Kevin (a young black guy with a strong Liverpool accent dressed in a green and white rugby shirt and khaki pants) asks the audience to help him solve 'Blue's clues' – clues left by his animated puppy pet, 'Blue'. Blue's clues can be identified by Blue's blue paw print. The problem or question is usually as simple as 'What can I do to get rid of the sniffles?' or 'What does Blue want to build?' There are three clues recorded in Kevin's notebook as he searches around his animated house and garden. On his quest, Kevin usually meets up with characters such as 'Bucket' and 'Spade' or 'Mrs Pepperpot' that are the objects their names suggest. Once all three clues have been located, Kevin returns to his 'thinking chair' and thinks of different ways that the three clues can be combined to give the 'answer'. For example, a sheet, a torch and a table can be combined to 'build' a tent. During the 'thinking' process the three clues as drawn by Kevin in his notebook are shown floating above his head. Throughout his journey Kevin also encounters smaller puzzles that need to be solved and live action sequences featuring children in related activities – such as building a playhouse. Kevin also asks for help at each stage and is guided by an unseen chorus of children who see the clues and solve the puzzles with him. Many of these elements are present in other children's programmes. What makes *Blue's Clues* distinctive, however, is the pacing and feel of the show. Malcolm Gladwell describes the American version presented by 'Steve':

> Steve, as a result, spends almost all his time on screen talking directly at the camera. When he enlists the audience's help, he actually enlists the audience's help. Often there are close-ups of his face, so it is as if he is almost in the room with his audience. Whenever he asks a question, he pauses. But it's not a normal pause. It's a preschooler's pause, several beats longer than any adult would ever wait for an answer. Eventually an unseen studio audience yells out a response.[23]

The British version painstakingly replicates this kind of pace and the relationship between viewer and presenter. For an adult viewer the programme is agonizingly slow, but it would seem that the pauses, whilst clearly designed to allow the child viewer to think, also give her or him time to look. Viewers are not obliged to progress or move on within the programme either through dialogue or through a change of scene. It may be that they are thus able to look *around* the screen for the clue, or to visually rehearse the way in which objects on screen might be combined. This emphasis on spatiality is encouraged by the mix of live action and cartoon; whilst Kevin (and presumably Steve) is 'real' (live action), the house, garden and other characters in *Blue's Clues* are simply drawn cartoon animations and, as such, extremely 'flat'. Whilst Kevin can open and shut drawers or sit on specific objects, the background, Blue, and other characters are as flat as book illustrations or icons on a computer screen. This flatness gives a sense of tangibility to the images on the television screen – as if they could be literally moved around by hand (or following the association with computers, by clicking and dragging). The world of *Blue's Clues*, then, is oriented through play and interaction that emphasize an ability to comprehend space and to think problems through visually. Furthermore, this kind of concrete thinking is literally enacted when Kevin also attempts to think a specific problem through. For example, in the 'building' episode, rather than immediately thinking of a tent, Kevin imagines that the torch will be wrapped in the sheet and then dance on the table. The three drawings above his head actually combine in this way, so that the images act as objects that can be literally rearranged, put together and pulled apart until they 'make sense'. Obviously in the multi-channel context I have described – and perhaps in the emerging multi-media environment more broadly – this kind of thinking seems to be increasingly foregrounded. Of course this way of approaching learning and thinking is not new in itself; but we may nevertheless be witnessing a shift from a verbal, frag-mented version of the world (*Sesame Street*) to a visual, ultimately holistic place (*Blue's Clues*).

The other aspect of the programme that conforms to the new multi-channel context is the programme's use of repetition. At the level of format, of course, the programme repeats the same essential narrative in each new episode. It uses the same rhymes, gestures, dances and catch-phrases time after time so that they create a familiar rhythm for the young viewer. What is interesting however is that the programme actually makes a feature of repeating the same episode, once a day over a week's viewing. At the start of each episode a blackboard is featured showing the numbers 1 to 5. One of these numbers is swinging; and a voice-over then confirms that the number swinging indicates how many times the child could (and, implicitly, should) have seen that particular episode. A voice then claims that the repeated opportunities to view the show occur because 'The more young children know, the more they learn and the more they feel better about themselves.' Daniel Anderson, one of the original American series' creators, claims:

> For younger kids, repetition is really valuable. They demand it. When they see a show over and over again, they not only are understanding it better, which is a form of power, but just by predicting what is going to happen, I think they feel a real sense of affirmation and self-worth. And *Blue's Clues* doubles that feeling, because they also feel like they are participating in something. They feel like they are helping Steve.[24]

In his analysis of the appeal of *Blue's Clues*, Malcolm Gladwell suggests that Nickelodeon executives weren't keen on this aspect, and claims that Anderson and his co-creator Tracy Santomero had to 'convince them'. Interestingly, however, in parentheses he notes that 'It also helped that Nickelodeon didn't have the money to produce a full season of *Blue's Clues* shows.'[25] In this instance then, repetition is unabashed, 'unpackaged', even actively promoted because it is arguably in tune with the needs of the younger audience: scheduling in this manner is legitimated as a special practice, 'just for them'. Conveniently, it also happens to fit in with the economics and scheduling practices of the new multi-channel context.

Conclusion

Any description of these new children's channels at this point can only function as a snapshot, which in turn will be limited by my relatively recent familiarity with the programmes and schedules. It is probably also clear that my own domestic situation – I have two children who are both under five years old – has determined the focus of my discussion. Within these constraints I have attempted to limit any speculation as to the future of the channels, particularly as their take-up within the UK is still relatively limited compared to other national contexts. All the channels are likely to undergo changes as take-up increases and audiences adjust to the multi-channel environment and negotiate the new economics of television. Indeed, BBC Choice in the form I describe it here will disappear under the BBC's current proposals for a series of digital channels. At this point of transition, however, it is possible to recognize shifts in the way the child audience is being invited to use and learn from television. In a context where there is a seeming proliferation of images, programmes and characters, global brands such as Cartoon Network, Nickelodeon and Disney work hard to make each UK-based 'franchise' a recognizable place within the domestic broadcasting landscape. I have suggested that branding, theme-ing and tweaking encourage older children to view by making the programmes appear novel, collectable and in certain instances 'camp'. For younger children, niche channels are promoted as special places that make a virtue out of necessity and present repetition as an opportunity for mastery. In different ways for both younger and older children, spatial and visual modes of cognition have become increasingly important. Other ways of seeing or comprehending the world have not been superseded; and such modes are by no means new, as my reference to pelmanism should have made clear. Nonetheless, there are some qualitative differences between the way in which my children will and do watch television and the experience I had as child. Yet, finally, to seek out the potential benefits or the learning that may be offered in this new context is perhaps to reflect my own needs at this point in time. Since, as Adam Phillips cautions, 'Children dream but adults want to, indeed need to, teach them; children know what interests them, but adults want them educated.'[26]

Notes

1. Hannah Davies, David Buckingham and Peter Kelley, 'Kids' time: childhood, television and the regulation of time', Journal of Educational Media 24, (1), 36, 1999.
2. This is explored in greater detail in David Buckingham, Hannah

Davies, Ken Jones and Peter Kelley, *Children's Television in Britain* (London: British Film Institute, 1999), particularly Chapter 3, 'Vision on: mapping the changes in children's programming', pp. 78–117.

3. For more on this see Sonia Livingstone's recent research, e.g. Sonia Livingstone, G. Gaskell and M. Bovill, 'European TV kids in a transformed media world: Findings of the UK study', in Paul Lohr and Manfred Meyer (eds), *Children, Television and the New Media* (Luton: University of Luton Press, 1999), pp. 8–25.
4. Although of course there is considerable variety in the styles of animation used in each programme.
5. Cartoon Network typically makes this practice excessive and offers heavily promoted 'superchunks' – two-hour stretches of the same programme.
6. See Marsha Kinder's introduction to her book, *Playing with Power in Movies, Television and Video Games* (Berkeley and Los Angeles: University of California Press, 1991), pp. 1–39.
7. This game (or joke) is one used frequently by popular magazines – two unrelated celebrities' photographs are printed side by side, with the question 'separated at birth?'
8. *The Powerpuff Girls* features three pre-school girls, Buttercup, Blossom and Bubbles, who also happen to be superheroes, committed to 'saving the day' for the folks of 'Townsville'. With their squeaky voices and excessively 'girly' mannerisms, they are clearly designed to reinvent and parody the superhero genre. As super-feminine crime fighters who commonly strike fantastic fighting poses, they also revisit the camp excesses of the original 'girl power' crime shows of the 1970s such as *Charlie's Angels* and *The Bionic Woman.*
9. Scooby Doo has been celebrated in this way by the film *Wayne's World.* The ending of this film which involves a series of bad guys/good guys being unmasked is an open parody of the way in which every episode of *Scooby Doo* concludes. In the film, as in the show, the unmasking of the bad guy is accompanied by the comment: 'I would have got away with it if it weren't for you pesky kids.'
10. *Top of the Pops* has another 'brand extension' aimed at an older audience – *TOTP2*, shown on BBC2 and BBC Choice (an obvious parallel would be the relationship of VH1 to MTV).
11. Both E4 – Channel 4's new digital/satellite channel – and the BBC's plan for a series of 'themed' channels demonstrate this tendency.
12. It is important to note that not everyone can afford to 'choose' to watch channels that require a regular financial commitment. It may also be the case that this branding 'frenzy' will be short-lived; the UK broadcasting system is still very much in a process of transition. Methods of purchase, as well as the kinds of package bought

(whether this is delivery systems, or the exact make-up of different 'bundles' of channels) have all yet to be definitively established.

13. The 'old maid' is therefore the one card left remaining, as it has no 'family'.
14. Peter Larsen, 'Imaginary spaces: television, technology and everyday consciousness', in Jostein Grisprud (ed.), *Television and Common Knowledge* (Routledge: London, 1999), p. 119.
15. *Ibid.*, p. 120.
16. On this particular Sunday, *Sabrina* trounced *Kenan and Kel* – Nickelodeon screened 11 episodes of *Sabrina* and just one of *Kenan and Kel* over the six-hour period.
17. This is something that the BBC's news programme for children, *Newsround*, has also encouraged, although the programme itself is still anchored by an adult presenter/reporter, as are the majority of the news items/reports.
18. Paddy Scannell, *Radio, Television and Modern Life* (Oxford: Blackwell, 1996), p. 176.
19. *Ibid.*, p. 177.
20. Although in *Sabrina* I have found that the status of the Aunts' relationships can sometimes cause confusion.
21. Susan Stewart, *On Longing* (Durham, NC: Duke University Press, 1993), p. 151.
22. *Ibid.*, p. 153.
23. Malcolm Gladwell, *The Tipping Point* (London: Little, Brown and Company, 2000), pp. 123–4.
24. *Ibid.*, p. 126.
25. *Ibid.*, p. 125.
26. Adam Phillips, *The Beast in the Nursery* (London: Faber and Faber, 1998), p. 59.

CHAPTER 3

Child-centred Television?

Teletubbies and the Educational Imperative

DAVID BUCKINGHAM

Teletubbies is one of the most successful and controversial children's programmes of all time. Since its launch in March 1997, it has been sold in more than sixty countries worldwide, and translated into over forty languages. Hundreds of millions of pounds have been generated from *Teletubbies* videos, magazines, computer games, toys and ancillary merchandise. Yet the bizarre day-glo figures of Tinky Winky, Dipsy, Laa-Laa and Po have also provoked a degree of outrage and irritation that is out of all proportion to their essentially mundane and harmless antics. Widely criticized by parents, politicians and journalists alike, *Teletubbies* seems to have become synonymous with the 'dumbing down' of contemporary childhood.

However valid such criticisms may be, the notoriety of this programme is also symptomatic of much broader tensions that characterize contemporary children's media culture.[1] As I will show in this chapter, *Teletubbies* blurs the boundaries between the public and the private; between education and entertainment; and between child and adult audiences. In this respect, it could perhaps be taken as merely another manifestation of postmodern culture. And yet the programme also displays significant continuities with children's programmes of the past. In some ways, *Teletubbies* represents something distinctively contemporary; yet paradoxically, a good deal about it is also far from new.

The public and the private

Teletubbies is commissioned and broadcast in Britain by the BBC – that is, by a non-commercial, public service broadcasting company. The particular characteristics of the programme, and the controversy it has aroused, need to be understood in the light of contemporary changes at the BBC – and indeed in terms of the broader move away from national public service broadcasting towards a global, market-led, multi-channel environment.

Successive Conservative governments of the 1980s and 1990s had exerted intensifying pressure on the BBC.[2] Margaret Thatcher, of course, was a powerful advocate of privatization; and while that did not eventually come to pass, many critics have argued that the Corporation effectively privatized itself – not least through the 'modernizing' policies of its notorious Director General, John Birt. Even under a more sympathetic government, the BBC is caught between the requirement to act as a national public service broadcaster – and hence to justify the retention of the licence fee through which it is funded – and the need to compete in a global commercial market. This tension is reflected across the whole range of its activities, from its screening of major sporting events to its involvement in digital broadcasting and 24-hour news.

Children's television is in a paradoxical position here. On the one hand, some critics and lobby groups argue that it is particularly at risk from what they regard as the BBC's abandonment of its public service traditions. They point to the increasing quantity of US animation programmes on British screens, and the reduction in factual programming for children – phenomena which they see as symptomatic of a more general cultural decline. The broadly 'educational' functions of children's television are, it is argued, being steadily undermined by the rise of poor quality entertainment. Such claims are, it should be emphasized, highly questionable, both in terms of their factual validity and in terms of their implicit assumptions about cultural value.[3] Yet children's television has undoubtedly become a symbolic 'test case' – if not quite a *cause célèbre* – in contemporary debates about the future of public broadcasting.

On the other hand, in this newly competitive broadcasting environment, children have also become an increasingly valuable market. In recent years, we have seen the introduction of several new specialist children's cable/satellite channels in the UK; and on terrestrial television, children's programmes have begun to spread to hitherto untouched areas of the schedule, such as breakfast times and Sunday mornings. Meanwhile, television is now ever more firmly caught up in global networks of multi-media marketing. Major US-based producers in the field such as Disney, Viacom and Murdoch's News Corporation are increasingly using integrated marketing strategies, which combine television, video, movies, computer games, records, toys and a whole range of other merchandise. In this context, some have argued that children are now much *better* served as an audience – at least in terms of quantity, if not necessarily in terms of diversity or quality; although others have spoken with growing alarm about the commercial 'exploitation' of children.

This new environment has ambivalent implications for pre-school programmes. The under-fives are, by definition, a small fraction of the overall viewing audience; and the more broadcasters seek to cater for distinctions *within* that audience, the smaller it becomes. To acknowledge the considerable differences between two-year-olds and five-year-olds is, in these terms, a very costly move. At the same time, the proportion of household income being spent on children – not least on catering to their tastes in media – has increased exponentially in recent years. The market in videotapes, 'edutainment' magazines and toys for pre-schoolers is currently booming.

Compelled to compete in order to justify the retention of the licence fee, yet simultaneously expected to uphold the public service tradition, the BBC is pulled in both directions at once. Perhaps particularly in the area of pre-school television, its decisions must have a commercial as well as an educational rationale. This was clearly apparent in the case of *Teletubbies*.

To some extent, the new show was conceived as a replacement for the BBC's long-running pre-school series *Playdays*. However, according to Anna Home, the Head of BBC Children's Programmes who commissioned the show, there was both a commercial and an educational logic for aiming at a much younger target audience.[4] Competitive pressure had forced the producers of *Playdays* to aim more at older children, in order to broaden their audience. Meanwhile, the new emphasis on testing in government education policy had led to growing anxiety among parents: the introduction of so-called 'baseline testing' at age four had led to increasing pressure to 'prepare' children even prior to them entering nursery school. For both reasons, *Teletubbies* was conceived as a programme that would be aimed at the very youngest age group; although it was recognized that it might also attract older children, up to the age of five.

The independent production company Ragdoll Productions, which was eventually commissioned to produce the new show, had a long track record in pre-school programming, with notable successes such as *Rosie and Jim* and *Tots TV* (both screened on commercial television). Ragdoll's work is informed by a broadly child-centred educational philosophy; and, as I shall indicate, this is strongly manifested in many aspects of *Teletubbies*. Yet with a new investment on this scale – 260 26-minute programmes were projected over the first two years – it was clear from the start that commercial concerns would have to play a major role. Significantly, *Teletubbies* was to be a joint venture between the BBC's Children's Department and its Schools Department – the first of its kind, and a clear indication of its educational emphasis. Yet it also had to attract support from BBC Worldwide, which is a wholly owned commercial subsidiary of the BBC with particular responsibility for merchandising and overseas sales. Here again, educational and commercial considerations were inextricably connected.

Spinning off

In fact, merchandising has been a significant aspect of children's television since its inception in the 1950s. Nevertheless, it has dramatically increased in scale in the past two decades, as children (like teenagers before them) have effectively been 'discovered' as a target market. The market of licensed goods based on TV and media characters is now worth more than £2.5 billion per year in the UK alone. The emergence of what were called 'programme-length commercials' – that is, cartoons explicitly designed to promote toys, such as *My Little Pony*, *Thundercats* and *Transformers*, which began in the USA in the 1980s – has been the most controversial aspect of this phenomenon. Yet merchandising has become a key imperative in children's television generally – not least at the BBC. Popular shows like the

Saturday morning magazine programme *Live and Kicking* have become showcases for new media products, as well as vehicles for selling the BBC's own merchandise: the *Live and Kicking* magazine, for example, is currently the market leader among pre-teens. Pre-school programmes have long been a key area for merchandising. In the UK and internationally, programmes like *Thomas the Tank Engine* (known in the USA as *Shining Time Station*) and *Postman Pat* continue to generate an extensive range of toys and other products.

In the case of *Teletubbies*, a major merchandising operation was planned from the very beginning – even if the scale of demand proved initially to be much greater than anticipated. The list of *Teletubbies* products either licensed by the BBC or marketed directly is ever-growing: it includes a magazine, books, audio and video tapes, computer games, posters, toys, clothing, watches, food and confectionery, mugs and crockery, stationery and games, as well as more unexpected artefacts like computer mouse mats. This is, of course, a global market; and there are many additional products deemed appropriate to specific national markets, such as *Teletubbies* rice bowls on sale in Singapore and *Teletubbies eau de toilette* in France. According to the BBC's annual report, £330 million was generated overall during the programme's first two years, with £23 million going directly to the BBC in 1998 (43 per cent of which came from sales of video-tapes).

This phenomenon raises several questions. To what extent does the potential for merchandising influence the programme itself? Producers and broadcasting executives routinely insist that it does not; but it is clear that these considerations now enter the process at a much earlier stage than they used to do. Thus, puppets or animated characters create greater opportunities for merchandising than live actors, for example in the form of toys. Teams of characters – four Teletubbies rather than one – generate what in the business is termed 'collectability'; and props that are regularly associated with the characters can also be marketed separately – as in the case of 'Tubby custard', recently licensed to St. Ivel. More generally, the unified 'look' of a programme – colours, design features, graphics – is crucial in defining a distinctive presence in shop displays. Ultimately, such considerations are bound to affect production decisions, although of course they may well conveniently coincide with producers' creative instincts.

Can this be seen simply as a way of 'exploiting' vulnerable children? Of course, BBC executives will firmly insist that it is not. There is certainly an element of puritanism about such charges: children's hankering for consumer goods is often seen as a problem – particularly if it is associated with 'low' cultural forms such as television – in a way that adults' similar desires are not.[5] Children, it seems to be implied, should somehow be kept innocent of the contamination of commerce. Nevertheless, the BBC does enjoy a privileged position here: since it does not carry advertising, it is able to promote its goods to what is effectively a captive audience. On the other hand, it also has a brand image for 'quality' products that it must struggle to retain – although whether or not it has overstepped the mark in this instance is certainly debatable.

Selling to the world

The second major dimension of BBC Worldwide's operation is overseas sales. Here again, *Teletubbies* has been an unprecedented success, particularly compared with other British productions; although it will be interesting to see whether it can rival the long-term international marketability of a programme like *Sesame Street*. As noted above, the programme is currently being purchased by over sixty countries; and those which were initially critical, such as Denmark and Norway, also seem to have come aboard. Perhaps most significantly, *Teletubbies* is being sold to the United States (albeit admittedly to PBS) – a country where children's programmes from overseas are almost entirely absent.

Here again, there are questions about the extent to which such considerations influence production decisions. Clearly, some kinds of programmes are much more marketable than others. It is generally much harder to sell programmes which are culturally specific than ones which are not. Thus, in the case of children's programmes, it is more difficult to sell non-fiction than fiction; and contemporary drama, particularly if it features non-standard accents, is less marketable than 'children's heritage culture' of the *Chronicles of Narnia* variety. Animation and puppet shows sell better because they can easily be dubbed into other languages, and also tend to be less culturally specific than those featuring real children. In many of these respects, *Teletubbies* would appear to be much more internationally marketable than, for example, the magazine format of a programme like its predecessor *Playdays.*

From the perspective of the purchasing countries, however, the dominance of a small number of multinational companies in the global marketplace inevitably raises concerns about cultural imperialism. Such criticisms apply as much to the BBC as they do, for example, to Disney. Thus, some overseas delegates at the 1998 World Summit on Television for Children, held in London, were critical of *Teletubbies* not only on the 'educational' grounds to be considered below, but also on the grounds of what they perceived as its cultural bias. On the other hand, as in the case of *Sesame Street*, the programme is designed to have the potential for national broadcasters to insert documentary-style material that is specific to their national context; and in countries that possess the necessary resources, such as Germany, approximately half the documentary material is locally produced.

A licence to print money?

The BBC has certainly been keen to boast of the success of its commercial exploitation of *Teletubbies*, although it remains sensitive to criticism. An advertising campaign in 1999 pointed out that such commercial activities were nothing new, and that the income from *Teletubbies* had been used to 'top up' the licence fee, 'helping us to invest more in programmes and services for you, the licence fee payer'. 'Of course you love them', the strap-line read. 'They helped us pay for *Blue Peter, Men Behaving Badly* and *Vanity Fair.*' Yet quite how much of this money was fed back into the production of *children's* programmes remains unclear.

Of course, the global success of *Teletubbies* could not have been predicted – and there were indications, as desperate parents battled to buy the rapidly dwindling stocks of dolls and other merchandise in the toy shops in late 1997, that the BBC and its licensees had drastically underestimated its market appeal. On the other hand, the fact that BBC Worldwide invested money at the planning stage – and thus inevitably influenced production decisions – rather gives the lie to claims that it was simply responding to consumer demand, or that commercial interests were merely a secondary consideration.

Ultimately, the commercial dimensions of *Teletubbies* are

merely symptomatic of the 'mixed economy' that now characterizes public broadcasting. Public broadcasters have increasingly argued that the production of children's programmes would
effectively be impossible if it were not for commercial involvement of this kind. This complex interweaving of commercial and
public service imperatives, and of national and global considerations, has become part of the conditions of existence of
contemporary television. Where the boundaries can and should
be drawn here is becoming an increasingly complex and difficult
issue for broadcasters, policy-makers and critics alike.

Cause for concern

The amount of press commentary that surrounded *Teletubbies* in
its early days threatened to rival that of the most popular soap
operas. Both in the tabloids and in the so-called 'quality' press,
any mention of the show seemed to guarantee headline news.
Teletubbies stories became a self-sustaining media phenomenon,
much of it based on the recycling of inaccuracies and hearsay.[6]
For the growing army of columnists and 'expert' commentators,
the expression of strong opinion about the programme became
de rigueur, although children's views were generally notable for
their absence from these reports.

Here again, the BBC is in a somewhat ambivalent position. On
the one hand, it is bound to seek publicity, in the hope of raising
both its audience and its public profile. At least some of the press
coverage is energetically 'spun' by the BBC Press Office; and it is
generally happy to provide interviews and illustrations, even to
publications whose interest seems somewhat unlikely. On the
other hand, the BBC is very sensitive to criticism from parents;
and any implication that it is being derelict in its public service
duties has to be strongly countered. At its peak, managing the
press coverage became an exercise in damage limitation.[7]
Meanwhile, for overseas broadcasters purchasing the show, the
existence of such a controversy can provide a very useful means
of generating advance interest.[8]

Some of this material is clearly regarded as light relief. Stories
such as the Reverend Jerry Falwell's condemnation of Tinky
Winky as a 'role model' for 'degenerate gay lifestyles' are reported
by the British press with considerable irony. Meanwhile, the *Sun*

launched a campaign against the sacking of the actor who originally played Tinky Winky – '59-year-old wrinkly [producer Anne Wood] K. O.'s Tinky Winky'; while the *Sport* hit back with 'scandalous' pictures taken from the internet of 'Teletubby Laa-Laa's Legover'. Elsewhere, writers claim to have detected references to hallucinogenic drugs in the programme (a giant letter 'E' descending from the sky), or to have evidence of its 'addictive' qualities. Such stories juxtaposing sex and drugs with childhood innocence are in a tradition that goes back at least to the ironic reception of *The Magic Roundabout* in the late 1960s; and they reflect the 'cult' appropriation of the programme by adults which I will consider in more detail below.

However, there is a more serious concern here too. Much of the debate has centred on the question that, according to the *Daily Mirror*, is 'on every parent's lips': 'The Teletubbies – are they harmless fun or bad for our children?' (23 May 1997). While *Mirror* readers were called upon to give their own views ('calls cost no more than 10p'), many newspapers have relied on academic 'experts' – mostly psychologists – to pronounce on the value of the programme. The *Observer* (12 September 1999) ran a story about the BBC's own research, which apparently suggests that *Teletubbies* is 'better for young children's education than the strict programme of formal learning being proposed by Education Secretary David Blunkett'. And in late 1999, there were reports about the German Academy of Paediatrics' condemnation of the programme's 'long-term addictive qualities'; and about British academics' research into its role in encouraging children to read and write.[9]

As this implies, the recurrent concern here is with *Teletubbies'* 'educational' merit. Thus, it has repeatedly been argued that the programme's use of 'baby talk' will undermine children's language development; that it is unnecessarily repetitive; that it takes place in an 'unreal' world; that there is too much play and 'dancing around doing meaningless things', and too little instructional content, for example in teaching letters and numbers. It is frequently alleged that the programme contains no 'real' language at all; and significantly, many critics seem concerned that the programme does not feature sufficient numbers of adults.

Many of these criticisms seem to be based on a rather superficial acquaintance with the programme – and indeed with the age group of children at whom it is aimed. At least some of them are simply inaccurate. For example, there is a considerable amount of 'real' language in the programme, particularly in the form of voice-over both by adults and by children; some estimates suggest that this is as high as 80 per cent. Nearly all the Teletubbies' 'baby talk' is repeated by the adult narrator. Likewise, while the Tele-tubbies themselves are clearly fantasy creations, the programme does contain documentary-style sequences featuring real children in real-world situations. Other criticisms seem to reflect a mis-understanding of the target age of the programme, and to be based on the comparison with *Playdays*, which was clearly aimed at older children. While it does contain some elements of early reading and maths, *Teletubbies* was not intended to serve as a direct form of preparation for school subjects. The BBC – and, in the USA, PBS – have done a great deal to counter these criticisms, and to explain the educational aims of the programme in relation to the two- and three-year-olds who make up its primary target audience.[10]

So why has there been so much criticism of this kind, or at least so much reporting of it in the press? To some degree, such reports can be seen as part of a time-honoured tradition of the press attacking its rival medium. The BBC is a favourite target of criticism, not least because many newspapers have financial interests in commercial television and resent what they see as the BBC's privileged position. Nevertheless, these responses also reveal a good deal about changing definitions of what counts as 'education' in the era of 'back to basics'. Indeed, it is significant that in July 1997 the incoming government's schools minister Stephen Byers made a high-profile speech in which he singled out *Teletubbies* as an example of the 'dumbing down' of British children – although (needless to say, perhaps) he was then bound to admit that he had never actually seen it. In Britain, as in many other countries, parents are increasingly being urged to partici-pate in their children's education: there is a growing sense, par-ticularly among middle-class parents, that state education is failing, and that they now have to supplement its inadequacies from their own resources. The renewed emphasis on homework and the massive boom in home computers and workbooks reflect the increasing competitiveness that has been created by national testing.

In some respects, of course, this is merely the latest stage in a backlash against what are seen as dangerous liberal-progressive ideas about education. The Labour government has followed the lead of its Conservative predecessor in arguing for a return to traditional methods – albeit, in this case, in the name of 'modernization'. In this context, television in general is largely defined as anti-educational. If it has a role, it is not to 'dumb down', but to 'brain up'. Television should not be entertaining children: on the contrary, it should be part of the 'work' they are expected to be doing when they are not at school. Insofar as it fails to provide rigorous drilling in letter and number recognition, a programme like *Teletubbies* is thus inevitably seen to be failing in its pedagogic duty.

Behind this concern is another, that lies even deeper. For some critics, the very existence of a programme aimed at such a young audience seems to represent an affront to their fundamental ideas or fantasies about childhood. From this perspective, early childhood must be preserved as a technology-free, commercial-free space – the last sanctuary from the corrupting world of adulthood. The American Academy of Paediatricians, for example, has recently announced that children under the age of two should not be exposed to television at all: television, it argued, should not be used as an 'electronic babysitter', a substitute for interaction with parents.[11] *Teletubbies* may be a particular target here, simply because it is one of the first programmes to be directed specifically at this younger age group. Even worse, it recognizes the fact that very young children do indeed watch television in any case. The programme assumes quite a developed degree of 'television literacy' on the part of its viewers; and makes implicit references to other programmes, not least the notorious *Mighty Morphin' Power Rangers*, whose lurid day-glo costumes may have provided the model for the colour-coding of the Teletubbies. While the programme frequently employs elements of traditional children's culture (such as songs and nursery rhymes), the potential offence here is compounded by its enthusiastic adoption of technological imagery. The Teletubbies are, on one level, simply gigantic soft toys, but they live in a kind of technological underground bunker, and even have televisions in their stomachs!

In addition, for adults who rarely see such programmes, *Teletubbies* is likely to be boring, irritating and difficult to understand. This is hardly surprising: what amuses and engages a two-year-old is, by definition, unlikely to hold much interest for us. By comparison with adult programmes, *Teletubbies* is indeed extremely slow and repetitive; much of its humour is basic slapstick; it uses strong primary colours rather than subtle pastels; and it is replete with silly noises and sound effects. In general, these are elements that programme-makers and researchers know have particular appeal to very young children; and this is broadly confirmed by Ragdoll's own research. The programme's imagery – the strangely 'hyper-real' landscape, the combination of nature and technology, and particularly the image of the baby's face in the sun with which the programme begins and ends – seems to be quite unsettling for many adults, although there is no evidence that it produces the same response in children.

Yet to make matters worse, the content of *Teletubbies* makes few concessions to potential adult viewers (parents or carers). In comparison with *Sesame Street*, for example, there are hardly any references or jokes that seem to be included for the benefit of adults; there are no adult presenters, and adults generally keep a low profile in its documentary sequences; and in comparison with *Playdays* or *Playschool*, its educational content is much less overtly didactic. In all these respects, the problem with *Tele-tubbies* is simply that it *excludes* adults – and thus, for some, represents a challenge to their authority.

Child-centred television?

As this implies, it may be the 'child-centredness' of *Teletubbies* that has made it so controversial – and indeed so popular with its target audience. Child-centred television is a problem, both for those who seek to return to educational 'basics' and (more paradoxically perhaps) for those who seek to defend traditional notions of childhood innocence.

Certainly, the philosophy of the show's creator, Anne Wood, is defiantly child-centred.[12] In interviews and articles, she consistently emphasizes the idea that children's programmes should 'take the child's point of view'. Young children, Wood argues, learn not through 'instruction' but through play; and they have a right to 'fun' and 'entertainment' just as much as adult viewers. Wood vehemently refuses to apologize for television as a medium, and refutes the suggestion that it is inherently inferior to more 'educational' media such as books. In line with child-centred educational philosophy, the emphasis in *Teletubbies* is on meeting what are seen as children's emotional and developmental 'needs'. According to official statements, the programme aims to build confidence and self-esteem; to celebrate individuality; to build children's imagination and sense of humour; and to encourage participation and movement. Wood strongly rejects the emphasis on target-setting that has increasingly characterized government education policy, and asserts young children's right to control their own learning.

These aims are reflected in several aspects of *Teletubbies*. On one level, the programme is highly ritualistic. Each edition contains a relatively inflexible sequence of items, with fixed moments or intervals in the structure. Following an introductory sequence, there is generally a short sketch or dance. The Teletubbies are then 'summoned' by a windmill-type transmitter that beams a short documentary sequence into the screens in their stomachs. To cries of 'Again! Again!' from the Teletubbies, this sequence is immediately repeated; and there is then a longer sketch or story featuring the Teletubbies, followed by a closing 'bedtime' sequence. Introductory, linking and closing sequences are repeated in each programme, with the same accompanying music, providing familiar, fixed landmarks. Of each 26-minute edition, only about half of the material is new. In addition, some sequences are repeated between programmes – notably some of the more expensively made computer animation pieces – and whole programmes themselves will of course be repeated in the normal run of the television schedule.

In keeping with the ritualistic emphasis, there is also much emphasis on 'hellos' and 'goodbyes', addressed to the viewer, to the other Teletubbies and to the children in the documentary sequences. The Teletubbies frequently appear in a fixed sequence, from the tallest (Tinky Winky) to the smallest (Po), or vice-versa; and the arrival of each Teletubby is generally 'announced' in the voice-over. Each is also always associated with a favourite (transitional) object, a particular song (often heard before they appear) and with certain characteristic dance movements.

Within each programme, there is also a considerable amount of repetition. Aside from the instant repeat of the documentary sequence, the longer sketches often involve a high degree of repetition. For example, each of the four Teletubbies might encounter a particular situation or problem, and respond in similar ways. Many of the shorter sketches involve variants of Freud's 'fort/da' game (or 'peekaboo'), or a 'lost and found' story-line. Both in the structure of the programme as a whole, and in the Teletubby sketches in particular, there is therefore a high degree of redundancy. Viewers, it is assumed, will be able to predict how a particular sequence of events will turn out: the viewer often knows more than the individual Teletubbies, and can see the solution to a problem ahead of time. For example, when the Teletubbies play a hide-and-seek game, we are shown where they are hiding; and when a rain cloud comes to Teletubby land, Po discovers what an umbrella is for, long after viewers will have worked this out for themselves. The overall aim here is clearly to induce a feeling of security and self-confidence.

The longer sketches frequently involve forms of learning or problem-solving on the part of the Teletubbies. While there is occasional frustration and a degree of 'naughtiness' (notably on the part of Noo-Noo, the Teletubbies' self-propelled vacuum cleaner), there is generally very little overt conflict. While two of the Teletubbies are male (and larger in size) and two female, and while one of them (Dipsy) is darker-skinned, these differences are never remarked upon, let alone used as the basis for disputes between them. Of course, potential conflicts do occasionally arise. But even when the other Teletubbies run away from Laa-Laa's 'delightful' song, she gets to perform a duet with Noo-Noo; and when, in one sequence, Laa-Laa and Po argue about the use of Po's scooter, they quickly decide to share and take turns. In general, overt moral messages of this kind (which are heavily emphasized, for example, in *Barney*) are very rare. For the most part, conflict is either avoided or left unresolved.

The documentary sequences often feature children under-taking activities independently, or with minimal guidance from adults. For instance, we see children going on a country walk, making carnival costumes or picking strawberries. In other instances, children are seen helping adults, for instance with digging potatoes, hay-making or looking for butterflies. Adults occasionally act as instructors, explaining what the children should do, but they are more frequently seen as facilitators. In the large majority of cases, we see adults and children doing things together, rather than adults performing and children watching. Only in a few instances do children act as a means of access to adult 'experts' (a musician, for example, or a doctor). Even in these latter cases, however, the voice-over is spoken by the children; and the sequence is often shot from the child's height and point-of-view. In general, the emphasis here is on children's competence and independence – although the children shown are generally a couple of years older than the programme's target audience.

Both in the documentary sequences, and in the world of the Teletubbies themselves, there is an emphasis on open space. The childhood that is represented is, by and large, rural rather than urban. Like the Teletubbies, the children are free to wander autonomously, rather than relying on adults to transport them. There are no dangers or threats here, and no arbitrary constraints imposed by adults.

At the same time, there is a great deal in the programme that invites response. At some points, viewers are implicitly invited to guess which Teletubby will appear or be chosen – for example, when the documentary is transmitted into one of their tummy-screens, or when one of them waves goodbye at the very end of the programme. Particular play routines are modelled and re-peated, implicitly inviting viewers to join in. The use of nonsense language, dance and movement, noises and comical sound effects, and the general anarchy that occasionally erupts, all implicitly invite viewers to mimic and participate. Music is also particularly crucial here, and much of it is strongly rhythmic, with an emphasis on drums and tubas. The Teletubbies themselves are highly physical: they are perpetually falling over, waving their legs in the air, sticking out their stomachs, bumping into each other, marching, running, dancing and clapping; and the sketches often culminate in a collective 'big hug'. However, while the pace is occasionally frenetic, there are also moments of stasis: the programme's use of silence as a marker of transition from one sequence to another is particularly striking.

As this implies, the programme is far from traditionally didactic. There are no adults in the world of the Teletubbies. A kind of quasi-adult authority is represented by the old-fashioned speaker-phones that occasionally rise – apparently quite at random – both in the Teletubbies' home-bunker and in the surrounding coun-tryside. It is often the speaker-phones that convey the elements of traditional children's culture (such as songs and nursery rhymes) as well as issuing instructions to the Teletubbies. However, this authority is not always accepted. In one notable sequence, the speaker-phones repeatedly instruct the Teletubbies to 'sing a song of four'. Frustrated and bored by the didactic repetition (reminiscent, it must be said, of *Sesame Street*), they eventually refuse to sing, and run away. The voice-over narrator is also a representative of adult authority – for example in announcing 'time for Tubby bye-byes' in the bedtime ritual that ends the programme; although here too, the Teletubbies appear as naughty children, refusing to go to bed at the first attempt. There is certainly an element of adult appeal in the deadpan voice of the narrator (which is quite reminiscent of that in *The Magic Roundabout*). Overt irony is rare, however – although we are told that 'the Teletubbies *liked* Laa-Laa's song' when it is clear from their behaviour that they did not. Broadly speaking, then, adult authority is far from wholly accepted in the world of the Teletubbies.

If there is an overall didactic message to *Teletubbies*, it is probably to do with 'love'. 'Teletubbies,' we are frequently told, 'love each other *very* much'. The world of the Teletubbies is one of mutual affection, warmth and security: it is a comfortable, safe world, effectively devoid of conflict. In some respects, this is the traditional domestic/pastoral world of young children's fiction, and indeed of earlier pre-school programmes. Nevertheless, it is also a world of fantasy. The Teletubbies home-bunker is provided with a range of anarchic technology, from Noo-Noo the vacuum cleaner with a mind of its own through to the always unpredictable Tubby toaster; and the improbably green rural landscape that surrounds it is populated with talking flowers. Interestingly, the programme moves from the fantasy space of the Teletubbies into the real world of children, via the documentary sequences, rather than the other way round. 'Home' is as much a space of fantasy as of domestic realism.

Tradition and innovation

Despite its innovative approach, *Teletubbies* can in fact be understood in relation to three parallel traditions in British pre-school programming. These might be labelled 'educative', 'storytelling' and 'entertaining'. While these traditions obviously change and overlap, the origins of each of them can be detected in one of the very earliest British pre-school programmes, *Watch with Mother*, first broadcast in the early 1950s. *Watch with Mother* consisted of five different programme strands, screened on different weekdays. *Picture Book*, presented direct to camera by a highly 'teacherly' adult, was the most overtly educative strand; *The Woodentops* featured puppets in broadly realistic storytelling about a farming family; while *Bill and Ben* involved more surreal, nonsense-based entertainment.

The educative tradition underwent a transformation in the 1960s, not least because of the influence of progressivist educational theories. The BBC's more child-centred *Playschool* (1964) was followed in the early 1970s by ITV's *Rainbow*, and subsequently by shows such as *Playdays*. While *Teletubbies* is not studio based, and does not have adult presenters like these programmes, it shares their broadly child-centred approach, characterized by the use of documentary inserts featuring 'real life' children, the emphasis on learning through play and the use of songs and rhymes. It is worth recalling here the controversy that surrounded the BBC's refusal to buy the US series *Sesame Street* in the late 1960s. While there were several issues at stake here (not least an implicit rejection of American influences), the BBC refused to buy the series largely because of its explicitly didactic approach: the 'drilling' of letters and numbers in *Sesame Street* was seen to be fundamentally incompatible with the more 'progressivist', less instructional approach of British education.[13] To compare *Teletubbies* with, for example, *Barney* is to be reminded that there is still a remarkable divergence between the dominant educational philosophies on either side of the Atlantic.

This tradition overlaps to some extent with the 'storytelling' tradition. A line can be traced here from *The Woodentops* through programmes like *Camberwick Green* and *Trumpton* in the 1960s and *Postman Pat* and *Cockleshell Bay* in the 1970s to *Rosie and Jim, Tots TV* and *Fireman Sam* in the 1980s and 1990s. Programmes in this tradition are predominantly based in domestic or pastoral settings, representing the idealized communities of 'middle England'. There is often an implicit pedagogy here – with lessons about tolerance and sharing – but moral messages are rarely laid on thick. While *Teletubbies* obviously does not share the 'realist' emphasis of these programmes, nor the strong narrative emphasis, it could be seen to represent an ideal, pastoral community, both in the Teletubby sketches (which often begin

'One day in Teletubby-land ... ') and in its documentary sequences.

Finally – and perhaps most strongly – *Teletubbies* can also be seen as the most recent inheritor of a more surreal tradition of entertainment programming for very young children. This tradition, consisting largely of animation and puppet shows, can be traced from *Bill and Ben* in the 1950s and *The Magic Roundabout* in the 1960s, through to the series of the 1970s and 1980s that are currently being revived as 'cult classics' on cable and satellite channels – shows such as *The Clangers, The Moomins, Bagpuss* and *The Wombles*. Frequently surrealistic and bizarre, these programmes spoke more directly to the imagination: they featured anthropomorphic characters in fantasy worlds, and traded in nonsense, repetition and absurd humour. *Teletubbies'* indebtedness to this tradition is, in many respects, extremely obvious.

Teletubbies clearly draws on each of these traditions; and in this respect, it is perhaps much less innovative than is often suggested. Ultimately, however, it may be its *combination* of these traditions that has made it so troubling for many of its critics. While it shares the broad pedagogic approach of the educative tradition, it also departs from it in several ways – for example, by its neglect of domestic 'realism' and of the teacherly mediation provided by adult presenters. And while it shares some of the surrealism and fantasy of the entertainment tradition, *Teletubbies* also claims to be explicitly educative in its approach. The programme combines 'education' and 'entertainment' as well as 'real' and 'unreal' elements in ways that are potentially quite unsettling. Thus, the Teletubbies are both 'real' toddlers and 'unreal' fantasy figures, with aerials on their heads and televisions in their stomachs; their world is both 'real', with its real grass and its real rabbits, and 'unreal', with its self-powered vacuum cleaner and its talking flowers.

In this respect, *Teletubbies* – and the controversy it has provoked – may also reflect much broader tendencies in children's media culture. Of course, entertainment is always educational, in the sense that it is bound to teach us *something*; and education has to be entertaining in some way, at least if it is to succeed in engaging learners. Perhaps this distinction can itself be seen as false, or at least as an over-simplification – as generations of educators and media producers have argued. Yet in many areas, the relations between 'education' and 'entertainment' appear to be undergoing a fundamental change. And for those who are most resistant to change, maintaining this distinction appears to have become a fundamental imperative.

Child and adult audiences

All the evidence would suggest that *Teletubbies* has been extraordinarily popular with its primary target audience. Independent research has found that children enjoy the 'ritualistic' elements identified above – the familiarity of the characters, the repeated movements, the noises and colours – rather more than the actual narratives. In general, they respond to the programme's invitation to 'active viewing': far from being glued to the screen, they are often moving around, dancing, playing and singing along, predicting what will happen, asking and answering questions, and so on. At the same time, the programme also seems to involve different modalities of viewing, and the documentary sequences in particular encourage a quieter, more reflective approach. While younger children can find the programme challenging, for most older children it serves as a welcome form of relaxation.[14]

However, at least in its early days, *Teletubbies* also acquired a substantial cult status among older viewers. For example, the programme was an unavoidable topic of conversation in the north London primary school where I undertook some research a couple of years ago. Children of six and seven were often keen to disavow any interest in the programme, fiercely condemning it as 'babyish'. Yet by the time they reached the safety of nine or ten, they seemed to be able to relate to it with a kind of subversive irony – although there was still often a passionate rejection among those who had younger siblings. As this implies, the children's judgments about *Teletubbies* were closely tied up with their attempts to project themselves as more or less 'adult'.[15]

Likewise, colleagues who teach in secondary schools reported that *Teletubbies* regalia often adorned their students' exercise books and bags, and that there were several scatological or obscene versions of the theme song in circulation. The programme also appeared to have a substantial audience among undergraduates. In the months after it was first screened, several unofficial 'fan' websites emerged, apparently produced by students; and many new sites have appeared following the export of the programme to the USA. The majority of these are heavily – and not always subtly – ironic. While some are relatively affectionate – 'Moosie's Noo-Noo Shrine' – many reflect characteristic preoccupations with sex, violence and conspiracy – as in 'Teletubbies ate my balls', 'the Teletubbies conspiracy site' and 'Teletubbies are the children of Satan' (featuring 'Noo-Noo, the angel of death'). As with Barney some years ago, it is comparatively easy to locate pictures of the Teletubbies engaged in sexual orgies or being killed and dismembered in various gruesome ways. Meanwhile, *Teletubbies'* ironic youth cultural cachet was reflected in stories in the popular music papers *Melody Maker* and *NME*. However, perhaps the ultimate seal of youth cultural approval was granted in July 1997, when the leading style magazine *The Face* ran a five-page story on 'Teleclubbers'. Watching *Teletubbies*, it asserted, was now the coolest accompaniment to 'post-club comedown', as young ravers unwind from the chemically induced frenzy of the previous night.

The BBC has done its best to discourage this 'cult' audience, for example by threatening to prosecute unofficial web sites and by refusing to license the characters for adult clothing. On one level, this is about protecting its pre-school audience; although it is also, of course, about protecting its copyright. Ultimately, however, it is doubtful whether the cult status of such a programme is likely to be sustained for very long. As I have suggested, there is actually very little in the programme that is designed to provide adult appeal – unlike, for instance, *Sesame Street*, which is partly intended to be viewed by parents. Beyond the visual aspects of the programme, there is little opportunity for narrative engagement; and indeed, one of the 'jokes' about *Teletubbies* is that you have to be on mind-bending drugs in order to be able to watch it. For some young people, it may have temporarily been 'cool' to say that you watched *Teletubbies*; and for some adults, it may have briefly been required to hold an opinion about the show's educational merits. But it is hard to imagine that many of these people were likely to have watched the programme over the longer term. In fact, the cult status of *Teletubbies* among older children and young adults is now well past its peak: while not yet completely uncool, an enthusiasm for the programme is now likely to be seen as distinctly *passé*.

Nevertheless, the adult appropriation of *Teletubbies* could be seen to reflect a more general sense of irony which increasingly

suffuses contemporary popular culture. As I argue in the introduction to this book, adults' relationships with children's culture
often display a complex mixture of nostalgic affection and ironic
disavowal. Responses to *Teletubbies* are symptomatic of this
ambivalence. On the one hand, the programme invites a comforting return to a 'cute' world of childhood innocence. Yet on the
other, it seems to encourage a degree of ironic distance, particularly by means of the deadpan delivery of the narrator and the
hyper-reality of its design and *mise en scène*.

From one perspective, the passing success of *Teletubbies* with
young people and adults could be seen as a form of regression or
infantilization – or at least, as further evidence of the blurring of
boundaries between children and adults. Yet it could also be
interpreted as a necessary process of recovering 'childlike' pleasures – in silly noises and games, in anarchy and absurdity – for
which irony provides a convenient alibi.

Conclusion

Interpreting any children's programme – and perhaps particularly
one aimed at a very young audience – is fraught with difficulties.
As adults, we are not the intended audience; and as such, there is
a significant risk of 'misreading', taking things too literally, or
simply lapsing into pretentiousness. It is all too easy to dismiss
such programmes as boring or simplistic, or alternatively to find
them cute or anarchic or surrealistic – responses which could be
seen as characteristic of how adults relate to children generally.
The danger here is that we end up simply imposing adult categories, and thereby making unwarranted assumptions about
viewers. Spotting the intertextual references and symbolic asso-
ciations, or alternatively 'hunting the stereotypes', are easy games
to play; but they tell us very little about how children themselves
interpret and relate to what they watch.

Perhaps it is this inherent instability – and the blurring of
boundaries that it seems to entail – that has made *Teletubbies* the
ideal vehicle for adults' concerns and fantasies. Yet in the end, our
responses to it may tell us much more about ourselves than they
do about its intended audience.

Acknowledgements

I would like to thank Peter Kelley and Hannah Davies for their assistance with the research for this chapter. This work was undertaken as part of an ESRC-funded project on 'Children's Media Culture' (L126251026), based at the Institute of Education, University of London.

Notes

1. I discuss these issues at much greater length in my book *After the Death of Childhood: Growing Up in the Age of Electronic Media* (Cambridge: Polity, 2000).
2. For a discussion of broadcasting policy under the Conservatives, see P. Goodwin, *Television Under the Tories* (London: British Film Institute, 1999).
3. For a critical review of these debates, and of the broader historical and economic context, see David Buckingham, Hannah Davies, Ken Jones and Peter Kelley, *Children's Television in Britain: History, Discourse and Policy* (London: British Film Institute, 1999).
4. Anna Home, 'Teletubbies', *TelevIZIon* 11 (2), 24–8, 1998.
5. For a useful discussion of this issue, see Ellen Seiter, *Sold Separately: Parents and Children in Consumer Culture* (New Brunswick: Rutgers University Press, 1993).
6. For discussions of the press coverage, see Anne White, 'To be blamed: the press in Britain' and Sue Howard and Susan Roberts, *Teletubbies* down under: the Australian experience', both in *TelevIZIon* 12 (2), 1999, pp. 15–19 and 19–25 respectively.
7. There are significant parallels here with the press coverage of *EastEnders*: see David Buckingham, *Public Secrets: EastEnders and its Audience* (London: British Film Institute, 1987), Chapter 3.
8. This was the case for Kinder Kanal in Germany, for instance: see 'It won't work without breaking taboos', an interview with Albert Schafer of Kinder Kanal, in *TelevIZIon* 12 (2), 5–7, 1999.
9. Again, some of this material is presented and discussed in *TelevIZIon* 12 (2), 1999.
10. See Horst Stipp, 'Under fire from American programme criticism', *TelevIZIon* 12 (2), 26–7, 1999; and the information provided on the PBS website, www.pbs.org/teletubbies.
11. See Stipp, 'Under Fire'.
12. These arguments are most clearly articulated on the web site, www.pbs.org/teletubbies. I am also drawing here on an interview

with Hannah Davies and Peter Kelley conducted in February 1997 as part of our ESRC project; and on a special feature in the *Radio Times*, 27 September 1997. For further discussion of child-centredness in television, see Buckingham *et al.*, *Children's Television in Britain*, Chapter 6; and my articles 'The construction of subjectivity in educational television. Part one: Towards a new Agenda', *Journal of Educational Television* 13 (2), 137–46, 1987, and 'Part two: *You and Me* – a case study', *Journal of Educational Television* 13 (3), 187–200, 1987.

13. This is discussed more fully in Buckingham *et al.*, *Children's Television in Britain*, Chapter 2. Máire Messenger Davies provides a definitive comparison between the British pedagogic tradition and that of *Sesame Street* in her piece 'Babes 'n' the hood: Preschool television and its audiences in the United States and Britain', in Cary Bazalgette and David Buckingham (eds), *In Front of the Children* (London: British Film Institute, 1995).

14. Again, see the studies contained in *TelevIZIon* 12 (2), 1999, particularly the article by Maya Götz, 'Children are enchanted, parents concerned', 50–9.

15. For further discussion, see Hannah Davies, David Buckingham and Peter Kelley, 'In the worst possible taste? Children, television and cultural value', *European Journal of Cultural Studies* 3 (1), 5–25, 2000.

CHAPTER 4

'Tell Me about Your Id, When You Was a Kid, Yah!'[1]

Animation and Children's Television Culture

PAUL WELLS

Often dismissed as a significant art-form and explicitly contextualized as 'merely' children's entertainment, animation has, in
recent years, received a greater degree of critical attention, foregrounding its distinctive language and its capacity to accommodate a range of potentially subversive or alternative meanings.[2]
Arguably, children have always enjoyed animation from this
perspective, engaging with the range of possibilities it offers, from
some of the more traumatic emotional effects in Disney features,[3]
through the 'gag' orientations of the cartoon, to the educational
constructs available in children's programmes like *Sesame Street*.

This chapter will be particularly concerned with the range of
generic approaches to animation that has characterized the output
in American television schedules since the 1950s, placing special
emphasis on the most popular forms, and those which have been
successful globally. Consideration will be given to the content and
impact of the early Disney series on ABC, and the rise of cheaply
made 'limited' or 'planned' animation[4] programming by Hanna–
Barbera. Further, some points will be made about the accom-
modation and influence of 'classic' animation – principally, the
Warner Bros. *Looney Tunes* and *Merrie Melodies* – as it established itself on television in what might nominally be regarded as
the 'post-theatrical' era. The chapter will also address the emergence of action-adventure cartoons (mainly based on 'superhero'
comic strips); quasi-sitcoms (echoing dominant models in live

action); 'cult' cartoons (often drawing from a classical tradition); and educational models which have maintained the presence of the independent production companies in the television output and economy. Central to this discussion, however, will be two key case studies pertinent to all of these areas. The first is a comparison of Hanna–Barbera's prime-time sitcom, *The Flintstones*, with the Fox Network's popular and ground-breaking series, *The Simpsons*; the second, an account of the relationship between Hanna–Barbera's classic *Tom and Jerry* MGM cartoons and the sometimes controversial *The Ren and Stimpy Show*, made by John Kricfalusi.

The continuing circulation of cartoons in television schedules has ensured that the aesthetic and socio-cultural agendas of the animated form established in what is now acknowledged as 'the golden era' of animation between 1928 and 1946[5] have remained central to debates about the art of animation and its maintenance, and bigger debates concerning its place within children's programming. These debates have fed into institutional approaches to the cost-effective production and execution of animation for television, and been informed by how animated programmes have been received and perceived by parents and children alike. An interesting example here is *The Ren and Stimpy Show*, discussed more fully below. Nickelodeon's market research test-screenings using sample audiences demonstrated that both adults and children uniformly preferred *Doug* and *Rugrats* as entertaining cartoon series, but Nickelodeon's commissioning editors retained the project on the basis that *The Ren and Stimpy Show* was the cartoon that observably and self-evidently children laughed at most.[6]

This immediately raises issues concerning the tensions between animation predicated on maintaining social and ideological consensus – effectively the premise of *Doug* and *Rugrats* – and the 'alternative' agendas and textual variations available in cartoons which potentially liberate children from a previously determined moral or cultural order – represented in this example by *The Ren and Stimpy Show*, but equally applicable to *The Simpsons* or *Beavis and Butthead*. A central aspect in this tension is the difference between what may be regarded as *creator-driven* projects and *process-driven* work, a key determinant which has characterized the whole history of production in animation, and which finds special purchase in the more limited exhibition context of television; though clearly, with the increasingly expansive number of channels available to viewers in the digital era, and vast amounts of broadcast space needing to be filled, the televisual context may enter a period of radical change. This in itself will necessitate a need to engage with aesthetic strategies; institutional and economic contexts; and the impact and effect of particular kinds of representation concerned with identity and social and/or educational achievement in a different light. The following discussion seeks to begin this process.

The rise of the television cartoon

In October 1954, *Disneyland* debuted on American television, ushering in a recognition that television was to compete with, and eventually surpass, film as a popular medium. The success of the show, and particularly in the first instance the appeal of the live-action 'Davy Crockett' saga, both enabled ABC to gain an established foothold in the struggles over ownership and control played out by the vying networks, and shift the emphasis of influence and effect from New York to Hollywood, back to the 'players' in the film community keen to establish themselves in the 'new' medium. *Disneyland* was a top ten ratings success, and essentially saved a financially ailing ABC through its appeal to a family audience, but most specifically to children. Scheduled against the work of artists like Arthur Godfrey, renowned for variety shows which drew an older demographic, *Disneyland* successfully found an adult audience who were re-familiarizing themselves with the cartoons they had seen in their own child-hoods (and at the zenith of Disney's public profile and popularity), and the children's audience who were seeing some of the Disney shorts for the first time in the comfort of their own homes. Significantly, Disney saw television as a way of marketing the rest of the Disney franchise, most notably the new theme park in Anaheim, California. The *Disneyland* programme itself was divided into four categories – 'Frontierland', 'Tomorrowland', 'Adventureland' and 'Fantasyland' – which echoed the four areas of the theme park, 'Fantasyland' mainly featuring cartoons. This ensured that there was also an enduring market for Disney's cinema output, which had become less successful by this time. The hour-long television version of the 75-minute feature *Alice in*

Wonderland (1951) was clear evidence of the way in which cartoons would be re-cycled through revision and repeat, speaking favourably to the new economies of television production. In 1958, the series moved to NBC, and became first *Walt Disney Presents*, and then *Walt Disney's Wonderful World of Color*, essentially a vehicle to promote NBC's parent company RCA's production of colour televisions, by once again foregrounding a mixture of classic cartoons and some startling nature photography. Crucially, Disney's output represented a 'modernization' of children's programming. *The Mickey Mouse Club*, for example, engaged with children in a different way from the homespun 'amateurism' of *Howdy Doody*. As Steven Stark has suggested:

> *Howdy Doody* was New York, live, with adult performers and a studio audience; *Mouse Club* was Hollywood, on film, with child performers but no studio audience. Because *Howdy Doody* was live (which meant no repeats) it was less profitable. Though both 'named' characters weren't real, one was a marionette, one was a cartoon character. The future belonged to the mouse.[7]

While the Disney studio embraced the television revolution, seeing the potential of re-defining their output accordingly, other studios were less enamoured, perceiving animation production in general as uneconomic, and closing units accordingly. William Hanna and Joseph Barbera, named heads of production at MGM in 1955, and seemingly secure in their reputation and achievements with the *Tom and Jerry* cartoons from the 1940s, suffered this fate early in 1957. Escalating costs of film production *per se* and, ironically, the increasing impact and effect of television in general, caused studios to re-think production in a cost-effective way. In halting the production of new cartoons, and selling the back catalogue of cartoon shorts, both MGM and later, Warner Bros., who finally closed their theatrical cartoon division in 1964, found the most economically efficient way of dealing with the crisis. Of greater significance, however, was the way Hanna–Barbera found production methods by which animation on television could be cost effective. At first suggesting new animation as 'bookends' to the re-packaging of old cartoons, Hanna–Barbera persuaded CBS's John Mitchell, Head of Sales at Screen Gems, to support the concept of 'limited' or 'planned' animation in the creation of new characters, 'Ruff' and 'Reddy', a cat and dog pairing allied against such villainous counterparts as Scary Harry

Safari and the Goon of Glocca Morra. Premièring in December 1957 on NBC, *The Ruff and Reddy Show*, hosted by Jimmy Blaine and a number of puppet characters, was broadcast in black and white, but the cartoons were made in colour in anticipation of the inevitability of colour television, and the equally inevitable profits made from syndication. As Barry Putterman has remarked: '[Hanna–Barbera's] financial success with this strategy unalterably changed the direction of Hollywood studio animation.'[8]

Warner Bros. began making direct-to-television cartoons in 1960, like MGM, re-packaging post-1948 cartoons with new 'bridging' animation. *The Bugs Bunny Show* premièred on ABC and was produced by veterans Chuck Jones and Friz Freleng. This served to showcase cartoon shorts to a new audience, and in some senses foregrounded the previous achievements of the 'golden era', arguably both pointing up the deficiencies of the new made-for-television animation that was to compete with it in the schedules, but also encouraging a reflexive relationship between the two 'styles'. Chuck Jones suggests that 'Saturday morning cartoons' were essentially 'illustrated radio' in which the dialogue had prominence over the visual and graphic elements, adding 'the drawings are different, but everybody acts the same way, moves their feet the same way, and runs the same way. It doesn't matter whether it's an alligator or a man or a baby or anything.'[9] Crucially, this emphasis on dialogue, and 'voice' rather than 'sound', is one of the key determining factors in the way 'animation' became subject to changing perceptions among its audience. The intonations and dynamics of Hanna–Barbera's voice artists – Daws Butler, Don Messick and June Foray – in defining 'characters' supplanted the urban *cacophony* of Warner Bros. and MGM cartoons and the more *symphonic* sound cultures of Disney films,[10] allying the cartoon to the model of theatrical performance which also dominated early television drama and situation comedy. This 'demotion' of the intrinsic vocabulary of animation in its own right has determined that 'animation' itself has been perceived differently by the generation who were ostensibly brought up on made-for-television cartoons, and those viewing generations thereafter, who use the Hanna–Barbera series from the late 1950s onwards as their point of comparison to new animation, and not the works of the 'golden era'.

From the late 1950s to the present day, the social and economic terrain of the 'Saturday morning cartoon' in the United States has been fiercely contested by the main networks, ABC, CBS and NBC.[11] Live-action series produced to appeal to children were often cancelled when it was realized that cartoons performed better in the re-run cycle, and thus became more cost effective, in the sense that fewer cartoons could be broadcast on more occasions over a longer time frame. In the early 1960s, NBC prospered with both *The Ruff and Ready Show* and *The Bullwinkle Show*, but by 1964 the latter show had transferred to ABC and was broadcast with *The Jetsons*, following its successful run in prime time. In the following season, ABC both consolidated and pioneered in their approach to the Saturday morning slots, premièring *The Beatles*, made in England by TVC, deliberately seeking to find the adult/child crossover audience already aware of, and participating in, the cultural success of the 'Fab Four'. This principle of producing cheaply made cartoons which sought to embrace cross-over audiences or already established demographics became an intrinsic approach within television animation in the United States, though interestingly, not in Britain.[12] Series about popular music groups followed with *The Jackson 5ive* in 1971 and *The Osmonds* in 1972. Again, in 1967, ABC broke new ground with the introduction of *The Fantastic Four* and *Spiderman*, animations based on popular comic books, which already had a committed fan base and market. Though CBS were partially successful in response with their comic-strip adaptation of *The Archies* in 1969, their competitive edge ironically returned in the re-packaging of classic Warner Bros. cartoons in *The Bugs Bunny/Roadrunner Show*; but ratings success for the network was properly achieved in the next season with the *Wacky Races* spin-offs, *Dastardly and Muttley* and *The Perils of Penelope Pitstop*, and the appeal of *Scooby Doo, Where Are You?*. Scooby survived on Saturday morning television for the next twenty years, and is still one of the most popular cartoon characters on Cartoon Network.

Crucial to the advances in the Saturday morning cartoon schedules, however, were animated versions of popular prime-time series. *The Brady Kids* followed on from the live-action *The Brady Bunch* in 1972; *The New Adventures of Gilligan, My Favorite Martians* and *Jeannie* based on the live-action sitcoms, *Gilligan's Island, My Favorite Martian* and *I Dream of Jeannie* were made between 1973 and 1974; *The Fonz and the Happy Days Gang* based on *Happy Days* debuted in 1980; versions of *Laverne and Shirley* and *Mork and Mindy* followed; and *The*

Dukes, based on *The Dukes of Hazzard*, began in 1982, interestingly scheduled against *Pac-man*, the first of the computer-game inspired animations that have reached their recent zenith with *Pokémon*. In general, though, the 1970s and 1980s were characterized by animation which was uninspired and aesthetically redundant. The form was merely employed as a graphic echo of live-action forms, extending the shelf-life of popular series by using what had become *the* visual language by which it was assumed children were addressed. The television generation only essentially understood 'animation' as 'the cartoon' as it had been produced for television and for the children's demographic. This became extended when television producers realized that the television generation were once again becoming a new movie generation in the 1980s with the rise of the multiplex, and that the line between fast-maturing children and 'young people' was increasingly blurred. Consequently, animated versions of *The Real Ghostbusters*, the Michael J. Fox vehicle *Teen Wolf* and *Beetlejuice* quickly followed on from their movie successes; a model that continues in the contemporary era with animations like *Men in Black* and *Jumanji*. The final cross-over area was inevitable. Will Vinton's *The California Raisins* graduated from their status as popular characters in commercials to secure their own series. Increasingly, the interface between a cartoon and its possible merchandising was effectively effaced in series like *Thundercats*, when concerns were raised by parents that series were only being created by and for toy manufacturers, working in their own interests.[13]

Subversive animation?

Cartoons had not lost their ability to be controversial, however. *Mighty Mouse*, which debuted in 1942, produced by Terrytoons, in its early years made an occasional nod to Fleischeresque sauciness in their bashful hero's engagement with feminine protagonists like Krakatoa Katy – 'She ain't no lady when she starts to shake her sarong!'. *Mighty Mouse* also moved with the times, his 'Superman'-like evolution in the 1940s and 1950s governed by everything from the consumption of foodstuffs newly available in the post-war period; the taking of vitamins in the suburbanite, health-conscious early 1950s; the absorption of atomic energy, still the currency of Cold War diplomacy; or through his acknowledged 'alien' powers, once again chiming with post-Roswell invasion anxieties. *Mighty Mouse* only featured in his own cartoons, however, in last minute appearances, when hollering 'Here I come to save the day!', and doing exactly that. The character became more central to the more melodramatic adventures that emerged throughout the 1950s, and in the reincarnations of the cartoon in the *Mighty Mouse Playhouse* in 1955 and *The Adventures of Mighty Mouse and Heckle & Jeckle* in 1979, where he was also used in educational contexts to advise children about the environment, encouraging them not to drop litter or sully forested areas. This morally sound, socially aware Mighty Mouse was to change slightly, however, in the more self-reflexive *Mighty Mouse: The New Adventures*, beginning in 1987.

These Ralph Bakshi-directed *Mighty Mouse* cartoons of the late 1980s were made by a team including a young John Kricfalusi, later the creator of *The Ren and Stimpy Show*, and they reflected a much more self-conscious appreciation of cartoon culture and tradition, most particularly in the ways that subversive representations and agendas could be 'invisibly' placed within the seemingly innocent and 'unregulatable' space of the cartoon form. In this, Bakshi was influenced by Jay Ward's *Rocky and his Friends*, which engaged in social satire, and provoked the censor with 'hidden' improprieties.[14] Bakshi, a Terrytoons veteran from 1956, often unsettled the studio with his claims to 'auteurism',[15] later fully justified, of course, through his work in *Fritz the Cat* (1972), *Heavy Traffic* (1973) and *Coonskin* (1975). Having achieved some success with his *Mighty Heroes* cartoons in the late 1960s, he was a self-evident choice to revive Mighty Mouse's fortunes. The new cartoons parodied other cartoons like *Alvin and the Chipmunks* (as Elwy and the Tree Weasels), *Batman* (Bat-Bat and Tick, the Bug-Wonder, who drove a Man-mobile) and *An American Tail* (Scrappy, an orphan mouse, a critical take on Spielberg's over-sentimentalized Fievel), and were clearly more 'adult' in their outlook. So much so, that the Reverend Wildmon of the American Family Association alleged that one cartoon, *The Little Tramp* (1989), depicted drug abuse in the act of inhaling cocaine, though to more innocent eyes this may look like the sniffing of a crushed flower.[16] This event did irreparable damage to the series: in spite of the fact that the offending three and a half seconds were removed, and (somewhat ironically) the series won an award from another parent watchdog group, Action for Children's Television (ACT), *Mighty Mouse: The New Adventures* was cancelled. These events alone are enough to show that the pedagogic role of the animated television cartoon has always been closely monitored by a variety of advocacy groups, on the one hand acknowledging the persuasiveness of animated characters in entertaining and educating children, and on the other, bringing 'adult' eyes to the censorship of imagery that is deemed unsuitable for children, yet which at the same time would not necessarily be noticed by them.

This was also the case with the apparently alternative agendas of *The Garbage Pail Kids*, who were perceived as endorsing misguided values which might adversely affect children and their behaviour. Even though these particular cartoons caused small-scale moral panics, this was largely uncommon as animators became self-censoring. Curiously, though, it remained the case that cartoons, however innocuous, were still viewed with suspicion, caution and sometimes overt hostility – issues seemingly emerging out of adult anxiety about an aesthetic which on the face of it seemed innocent and child-centred, but which was nevertheless an aesthetic produced by adults. Clearly, there was some recognition by advocacy groups – among them The National Coalition on Television Violence and the National Federation for Decency – that theatrical cartoons of 'the golden era' did have adult themes, and that Warner Bros. shorts did deliberately 'play' to adults. The Fleischer Brothers were also notorious for the sexual imagery of their Betty Boop cartoons.[17] The legacy of the racier, more surreal, more 'cartoonal' aesthetic of the 1930s and 1940s was an underlying suspicion about the motives of the artists and an anxiety about the apparent freedoms of the graphic idiom. Even though it was quite clear that the television aesthetic could not share these qualities, and that the artists responsible for the new era of television cartoons were fully aware of the moral and social constraints imposed upon representation in programmes by the Broadcast Standards and Practices Department, the threat of 'anarchy' in the cartoon remained. In some contexts, this view was critically endorsed. Radical critic Harlan Ellison passionately opposed the regulatory apparatus for comics, inspired by the campaigns of Dr Frederic Wertham, and spoke out in defence of television cartoons which seemingly raised the same concerns among parents. Writing in 1968, Ellison claimed that cartoons worked as 'a genuine training ground for [children's] thinking' and contained 'tolerable terror' and useful 'simplifications of the complex world of good-and-bad, when they are at an intellectual age when they cannot grasp the subtleties of inter-personal relationships and global politics', adding 'there is nothing on prime time to compare with the social comment and satire' in some children's cartoons.[18]

Ben Crawford has noted that this 'television aesthetic', though, has consequently had significant effects, both in the ways that such cartoons have since been evaluated and understood, and in the subsequent ways that animation has been made for television. He notes that 'almost all discussion of TV cartoons for kids adheres to a single model and participates in a single discourse – the condemnation of cartoons on TV on the basis that they contribute to the corruption of children, to a televisual *détournement de mineurs*'.[19] More controversially, he adds that the generation first watching television cartoons has a sensibility which is directly reflected in these animations:

> . . . that generation wants and receives a culture which is high on impact and low on significance, without any basis or need for justification; . . . their response to the imperatives of any system of values is cynical at its most energetic and usually exaggeratedly phlegmatic or insouciant. They live precisely beyond freedom and dignity, contemptuous of both the discipline of non-violence and the structures of meaning. In short their desires correspond to the features of the Saturday morning cartoons on which they were raised.[20]

Though self-evidently a highly contentious generalization, this perspective does suggest some points which are worthy of address, and serves once again to inform an analysis of how animation on television has changed, but also remained responsive to the new (sub-)cultural contexts in which it finds itself.

If, as Crawford implies, cartoons engage with, promote and endorse an ideologically charged and seemingly amoral model of cultural 'difference' or 'otherness', it is crucial to identify whether this argument can be sustained, both in relation to what is now regarded as the finest period of television animation, the 1960s and early 1970s, and the subsequent evolution of the television cartoon in the 1980s and 1990s. For example, and in anticipation of my later discussion, *The Simpsons* is arguably an inevitable product of the cultural influence exerted by the 'baby-boomer' generation Crawford speaks of, while *The Ren and Stimpy Show* works as a self-conscious parody of the aesthetic codes and conventions of the animation-for-television era, played out through the cultural identities of the late millennium. Further, the brutalist minimalism of *Beavis and Butthead* and its correspondence to the 'slacker' generation may be both an anti-culture critique and a statement about the redundancy of visual cultures[21] in the same way that *King of the Hill* reveals the limitations of 'naturalism' and 'gags' within the (live-action) sitcom. It remains then to trace how the television cartoon has addressed its material and engaged with its adult/child audiences, and assess what effects may be identified through this process.

From 'yabba dabba do' to 'yabba dabba don't'

In 1956, Alberta Siegal published her findings on the relationship between aggressive behaviour in children and the viewing of animated cartoons. Simply, she concluded that children who had viewed the slapstick violence of *Woody Woodpecker* behaved no differently from those who had viewed *The Little Red Hen*, a non-violent cartoon.[22] This report proved unusual in the sense that most studies sought to conclude that animated cartoons were harmful and encouraged imitative behaviour. Most influential in this respect were Albert Bandura's famous 'bobo doll' studies during the 1960s, which simplistically suggested that children aped the violent behaviour of a cartoon-like clown character by re-enacting similar kinds of aggression towards a bobo-doll after viewing the clown in a quasi-televisual context.[23] This tension between the influence and effects of cartoons, and their subsequent uses and gratifications, has informed debates about the genre since its absorption into television culture, and little has been resolved. However, one of the most significant developments which shifted the terms and conditions of the debate was the emergence of *The Flintstones* as the first 'prime-time' animation.

If child psychologists had been concerned with effects, a continuing lobby remained concerned about the art of animation. Leonard Maltin argues 'the cartoons produced by Hanna Barbera and their legion of imitators are consciously bad: assembly line shorts grudgingly executed by cartoon veterans who hate what they're doing', adding that 'the same canned music, the same gags, the same sound effects and gimmicks, and the same characters in different guises ... [most notably] the tall and a short sidekick wore out its welcome'.[24] Self-evidently, William Hanna and Joe Barbera did not set out to make 'consciously bad' cartoons – their credentials had long been established in the classic *Tom and Jerry* cartoons of the 1940s – but they recognized that 'limited animation', a drastically different and comparatively 'artless' approach, was their only alternative in sustaining 'cartoons' of any sort in a major marketplace. The emphasis was placed less on 'animation' (i.e. the execution and quality of 'movement') and more on comic writing and engaging design. Accents, catchphrases, rhymes and verbal jokes became more important than any complex 'physical' sight-gags, while character design was predicated on what William Hanna describes as 'a pleasing and congenial appearance that would appeal to children ... [a look that would] arouse interest or excitement in a child but never fear or revulsion', and whose personality may be likened to the charisma of a live-action actor, 'a quality composed of both an intangible essence and specific mechanics'.[25] There is little here that suggests any of the subversion that previously was arguably almost inherent in the cartoon short; and indeed, there is significant concession to the needs and demands of television – a simple sense of 'flat', two-dimensional theatricality, played out through the 'proscenium arch' of the television screen; and an enhanced sense of performance by predictable and consistent characters, who exchange personality for 'celebrity' in acting as a cipher for simple and accessible ideological, ethical or moral archetypes. Huckleberry Hound did not possess the moral ambivalence of Bugs Bunny; Yogi Bear does not engage in the social disruption on the scale of the not infrequently 'insane' Daffy Duck. The reference point of the Hanna–Barbera cartoon was not its own instability but the certainties of the material world.

The Huckleberry Hound Show won an Emmy in 1959, and featured not merely the multi-identitied Huckleberry Hound, but two other popular stalwarts of the Hanna–Barbera output, Pixie and Dixie (with Jinx, the cat) and Yogi Bear. Yogi was part-modelled on Art Carney's Ed Norton from *The Honeymooners*, and represents the first direct referencing to sitcoms of the period, and an example of the symbiotic relationship between television animation and the sitcom thereafter. Quick Draw McGraw, Snooper and Blabber, and Augie Doggie and Doggie Daddy (1959–1963) became equally popular characters, foregrounding the talents of story-men like Michael Maltese and Warren Foster, who were merely secondary figures to the director in the hey-day of the cartoon short. Sponsored by Kelloggs, Hanna–Barbera cartoons featured on over one hundred stations and enjoyed a circulation throughout the day, often being broadcast in early evening slots which anticipated a prime-time scheduling position. Screen Gems' John Mitchell approached Hanna–Barbera and asked them to consider creating a half-hour series, using animated people rather than animals, which might have the potential longevity of a situation comedy. *The Flintstones* (1960–6), directly predicated on the already successful series, *The Honeymooners*, featuring Jackie Gleason as Ralph Kramden, was essentially root-ed in the suburban family narratives of the early 1950s sitcom (such as *I Love Lucy* and *Father Knows Best*) but enjoyed the comic incongruity of playing out the consumer artefacts of post-war modernity in the context of the Stone Age. Equally incon-gruous were the show's initial sponsors – Winston Cigarettes (Reynolds Tobacco Company) and One-a-Day Vitamins (Miles Laboratories) – who recognized and invested in the originality of the concept, believing it to have an intrinsic 'difference' yet a culturally acceptable 'familiarity' which made it commercially appealing.

Though broadcast in prime-time, *The Flintstones* retained its children's audience. Though critics were initially hostile,[26] it also gained its intended adult audience. Fundamental to the pro-gramme's success (and repeated later in *The Simpsons*) is the importance of the role played by what Richard Butsch has termed 'the White Male Working-Class Buffoon'.[27] Fred Flintstone represented one of the few portrayals of working-class fathers in the 1960s, a mark of the predominance of a middle-class con-sumer ethos in most programming. Sponsors were assured that the representation of affluence and comfort would encourage viewers to aspire to these conditions and buy the relevant household items. *The Flintstones*, in not actually portraying the post-war suburban home and, indeed, using many of its tenets for satiric or parodic effect, needed to create an empathetic character who illustrated the vicissitudes of paternalist aspiration as well as domestic achievement. Fred and his neighbour Barney are at their most sympathetic when trying to improve their social status and move into other realms of 'culture'. Similarly, their schemes to get more money, or evade the threat of unemployment, play out anxieties about how the roles and functions of family and social life may be defined and acted out. Their recurrent 'failure' – essentially an acceptance of, and need for, the status quo – reinforces a consensual view of domestic order which casts Wilma and Betty, their wives, as sensible, supportive and pragmatic; the workplace as a context in which the established hierarchy is rarely challenged; and 'society' as a mechanism which can generate and secure the populist notions of individual achievement, good neighbourliness, community support and institutional success, as long as power remains in the right hands.

Though the limited animation style of the Hanna–Barbera studio was much criticized, the very language of animation as the facilitator of impossible events and situations was self-evidently crucial in creating a pre-historic environment in which the modern physical and material world is re-determined through visual puns and the free use of graphic illusion. Elephant trunks become gasoline pumps; bird-beaks become hi-fi styli; a pterodactyl (a creature that only exists through graphic representation) becomes an aeroplane; and so on. The 'gags' essentially emerge from the exploitation of incongruous pictorial similarities in the *mise en scène* and the collapse of the historically determined social functions of objects as they are understood in the 'modern' world. Arguably, this in some senses distracts from the quasi-hegemonic project being played out in *The Flintstones*, which is later fore-grounded and self-consciously parodied in *The Simpsons*. The playfulness of the narrative context, and the exploitation of a basic 'cartoonalness', most notably in the caricatural paradigms and 'fantastic' juxtapositions, is also enhanced by the linguistic aspects of the programme in which verbal puns and language-based sight gags are predicated on an often wonderfully tenuous relationship to rocks, stones, pebbles, and so on. This centrality of the visual pun often undermines the narrational and thematic consistencies which may be drawn from the text. Hollywood actor Tony Curtis inevitably becomes Stoney Curtis; Leonard Bernstein becomes Leonard Bernstone, and so on. Popular culture is drawn upon as the vehicle by which to secure adult identification, a strategy adopted much earlier, for example by Warner Bros. in the 1930s and 1940s, whose cartoons parodied their own live-action artists. This level of identification tends to heighten the comic elements of the cartoon while demoting some of the overt situational tensions about class and social aspiration, which become more readily understood as 'sentimental' issues.

Children, visually literate in the modes of graphic caricature as a result of their engagement with a range of illustrative tropes in children's literature and, indeed, well versed in their engagement with various modes of 'the cartoon' (rarely subject to any sense of variousness or distinction within the genre, or across styles, by adult audiences), readily engage with the aesthetic space of *The Flintstones* and its contingent familiarity. This, after all, is an imaginative reconstruction of the family, the domestic environment, and contemporary culture, but one enjoyed from the safe position afforded both by its displacement from its apparent historical context – the Stone Age – and by its recognizable status as cartoonal artifice. It is in this aspect that children as an audience have often been misrepresented, in the sense that they have always constituted a more sophisticated audience than is sometimes acknowledged. A recent study undertaken by the Independent Television Commission in Britain confirmed once more that children could distinguish between 'reality' and its cartoonal representation, and recognized that the artifice of the graphic space contextualized the characters, situations and experience that they were viewing.[28] Though, unsurprisingly, boys and girls viewed differently, and displayed different levels of investment and identification, it was clear that cartoonal 'behaviours' exemplified in certain characters emerged as a consequence of their status as 'cartoon' characters and not 'real' people. This enables children to accept conflict and confrontation in shows like *The Flintstones* as being intrinsically different from its representation in a live-action situation comedy or soap opera. In being an art of the 'unreal', animation, in however a basic a form, converts physical and material 'contexts' into mutable and ephemeral 'texts'. Children therefore readily perceive cartoon violence as slapstick; understand cartoon conflict as the vehicle for humour; and enjoy cartoon confrontation as a mode in which opposing 'forces' seem to symbolize an abstract tension between different ideas and issues. It is in the latter area that children may engage with the moral and ethical framework in which the ideas and issues may be couched; but it is likely that this level of engagement will work predominantly at a more personal, and potentially idiosyncratic, level, since it still needs to transcend the 'distanciation' caused by its cartoonal context.

It is inevitable that adults viewing the same texts will in many senses be watching something entirely different. The scale of adult socialization distanciates the cartoon from 'reality' in another way. The 'cartoon' is not regarded as different because it represents an intrinsic artifice, but because it is a thing of another time and place, a childhood 'text', now watched in a spirit of 'pastness', and possibly nostalgia, but most importantly, with an adult sensibility. The adult viewer watches differently, articulating sub-texts and other levels of meaning, noting the reference points, and participating in a way that acknowledges the capacity of the animation medium to use graphic artifice for the purposes of offering alternative perspectives on the material world. This means that on the one hand, for example, when Fred tries to surprise Wilma with a tenth anniversary wedding gift of a 'Stoneway' piano, purchased for $50 from a streetside shyster, '88 Fingers Louis', this can degenerate into a set of 'runaway' piano gags in the spirit of Laurel and Hardy's *The Music Box* (1932); while on the other hand, there is a gag where Wilma believes she witnesses a piano passing by, but is reassured by Fred with the words, 'A piano? It's merely a manifestation of your sub-conscious clashing with your conscious, which in turn is a logical outgrowth of a possible musical frustration, coupled with the cucumbers you had for dinner!' An 'everyday' scenario of a well-intended anniversary surprise demonstrates Fred's aspiration, naivety, integrity and foolhardiness, but it also signals the 'knowingness' of the creators of *The Flintstones* in foregrounding a parody of psychoanalytic explanation for a 'dream', which had in effect been a surreal moment of 'actuality' in the narrative. This one example signals a self-conscious knowledge of the parameters of the animated terrain, simultaneously illustrating its capacity for overfictive excess (essentially the capability to represent the impossible, the exaggerated, the unreal), and its orthodoxy in referencing the *received* knowledges which shape the consensual frame of lived experience.

This occurs almost uniformly in animated films, but is especially pronounced in *The Flintstones* because it has a representational reference point in the American sitcom, and its configuration of suburbanite normality. Though nominally based on 'blue collar' culture, the context embraces the variousness of 'middle classness'. By this I mean that the capacity (and commercial necessity) for animation to represent the widest range of 'imagined' perspectives and possibilities *inevitably* liberates Fred, Wilma, Barney and Betty from the economic constraints that would otherwise inhibit their existence, and which would locate them representationally within a class coding intrinsically linked to 'realist' aesthetics. Though Fred and Barney nominally seek 'the good life', they remain within their blue-collar culture, nevertheless enjoying a variety of experiences legitimized by the aesthetic possibility in which they are represented, rather than the context and circumstances in which they supposedly live. Wilma suggests 'Fred's a diamond in the rough, but even diamonds can stand a polish'. In one episode, a concussed Fred is transformed into an upper-class Englishman 'Frederick', who notes 'I've heard *Ode to a Lark* so many times, I could build a nest and lay eggs', and comments when listening to an operatic aria, 'the tonal counterpoint is too pianissimo', while also criticizing his beloved bowling as 'truly monotonous'. Fred is hit by a rock, of course, and returns to his irascible, Barney-patronizing, bowling-loving self, fully endorsed by a relieved Wilma. Though a clichéd narrative device, the concussion liberates Fred, and the cartoon itself, into aspirant narratives that rejoice in their 'difference' but celebrate their return to comforting orthodoxies. Whether at Stoneyside Country Club, or at the Order of the Dinosaurs, or on the Boss's yacht, Fred is given the opportunity to 'perform' a new social identity, for example as a musician, a golfer, and so on, but is ultimately returned to the site of his consensually accepted social place. Animation enables the 'fantasy' of difference to gain an ontological equivalence to the more 'realistic' premises of each episode, and consequently closes the gap between the modes of existence that are seemingly played out. This sense of continuity within the text despite its contextual flux further enables both children and adults to participate in the realization of a 'parallel' and potentially alternative world, constructed entirely upon its own terms and conditions, while also recognizing their own place outside it.

The Flintstones effectively establishes a paradigm which is much drawn upon by *The Simpsons*; the essential difference being that Matt Groening and his fellow artists, in making *The Simpsons*, are not merely content to reference the received knowledges of their social space but also seek to challenge them. Indeed, their approach readily questions the Crawford perspective cited earlier, wholly engaging with the notion of a 'culture which is high on impact, low on significance', and the mode of indifference and cynicism supposedly underpinning this. It is clear that *The Flintstones*, and indeed much of the Hanna–Barbera output, cannot be accused of the reductive mode of attitude and experience Crawford describes; and it is also the case that his claim rests on a supposition and generalization about the nature of cartoons that is seemingly based on not having paid any real attention to them. As is so often the case, the 'purpose' or 'intentionality' underpinning an approach to material is mistaken or ignored in favour of the attention to the 'subject' it is supposedly addressing. The structural determination of *The Flintstones*, for example, in spite of all its variousness, tends to maintain an overall conviction of 'cartoonalness' as a prevailing 'message' in its own right. Seemingly, both the audience and the artists who now recollect, still watch and claim reference to these previous modes of television animation remember the subversiveness of their graphic style and representation rather than the prevailing codes of reference to the supposedly 'familiar', and its ideological claims. Groening and the makers of *The Simpsons* essentially insist upon the recovery of an overt, if ideologically inconsistent or incoherent agenda. This is not a criticism, but merely an evaluation of the ways in which *The Simpsons* recognises that the kind of naturalised ideological orthodoxies implied in *The Flintstones* have collapsed in the light of postmodern relativism, and have been replaced by more open discourses which can challenge established orthodoxies. Matt Groening's counterculture credentials underpin *The Simpsons* and encourage scepticism and mistrust in the received models of social order. The emergence and establishing premise of *The Simpsons*, for example, was highly charged in its resistance to the more right wing agenda of its immediate rival in the schedules, *The Cosby Show*.

Bill Cosby, long an advocate of the positive pedagogic possibilities of television, and highly invested in creating morally sound and socially responsible programmes which seek to influence and effect family unity, was critical of the approach adopted by *The Simpsons*. Cosby argued that Bart was attractive to children from lower socio-economic backgrounds because his aggression was a signal that he knew he was marginalized, unfocused and without direction, but apparently triumphed over this because he didn't care.[29] Cosby identified this as a learning difficulty that the programme had a responsibility to address, showing the social infrastructure as a potentially enabling system, rather than one perpetuating failure, disillusion and 'smart-arse' cynicism. The producer of *The Simpsons*, James L. Brooks, in reply to this observation, noted that to make a programme which sought to provide role models was inherently dangerous, suggesting that 'My role model may not be somebody else's role model', but more importantly, that such an approach was 'so nakedly anti-art and pro-propaganda' that it was unacceptable to the artists making the programme. Brooks and Groening were concerned about taking into account the variability of the characters, the vicissitudes of everyday experience and the flux of ideologically charged tensions, rather than offering a version of experience determined by one ideological preference. Even if this had been their intention, this would have been difficult to sustain in the light of the variables inherent in the animated form. As I have already suggested, even a text determined by limited animation, like *The Flintstones*, becomes a more open text when these credentials are properly acknowledged; and the heightened self-consciousness of *The Simpsons* merely exacerbates this.

Most notable in this regard is the show's cartoon-within-a-cartoon, 'The Itchy and Scratchy Show', initially the subject of Marge Simpson's concern about the influence of the programme on her children's violent behaviour. Suddenly a key media figure in her condemnation of cartoon violence, winning the support of other viewers and advocacy groups, her recommendations to the producers of 'The Itchy and Scratchy Show' sanitize the cartoon, prompting hordes of children to stop watching the show and engage in interactive play and idyllic, socially acceptable behaviour. There is some irony here, in the sense that this was actually the fate of the late *Tom and Jerry* cartoons under different circumstances. Chuck Jones's more literate and lyrical style essentially removed the speed and conflict from the cartoons, in effect sentimentalizing the relationship between the two characters, and removing much of the kinetic appeal of their narratives. (Whether children engaged in idyllic play thereafter is unknown, though!) Marge, however, while gaining considerable kudos for standing up to cartoon 'content', is ultimately undone by the recognition of 'aesthetics'. The arrival of Michelangelo's 'David' at the Springfield Museum prompts a campaign against full frontal nudity, and once more, appearing on 'Smartline', a local current affairs magazine programme, Marge has to concede that in spite of hating cartoons and their possible effects, she supports the principle of freedom of expression, as 'David' is clearly a work of art. *The Simpsons'* reflexivity about the ideological currency of its own animated aesthetic is the key to its success, and ultimately, its profile as a politically engaged programme.

The focus of this political engagement and the key site of both aesthetic and comic issues in *The Simpsons* is 'the body' and anxiety about 'cerebral' achievement. 'Discouraging the airy humanistic conceit of our species,' notes Peter Conrad, '*The Simpsons* tugs us back to earth by confronting us with the paterfamilias, Homer ... '[30] and the nihilism of his near animality. His scale of consumption and level of ambivalence is a reminder of the absurdity and indifference of contemporary American culture and, in this context, a comment upon the radical change in the response to material culture as it was evidenced and celebrated in *The Flintstones*. Further, Fred and Barney's sense of aspiration, energy and ability has been replaced by a considerable scepticism about the value and purpose of particular kinds of attainment, especially in regard to the view that 'knowledge' and the cultivation of an 'intellect' will lead to upward mobility. Homer's brain literally floats away and collapses when he is bored by neighbour Ned Flanders; Bart cries in utter frustration when, even after considerable effort, he fails his history examination;[31] and Lisa's gifts are all but ignored in the context from which they emerge. This articulation of 'underachievement' is played out, however, through the extraordinary literateness and aesthetic ingenuity of Groening and his team. Conrad again notes how the programme-makers consistently reference the myth of Prometheus in recognition of their own self-conscious act of bringing characters to life and, ultimately, creating their own 'populist' context for metaphysical enquiry.[32] This enquiry is largely concerned with the oppressive effects of consumerism and its seemingly symbiotic relationship with television itself. Unlike the Flintstones and the Rubbles, the Simpson family cannot escape the limits of their cultural conditioning; and this is used both to exemplify the 'wit' of Groening *et al.* in exposing the illusion of stability and contentment in relation to an assumed ideological orthodoxy within consumer capitalism; and to illustrate this literally through the intrinsic flux of the animated image and the confluence of often conflicting and random cultural resources mobilized to create its text.

Adult engagement with the sophistication of *The Simpsons* may be assumed, but it is important to consider once again what children may draw from this agenda. Phil Hogan has argued that children 'love the novelty of an adult with the appetites and impulses of a child', but laugh at Homer not because he is intrinsically offensive, or in some instances fundamentally 'wrong', but because he is 'funny'[33] – the incongruity at the heart of the character, heightened again by the caricatural excess of animation, merely exacerbates the comic potential of the imagery rather than the socio-cultural function of 'the parent'. Even if such depictions serve as a potential representation of human flaws, these may be more readily understood and accepted by children as 'foibles' rather than as something which may be viewed as intrinsically unacceptable. After all, the unconditional acceptance of those we love and admire is as much about the acceptance of their flaws and self-delusion as it is their particular qualities and attractiveness. Further, such recognition may be a significant contribution to the maturing process by which children try to bridge their own understanding of the text with that of their parents or other adults. In this respect, cartoonal caricature creates a possible space both for laughing at, and laughing with, the characters, and a place by which these may be distinguished for explanatory and exploratory purposes. The questioning process which often arises when children seek to enhance their already established enjoyment of the programme and its 'cartoonal attractions',[34] may be the most effective educational vehicle, and one which transcends the dominant discourse of the assumed harm that may be caused by representing 'dysfunctionality' – though under these circumstances, such a term is highly contentious and questionable, and effectively collapses if the audience is viewed (and indeed views) in a different light.

'Is you is, or is you ain't my baby?'

For many years, cartoons have only been perceived in the light of their 'process-driven' presence; a genre seemingly without authorship; a variety of funny narratives in which the characters seemed self-determining rather than the product of known artists. This in itself is ironic given the intrinsic artifice of the form. A great recognition of this artifice in recent times, however, has not merely recovered modes of authorship, but aspects of what Mark Langer has termed 'animatophilia', and the identification of 'animatophiles' – 'a taste group characterised by a high degree of knowledge about animation [who include] animation company owners and employees, animation scholars, devoted fans and obsessive consumers of animation and its ancillary products'.[35] Both the children who grew up watching cartoons and their children, who are often joined by their parents in their participation with the same repeated cartoons, or ones like them, may be defined as part of this group. As Mimi White has noted, they operate as an audience which counters the claims of those championing the dominant bourgeois values supposedly under attack in shows like *The Simpsons* by being 'smart enough to recognize a joke when they see one'.[36] She also suggests that the self-reflexive aspects which link the cartoon, consumer culture and television itself also play out a critique of the allegedly 'therapeutic' functions of television. Thus, in a range of programmes from *The Oprah Winfrey Show* to *Friends* to *The Sopranos*, it has been suggested that narratives are underpinned by discourses which offer viewers implied models of therapy for their own personal and social difficulties. Often these discourses are merely the by-product of the narrative, and not its rationale, but nevertheless American viewers have enjoyed the quasi-counselling offered by their most popular television texts. By contrast, *The Simpsons* deliberately foregrounds its 'cartoonalness' in order to expose the limits of this therapeutic discourse, and the fallacy of its project in the face of modes of ownership and control which privilege the commercial agendas of broadcast output first and foremost. Likewise, John Kricfalusi's *The Ren and Stimpy Show* becomes a significant example of this tension, as 'animatophile' Kricfalusi used his show to bespeak an 'animatophilia' that was increasingly at odds with the commercial and ethical tensions of groups unable to engage with the self-conscious approach of a 'creator-driven' project, which sought to accommodate cartoon aesthetics to a known model of 'spectatorship'.

Kricfalusi has become one of the most outspoken advocates of the cartoon form. His Spümcø web site is a combination of his own webcast animation, including 'Jimmy the Idiot Boy', 'George Liquor' and 'Sody Pop', and short essays on aspects of cartoon history. Kricfalusi suggests 'I've always taken it for granted that cartoons were for everybody – young, old, all sexes, rich, poor, smart, stupid, clean-living and morally-depraved alike. Cartoons, like Rock 'n' Roll, are Pop Culture'.[37] This perspective is predicated on the idea that animation reaches a wide audience because it is fundamentally informed by 'funny drawings' – a caricaturist's eye for exaggeration and redefinition of space, time and above all physical properties, most specifically in relation to the body. In prioritizing the inherent properties of the medium and speaking to a *visual* literacy in his assumed audience, Kricfalusi once more re-oriented the television cartoon to reflect the contingency and aesthetics of 'the golden era'. It was this, more than anything else that led him to fall foul of Nickelodeon and MTV, who in owning the rights to *The Ren and Stimpy Show*, felt that Kricfalusi's work did not meet their criteria, and thus removed him from the show, even though it was he who created the cartoon's distinctive signature style. As Kricfalusi laments, 'Cartoonists are given their creative duties by people who aren't cartoonists ... This is why the term "Saturday Morning Cartoons" is practically a swear word to anybody who remembers real cartoons'.[38] Kricfalusi cites Dave Fleischer's 1930s 'Talkatoons', Grim Natwick's 'Betty Boop' designs, movement cycles in the 'Popeye' cartoons, Bob Clampett's *The Great Piggy Bank Robbery* (1946) and Hanna–Barbera's *Tom and Jerry* cartoons as the key influences that underpin his work. These provoke his dictums 'Symmetry is ungodly', 'No sharp angles, points or straight lines' and 'Need shit-eating grin',[39] the latter a recognition of the satisfaction that the cartoon medium offers in breaking taboo areas through the artifice of the graphic medium – anything you see is not *really* happening, but demonstrates what happens if it might have. As John Patterson notes, 'Anyone who loved the psychotic chihuahua and his fat feline bosom buddy [Ren and Stimpy] and their unyielding devotion to farts, vomit, shit, piss and Tom and Jerry-esque violence is sure to love George [Liquor] and Jimmy [the Idiot Boy]'[40] – the latter pairing a quasi-redneck, who loves meat and close haircuts, and his retarded nephew, whose erections retract *inwards*. Kricfalusi's commitment to web-cast animation seeks to transcend the corporate inhibitions he encountered with his broadcast work.

The Ren and Stimpy Show may be viewed as Kricalfusi's stand against what may be regarded as the least successful television cartoons, most notably the work of Filmation, who produced *The*

Archies and *Gilligan's Planet*, and unpersuasive 'superhero' cartoons which were both a travesty to their sources and an explicit illustration of the lack of 'animation' technique present in the work. His explicit role as author, and his application of classical cartoonal aesthetics as an 'explicit' art within a popular form, marks *The Ren and Stimpy Show* out even from successful contemporaries like Mike Judge's *Beavis and Butthead*, which in once again prioritizing dialogue over animation only reflects Filmation-style diminution. Kricfalusi simultaneously wishes to recall, reappraise and revive the work of Chuck Jones, Tex Avery, Bob Clampett and, most specifically, Joe Barbera, while critiquing both the production context and history of the late television cartoon. This is achieved by using the extremes of representational possibility available within the classical animation vocabulary, particularly as it was executed within Warner Bros. and MGM cartoons of the 1940s, to portray the potential extremes of behavioural conduct and cultural mores in the late millennial period. Kricfalusi essentially uses his 'animatophilia' as a critical tool, and as Langer has suggested, '[I]n this sense, animatophilia becomes a trash aesthetic (or perhaps, more correctly, a trash practice), which examines the detritus of mass culture and recombines it to produce cultural capital. The violation of taste norms becomes a key element of this animatophile practice.'[41] Crucially, though, this mode of cultural capital is intrinsically related to the self-conscious knowledge of the assumed audience: children *know* that they are being addressed through forms of physical and excessive humour; adults *know* that they are being addressed through their recall of childhood cartoons, and their understanding of the incongruity between the sophistication and explicitness of cartoonal expression and the supposed 'innocence' of the medium.

Furthermore, this was also known by Nickelodeon as they initially sought to exploit the retro-styling of the cartoon in the assured knowledge that the best animation had longevity – *Looney Tunes* and *Tom and Jerry* still play after fifty years – and that the adult/child crossover audience would engage with the known constituency of established appeal. Kricfalusi's work, however, moved beyond the 'knowing' cultural critique of *The Simpsons*, or the 'dumbed down' irony of *Beavis and Butthead*, and sought to reconfigure the design and spirit of the cartoon as a comic tension between *noir* foreboding and surreal brutalism, which signified television culture as the repository (or should this be 'supposi-tory') of definitions of post-war cultural orthodoxy. Kricalfusi's use of catch-phrases from cartoons – Mr Jinx's 'I hate meeses to pieces' or Elmer Fudd's 'I'm huntin'for a wabbit' – work as aural fragments which offer a casual reminder of the way in which the cartoon re-states its credentials within the populist frame, but are necessarily redefined within the Kricalfusi universe in order to remind the contemporary audience of the nature of their sub-versiveness. Effectively, Kricalfusi recognizes that the socio-cul-tural 'amoeba' ultimately absorbs and emaciates all challenges, necessitating that new forms (albeit ironically, based on *received* knowledges) must find a fresh context in relation to competing texts. *The Ren and Stimpy Show* is effectively an example of the ways in which its celebration and critique of the *Tom and Jerry* cartoons re-defines modes of *reception* as codes of *perception*.

From 1940 to 1967, 161 *Tom and Jerry* cartoons were made. William Hanna and Joe Barbera working at MGM made the series for the first 17 years of its incarnation, before the characters briefly passed into the hands of Gene Dietch and later Chuck Jones. The Dietch and Jones years merely exemplify the distinctiveness of the Hanna–Barbera period: Dietch's work a surreal shadow of MGM's output, of which he had seen but five examples, and Jones's work a lyrical re-definition of the characters, which in effect changed both the relationship between Tom and Jerry, and their narrative circumstances. Jones, one of the more cerebral and literary-oriented cartoon directors, re-thought *Tom and Jerry* but con-cluded:

> I was never able to give [Jerry] as much character [as Hanna Bar-bera]. I probably got more human personality out of Tom than they did, but not the same character. Tom was pretty vicious in their stuff, and was a clear cut villain. I used the idea that nothing's clear cut because in comedy you should be able to understand the vil-lain and the hero.[42]

Kricfalusi essentially uses Jones's idea about comic ambivalence, but abandons any notion of moral archetypes in favour of extending both the *mise en scène* and the dramatic environment of the *Tom and Jerry* cartoon to explore more 'exploitative' modes of representation. I have written elsewhere[43] that *Tom and Jerry* cartoons called not merely upon comic ambivalence but upon the ontological ambivalence of the cartoon vocabulary to play out a flux of gender positions and cross-species couplings. Kricfalusi takes the nature of these implications to their logical extreme, illustrating the physiognomic explicitness of bodily functions as a contentious site where the adult/child crossover appeal may best be explained. Simply, Kricalfusi exploits the 'openness' of the child's exploration of, pleasure in, yet embarrassment about, the body and its excretions, coupled with the supposedly 'closed', arguably repressed, adult engagement with the limits and dis-solution of physical being, to resource his own playful re-working of 'cartoonalness'. *Tom and Jerry* effectively facilitated a view of the body as infinitely malleable, re-configurable, indestructible; somehow something 'external' to be lived *within. Ren and Stimpy* takes this one stage further, and demonstrate how the body is lived *through.*

This shift also takes into account the movement from 'per-sonality as pantomime' to 'personality as (polymorphous) per-versity'. William Hanna notes while Warner Bros. specialized in the development of character through wisecrack, *Tom and Jerry* prioritized the physical humour of pantomime:

> The zips, scrambles, chases, falls, fights, and frolics of Tom and Jerry could be laughed at and appreciated by anyone who could identify with human frailties, daily dilemmas, and the overall absurdities of life … Tom, as the antagonist, displays a pretty standard stock of expressions ranging from sly and sinister to outraged or terrified. Jerry, on the other hand, provided the pan-tomime wit of the shows, enacting a much greater variety of atti-tudes in which he could by turns be cunning, innocent, fearful, valiant, determined, impatient, mirthful, bewildered and wise.[44]

The influence of Tex Avery is self-evident in these pantomimic exchanges, as his visual tropes concerning 'action' (for example, Tom's body as a series of separate but seemingly related moving parts in *Two Little Indians* (1953)) and 'reaction' (for example, the multiplication and enlargement of Tom's eyes in shock during *Puss 'n' Toots* (1942)) are drawn from Avery's Warner Bros. period. More than this, Avery's graphic effects legitimate an adultness in the 'sensual' extremes being played out in the rela-tionship between the cat and mouse. The longevity of the series is not merely about comic timing, but about the ways narratives accommodate and illustrate what may be described as melodra-matic excesses of emotional interaction. Tom's fear of ghosts in

Fraidy Cat (1942); Jerry's feminized embarrassment in *Baby Puss* (1943); Tom's blistering performance of 'Is you is or is you ain't my baby?' in *Solid Serenade* (1946); and Jerry's playful exuberance in *Little Runaway* (1952) are but a few examples of the overt projection of self-consciously pantomimic emotions. It is this which sustains the cartoons in the light of what are often for-mulaic, if inventive, plot structures, and overrides potential con-cerns about the sometimes violent slapstick of the conflict and confrontation which Tom and Jerry endure. The emotions are affecting and amusing; the action is 'arbitrary' in the sense that it is understood as a set of performance conventions. Crucially, it is in this respect that children have consistently displayed their sophistication in understanding how the 'melodramatic' facilitates the emotive currencies of the narrative, while the exaggerated, caricaturial tendencies of the 'pantomimic' are mere signifiers of the artificial performance of the codes and conventions of engagement between the characters.

Kricfalusi's redefinition of the graphic space, the 'melodra-matic' and the 'pantomimic' are crucial here, because he makes clear distinctions between his acknowledgement of these codes and conventions in performance, and the challenging ethical and ideologically charged representational ideas he wishes to explore and 'exploit'. If Hanna–Barbera used the graphic freedom of the cartoon to enhance 'personality' through emotion, Kricfalusi wishes to engage in a much more postmodern idiom of perver-sity, sometimes for its own sake. At one level, all cartoonal representations are 'abstract' in the sense that they are artificially constructed, two-dimensional, graphic representations, but while Hanna–Barbera grounds this abstraction in known and quantifi-able 'performance' indicators, Kricfalusi deliberately uses his 'abstraction' to simultaneously acknowledge the forebears of 'cartoonal' vocabulary and stretch the parameters of what the medium can express in an inviolate but contentious way. Both children and adults understand that Kricfalusi is asking the spectator to enjoy the site he interrogates which is situated between the cartoonal language explored at MGM and the excesses of physical extremism played out in live-action exploi-tation cinema.

Two pertinent examples to engage with in this respect are *Son of Stimpy* and *Fake Dad*, both of which deal with the parent/child relationship, but from 'perverse' angles which re-determine their 'pantomimic' and 'melodramatic' credentials. Both cartoons were also the subject of some small focus-group work with twelve 6–8-year-old children (six boys, six girls) from a variety of ethnic and social backgrounds in Leicester;[45] and though this constitutes an unrepresentative sample of potential viewers, some material which emerged from the session usefully underpins some of the issues raised here.

Son of Stimpy, the saga of Stimpy's search for 'Stinky', his fart-child, in its scenario alone stretches notions of credibility and taste. Kricfalusi opens the cartoon with Stimpy watching cartoons on the television (the audience can only assume this fact, from the soundtrack, however, as no images are seen) and engaging in a ritualistic act of flatulence; in Stimpy's eyes, the protracted performance and the small 'skidmarks' left on the floor are evidence of the 'birth' of a child. From here, sustained only by the internal logic of the cartoon itself, Stimpy's 'fart-child', Stinky, is assumed to be a real, living entity. The fart's status as a gas, however, means that it apparently disappears as soon as it is born, and it is only Stimpy's faith in the existence of his 'son' that transcends Ren's scepticism about Stimpy's 'stinky fantasies', and the patronizing 'just-agree-with-him, he's-mad' sensibility of the 'magic nose goblins' still living beneath a chair under which they have been wiped, whom Stimpy consults about Stinky's possible whereabouts. Stimpy slumps into protracted depression about Stinky's absence, provoking Ren to note, 'It's been three years, I'm starting to worry about you'. Ren tries to comfort Stimpy at Christmas, offering to kiss under the mistletoe, but Stimpy angrily rejects him, and heads off out into the snowy night to find Stinky. Putting up 'Have you smelled me?' posters of Stinky, Stimpy lives through urban oppressiveness, false alarms (he thinks he has found Stinky at a stable selling fresh manure) and the excessive cold, ultimately returning home in an iceblock. Stinky, meanwhile is also searching, escaping two hobos who attempt to 'light' him – a reference to the schoolboy prank of attempting to ignite 'fart' gas – and living underground. Finally, however, he is re-united with Stimpy in the 'squelch' of an embrace, but almost immediately he claims his independence in order to be married to a dead cod-head. The marriage takes place, and Stimpy enjoys 'a happy ending'.

Kricfalusi legitimates his narrative by bringing the melodramatic 'lost son' motif to an otherwise taboo subject: the breaking of wind, and the intimation of the emission of bodily waste. Stimpy 'values' this *reductive* act as a *productive* act. The 'fart' is now a 'figure', and with this transformation comes the address of a 'subject', rather than the abstract retention of an 'object'. The children watching this cartoon especially embraced this transition, laughing initially at the over-determined performance of 'farting', but then enjoying the absurdity of being amused by and caring for 'a fart-child', and further, hoping for its reconciliation with its 'father'. Their amusement was also derived from the idea that the central currency of the whole cartoon was that it was predicated on things that were impolite to talk about, but *actually* the object of amusement for both children and adults alike in 'real life' – farting, nose-picking, body odour, and so on. The 'Son of God' motif which underpins the cartoon, signalled in its title and its Christmas setting and soundtrack, went unrecognized by children, but is freely acknowledged by adults as allying the sacred and profane in a way that some might find provocative. Kricfalusi does not make this a coherent analogy, however, but self-evidently uses the 'openness' of the animated vocabulary for subversive purposes.

The animatophiles will find much to enjoy, too. Ren's 'Peter Lorre-esque' inflections – Kricfalusi's tribute to Bob Clampett – is but one example of the classic cartoon vocabulary he constantly references. More pertinently, though, Kricfalusi's major achievement is in referencing the stylistic bravura and modes of cartoon-alness from the Fleischer and Warner studios, by extending the timing for, and using static 'holds' in relation to, the graphic extremes and excessive emotions he depicts. In the case of *Son of Stimpy*, this is especially so in relation to the revision of panto-mimic gestures and melodramatic expression. Stimpy's tears are so excessive that they invite no sense of sentiment; his deflated bottom, as a result of his exaggerated attempts to break wind, creates a bizarre bathos, and ultimately, like the former example, a critique of Disneyesque pathos. For children, this was amusing because they readily perceived that they were being asked to laugh at the 'silliness' of the situation, rather than any of its 'plausible' outcomes. Animatophiles recognized the deconstruction of modes of cartoonal expression which had been successful during 'the golden era', and which Kricfalusi was now half-celebrating, half-subverting in the re-invention of the cartoon.

Fake Dad deals with Ren and Stimpy fostering 'a 7-year-old child' for the weekend. The child in this cartoon is actually a huge prison inmate named Kowolski, already sentenced to 30 years in prison for crimes against humanity. The whole cartoon is concerned with Ren's inability to deal with 'the child', trying to 'burp him' over a period of 36 weeks, for example, only at the point when he admits failure for Kowolski to violently break wind on him, blowing Ren's fur off. Once more, Kricalfusi's taboo-breaking agenda informs his approach, using the deep-rooted cultural fear of the body and the anxiety about parent/child bonds to facilitate a fresh approach to representation. Fully exposing the arbitrary construction of the contemporary family and the fissures at its heart, Kricfalusi also shows 'arbitrariness' and 'fissure' as central components in the new configuration of the cartoon, which inevitably recalls the approach of the animators of the classic period. By reducing dialogue, and heightening and holding the 'extreme' takes of his characters, Kricfalusi calls attention to the form, but also the representational codes which have become naturalized within it. Children watching this cartoon noted an uneasy tension caused by its pace and the 'non-' events it dwelt on, most notably Ren's insistence that he will beat Kowolski on the bottom, only to change his mind in a fit of excessive emotional guilt. All the children in the focus group felt that this moment was supposed to be funny, but wasn't. Arguably, Kricfalusi had denied the children their comic 'pay-off' to raise an issue; more likely, though, this was done in the spirit of re-defining the cartoon. A similar situation arises in the 'Sven Hoek' episode, when Ren is visited by his cousin, Sven, who unfortunately looks and behaves as stupidly as Stimpy. Ren returns home to find that among other things, his opera records have been covered in bubblegum, and his precious dinosaur eggs painted in lurid colours. This provokes him beyond extreme, leading him to detail just how violent he will be with Stimpy and Sven, only to not fulfil his actions, taking time out instead for a 'wiz'. The delayed 'pay-off' comes when the house is detonated and the trio find themselves in hell, and Ren is cautioned for having urinated on the electrified fence of a children's boardgame, which parodies 'Operation'. Lessons can be absorbed in a number of ways and, clearly, Kricfalusi's sense of the 'perverse' might be one of them.

Conclusion: Rubber band reality

When effectively fired from his own creation, Kricfalusi ironically claimed that 'farts are behind me'.[46] His place in contemporary cartoon culture is assured, however, in two respects. Firstly, *The Ren and Stimpy Show* was an incredible ratings success, doubling the 2–11-year-old demographic, and generating an audience of 1.2 million, which also included a 35 per cent share of over 18-year-old viewers.[47] This was followed by prime-time showing on MTV which added a further million viewers, and firmly established the show in the public imagination. Secondly, Kricfalusi's achievement has been to properly recall the work of cartoon luminaries like Bob Clampett, Tex Avery and Dave Fleischer, but most importantly, Joe Barbera, whose work in the *Tom and Jerry* cartoons, and in *The Flintstones* and others, Kricfalusi is ultimately hybridizing and re-inventing for a new culture. Groening's work, too, embraces this challenge, using *The Simpsons* as an on-going litmus test of the values and tastes of an American society now far more aware of the fallibility of its own myths and the redundancy of its claims to populist consensus. This culture, more knowing, more sophisticated, less easy to please, is perhaps epitomized in a statement from the episode of *The Simpsons* dealing with the 'Itchy and Scratchy' issue. Speaking of Michelangelo's 'David', the news programme 'Smartline' poses the question, 'Is this a masterpiece, or just some guy with his pants down?'. An amusing line, but also an interrogation of a whole taken-for-granted system of values, ethics and creative ideas; an interrogation that popular animation in the hands of creator figures like Kricfalusi and Groening is eager and able to properly explore. Finally, it is important to note that children and adults alike have clearly grasped Groening's concept of 'rubber band reality' in animation. In the contemporary era, viewers recognize that the known and trusted variables of physical and emotional experience are literally stretched and distorted in the cartoon in order to achieve three things: first, to see if the ideas and issues explored remain robust, stable and knowable; second, to redefine the terms of these ideas under new conditions; and third, to foreground the distinctiveness of the animated cartoon as an interrogative tool that can return things to their previous form, or change them irrevocably and irredeemably.

Notes

1. From Robert McKimson's 1964 cartoon *Dr Devil and Mr Hare*, in which Bugs Bunny, dressed as an archetypical German psychiatrist, psychoanalyses the Tasmanian devil.
2. See P. Wells, *Understanding Animation* (London: Routledge, 1998); K. Sandler (ed.), *Reading the Rabbit: Explorations in Warner Bros. Animation* (New Brunswick, NJ: Rutgers University Press, 1998); M. Furniss, *Art in Motion* (London: John Libbey, 1998).
3. See Wells, *Understanding Animation*, pp. 222–43.
4. 'Limited' or 'planned' animation in the American context operates as a more economic form of animation by using fewer and less detailed backgrounds; creating fewer animated movements – often only the movement of eyes, mouth and functional limbs on key characters; employing simple, repeatable movement cycles; and by stressing dialogue over action.
5. This period effectively begins with the emergence of Disney's *Steamboat Willie* (1928) and *Plane Crazy* (1928) and ends with *The Three Cabelleros* (1946), and is notable for the major achievements of the Disney studio in feature-length production and for the innovations in the cartoon-short by the animators at Warner Bros., Fleischer Brothers and MGM. While it should be quite rightly regarded as a 'heyday' in the prominence and development of the genre, it is perhaps worthwhile noting that it excludes pioneering work by Winsor McCay, Otto Messmer, Earl Hurd, Raoul Barré and Charles Bowers in the pre-1928 context in the United States; significant achievements in other non-cartoonal forms of animation elsewhere; and indeed, the 'taken-for-granted' uses of animation in 'live-action' cinema as special effects.
6. See P. Brophy, 'John Kricfalusi: Profile and interview', in P. Brophy (ed.), *Kaboom!: Explosive Animation from America and Japan* (Sydney: Museum of Contemporary Art/ Power, 1994), p. 100.
7. S. Stark, *Glued to the Set* (New York: Simon and Schuster, 1997), p. 19.
8. B. Putterman, 'A short critical history of Warner Bros. cartoons', in K. Sandler (ed.), *Reading the Rabbit*, p. 35.
9. J. Adamson, 'Chuck Jones interviewed', in G. Peary and D. Peary (eds), *The American Animated Cartoon* (New York: E. P. Dutton, 1980), pp. 140–1.
10. See P. Brophy, 'The animation of sound', in A. Cholodenko (ed.), *The Illusion of Life: Essays on Animation* (Sydney: Power/AFC, 1991), pp. 67–112.
11. See M. E.Shapiro, *Television Network Weekend Programming 1959–1990* (Jefferson, NC: McFarland & Company Inc., 1992).

12. British animation for children has largely been characterized by what may be described as the legacy of 'Postgate–Woodism' – the influence of Oliver Postgate (*Bagpuss, Pogle's Wood, The Clangers, Ivor the Engine*) and Ivor Wood (*The Herbs, Postman Pat, Paddington Bear*). The work here is largely characterized by benign, paternalist communities; middle-England pastoral nostalgia; and small-scale eccentric heroes, promoting consensus, ritual and restraint. The social and moral codings in these animations have survived in more contemporary animation from *Bob the Builder* to Nick Park's 'Wallace and Gromit' films and *Chicken Run*. For an extended discussion of these issues see P. Wells, *British Animation: An Industry of Innovation* (London: BFI, forthcoming). Some of these programmes are also discussed by Helen Bromley in Chapter 10 of this volume.

13. See A. Horrox and V. Nyberg, 'Square Eyes', in P. Simpson (ed.), *Parents Talking Television* (London: Comedia, 1987), pp. 26–30.

14. For a full disussion of this issue, and all aspects of censorship in the American animated cartoon, see K. Cohen, *Forbidden Animation* (Jefferson, NC: McFarland & Co., 1997).

15. See L. Maltin, *Of Mice and Magic: A History of Animated Cartoons* (New York: Plume, 1987), pp. 154–5.

16. J. Korkis and J. Cawley, *The Encyclopaedia of Cartoon Superstars* (Las Vegas: Pioneer, 1990), p. 137.

17. See L. Cabarga, *The Fleischer Story* (New York: Da Capo, 1988).

18. H. Ellison, *The Glass Teat* (Manchester: Savoy, 1968), pp. 53–5.

19. B. Crawford, 'Saturday morning fever', in Cholodenko (ed.), 'The Illusion of Life', p. 113.

20. *Ibid.*, p. 114.

21. See D. Kellner, '*Beavis and Butthead*: No future for postmodern youth', in S. Steinberg and J. Kincheloe (eds), *Kindercultur: The Corporate Construction of Childhood* (Boulder, CO: Westview Press, 1997), pp. 85–103.

22. See A. Siegal, 'Film-mediated fantasy aggression and strength of aggressive drive', 'Child Development' 27, 365–78, 1956.

23. See A. Bandura, D. Ross and S. Ross, 'Imitation of film-mediated aggressive models', 'Journal of Abnormal and Social Psychology' 66, 3–11, 1963.

24. Quoted in E. Slafer, 'A conversation with Bill Hanna', in Peary and Peary (eds), 'The American Animated Cartoon', p. 255.

25. W. Hanna, *A Cast of Friends* (Dallas, TX: Taylor Publishing Co., 1997), p. 105.

26. See T. Sennett, *The Art of Hanna Barbera* (New York and London: Viking Penguin, 1989), pp. 83–4.

27. R. Butsch, 'Ralph, Fred, Archie and Homer: Why television keeps

recreating the white, male, working class buffoon', in G. Dines and J. M. Humez (eds), *Gender, Race and Class in Media: A Text Reader* (London: Sage, 1995), pp. 403–12.

28. See S. Chambers, N. Karet, N. Sampson and J. Sancho-Aldridge, *Cartoon Crazy? Children's Perception of 'Action' Cartoons* (London: ITC, 1998).

29. See D. Bianculli, *Teleliteracy* (New York: Simon and Schuster, 1994), pp. 174–83.

30. P. Conrad, 'They've got Yellow skin and not enough fingers. Still, they're only human ... ', *Observer* 'Review', 31 May 1998, pp. 2–3.

31. Only to pass by default when he cites the circumstance of George Washington's surrender to the French in 1754 as a point of empathy, and is granted extra marks for 'applied knowledge'.

32. Conrad, 'They've got Yellow skin', p. 3.

33. P. Hogan, 'Actually, I tell my kids that it's like Jacobean theatre', *Observer* 'Review,' 31 May 1998, p. 3.

34. Tom Gunning has posited a view of early cinema which is predicated on what he calls a 'cinema of attractions'; essentially a reworking of a conception of film construction 'less as a way of telling stories than as a way of presenting a series of views to an audience, fascinating because of their illusory power ... and exoticism'. See T. Gunning, 'The cinema of attractions: Early film, its spectators and the avant garde', in T. Elsaesser (ed.), *Early Cinema: Space, Frame, Narrative* (London: BFI, 1990), p. 57. I wish to provisionally suggest here that 'cartoonal attractions' also forfeit the determinants of narrative to foreground the distinctive vocabulary of graphic visualization in motion, and its non-objective, non-linear aesthetic as the carrier of complex personal symbolic and/or ideologically charged meanings.

35. M. Langer, 'Animatophilia, cultural production and corporate interests: The case of *Ren and Stimpy*', in J. Pilling (ed.), *A Reader in Animation Studies* (London: John Libbey & Co., 1997), p. 146.

36. M. White, *Teleadvising: Therapeutic Discourse in American Television* (Chapel Hill, NC: University of North Carolina Press, 1992), p. 174.

37. http://www.spumco.com/magazine/jkfleischer/jkfleischer01.html

38. http://www.spumco.com/magazine/jkfleischer/jkfleischer05.html

39. See J. Patterson, 'Turned on, and tooned in', *Guardian* Guide, July 26 1997, pp. 5–8.

40. *Ibid.*, p. 6.

41. Langer, 'Animatophilia', p. 149.

42. Quoted in J. Adamson, 'Chuck Jones interviewed', in Peary and Peary (eds), *The American Animated Cartoon*, pp. 131–2.

43. Wells, *Understanding Animation*, pp. 208–15.

44. Hanna, *A Cast of Friends*, pp. 46–7.
45. This small focus group was set up using the younger siblings of some locally based Media Studies students attending De Montfort University in Leicester during 1998. The students had become interested in how young children engaged with animations like *The Ren and Stimpy Show* as a result of their work in Animation Studies and Children's Media and Youth Culture, and 'volunteered' their younger brothers and sisters into a session, led by myself, which asked them to view examples from *The Ren and Stimpy Show*, and to respond to a set of predetermined questions, which would prompt further questions and discussion after initial responses.
46. Quoted in J. Pendleton, 'Ren and Stimpy goes to camp', *Variety*, 5 October 1992, p. 26.
47. Langer, 'Animatophilia', p. 155.

CHAPTER 5

South Park

Not in Front of the Children

HELEN NIXON

During the late 1990s, the popularity among children and teenage viewers of the 'adult' animated television programme *South Park* once again brought to the fore the vexed question of what constitutes 'appropriate' viewing for children. Public discussion of *South Park* focused on two main issues. First, concern was expressed at the treatment of 'adult' topics and the use of 'adult' language in a cartoon based on the lives of 8-year-old children. The apparent problem here was the use of child protagonists in a programme based on 'adult' content. Second, concern was expressed about children's desire to watch what was intended to be 'adult' material. The apparent problem here was the appeal for children of a programme that contains content considered suitable only for older audiences. There is much about *South Park* that is unlike what has traditionally been thought of as 'children's television'. This chapter addresses both these issues as it explores the texts of *South Park*. It suggests that both the broad appeal of *South Park* texts, as well as the anxiety they arouse, are due to their play on 'typical' as well as more controversial images of childhood, and their tendency to cross the boundaries between childhood and adulthood.

South Park: The television series

South Park is an animated television series produced in the USA and set in the small village of South Park, Colorado. Unlike its popular counterpart *The Simpsons*, whose story-lines are built around the lives of the Simpson family, *South Park* is not a variation on that American television staple, the family sitcom. Rather, the series focuses on the seasonal lives of an isolated rural community, with a particular focus on four 8-year-old boys. These characters, described by *Time* magazine as having 'grating voices and feeble minds',[1] are the fat and self-centred Eric Cartman, the wussy Stan Marsh, the Jewish Kyle Broflovski and the poverty-stricken Kenny McCormick. As these descriptions suggest, the characters are in many ways stereotypical, a fact emphasized by the naive, two-dimensional and crude style of *South Park*'s animation.

Other regular characters in the *South Park* cartoon include key members of the South Park Elementary School community: the children's strange teacher, Mr. Garrison; the school's grouchy bus driver, Mrs. Crabtree; the school counsellor Mr. Mackie; and the town's only African-American, the lovable school chef known simply as Chef. Some of the more unusual regular characters in the series include Mr. Hankey, the talking Christmas poo; Mr. Garrison's talking glove puppet, Mr. Hat (replaced in several episodes by Mr. Twig); the genetic scientist Dr. Alphonse Mephisto; and Jesus Christ, the host of the public access cable programme *Jesus and Pals*. The names of these characters, as well as the recurring story-lines of Kenny's weekly and often violent death and Mr. Garrison's mental instability and homosexuality, together point to some of the sources of controversy surrounding what has been called *South Park*'s 'political incorrectness'.

Reportedly first made in 1997 for about US$300,000 an episode, a third of the cost of *The Simpsons*, *South Park* was created by young Americans Trey Parker and Matt Stone, then in their mid-twenties. *Newsweek* reported that Parker and Stone turned down development deals with major studios such as New Line, Warner Brothers and Dream Works before signing over the screening rights to cable channel Comedy Central, who guaranteed them creative control of the series.[2] Still heavily involved in programme production during the fourth series produced in 2000, Parker voices the characters of Cartman, Stan and Mr. Garrison, whilst Stone voices the characters of Kyle, Kenny, Jesus and Jimbo, Stanley's uncle and a veteran of the Vietnam war. In one of the most outrageous but amusing twists in the series, musician and record producer Isaac Hayes provides the voice of Chef, a character who regularly bursts into sexually suggestive R&B tunes while cooking such specialities as Chef's Salty Chocolate Balls and giving advice to the children about life, love and growing up.

Considered by its reviewers as 'too hot for mainstream television', the first series of *South Park* went to air in the USA in August 1997 on cable television's Comedy Central channel in a late-night time slot. There it has been an outstanding ratings success, regularly producing viewing figures of up to triple the previous records set by such programmes as *Absolutely Fabulous*. However, according to the programme's producers, *South Park* has been even more successful in the UK and Australia.[3] Creators Parker and Stone suggest that this may be because their humour has been heavily influenced by the British absurdist comedy practised by *Monty Python's Flying Circus*, whose dictum was 'life wasn't meant to be serious'. With the release of the fourth series in 2000, the creators used the opening sequence of the programme to make ironic references to the way the show was changing in line with the technological advances of the twenty-first century. In this sequence the four original main characters and the new main character Timmy – who is physically and intellectually challenged and confined to a wheelchair – are introduced by name. They are represented as 3-D computer-generated figures revolving in slow motion above still frames that show them in various scenarios from season four episodes. Running across the screen are subtitles that introduce this series as 'faster', 'cooler', and 'smarter', and indicate that viewers can expect to see in *South Park* 'more explosions', 'more animation' and 'improved walk cycles'. The absurd opening proviso remains the same as for earlier series: 'All characters in the show – even those based on real people – are entirely fictional. All celebrity voices are impersonated – poorly. The following program contains coarse language and due to its content should not be viewed by anyone.'

These characteristics alone point to at least two of the difficulties of writing about *South Park*. Firstly, the anarchic randomness of its humour serves to keeps much of the programme outside the bounds of mainstream discussion and analysis. Like most cartoons, *South Park* relies heavily on spectacle. Much of its humour is conveyed in silly sounds, sight gags and frequent pregnant pauses in which the child characters stare blankly at the viewer, nonplussed by the silly antics of the mostly adult people around them. This is immediate, visual and sometimes visceral entertainment. Secondly, when the 'content' of *South Park* is written down, it appears so outrageously silly, sexist, racist or crude that one cannot easily justify repeating it. When translated literally, much of *South Park* must at best be described as in extreme bad taste. As one local newspaper put it, even mass-media reviews of *South Park* 'simply dare not allude to most of the programme's dialogue, double entendres, and sight gags'. In their view, this is 'hysterical adults only viewing which simply has to be seen to be believed'.[4] *South Park* is of interest in the context of this book precisely because it is a programme that is often crude, shocking and humorously offensive and yet has enormous appeal for older and younger viewers alike.

The cross-age and cross-media appeal of *South Park*

When is a television programme 'for' children and when is it not? When they have been asked to comment, children have simply said that a television show or film is for them if they enjoy watching it.[5] Although it was designed as a satirical cartoon for adults, market research and everyday experience suggested that *South Park* quickly established a strong following with much younger viewers than its target audience of 18–39-year-olds. As was the case with *The Simpsons*, the language and other semiotic codes associated with *South Park* entered the everyday lives of young people the world over. In both the UK and Australia, despite its mid- to late-night screening slot, by its second season *South Park* was regularly watched by children as young as eight and nine, and was also extremely popular with young people in their early and mid-teens.[6]

At the height of its popularity during the screening of series two and three, teaching colleagues of mine reported that the conversations of their children and students were sprinkled with such terms from *South Park* (and *Beavis and Butthead* before that) as 'cool', 'dude' and 'that sucks!' I had first-hand evidence of children's take-up of *South Park* language and mannerisms when I was entertained in rural South Australia by a friend's 8-year-old daughter and her 12-year-old sister. They performed for me improvised routines in the personae of Terrance and Phillip, the cartoon characters who star in the *South Park* children's favourite TV programme *The Terrance and Phillip Show*. The girls' improvisations skilfully combined satirical comments about their daily school lives with Terrance and Phillip's two trademarks of high-pitched monotone laughter and obsession with flatulence. Similarly, a Canadian colleague reported that the *South Park* character Kenny was frequently the subject of school-yard chat and improvised conversation among his 14-year-old students.

One possible explanation for the supposedly large numbers of young *South Park* viewers is that adult constructs of the age range of 'childhood' are out of date, with 'the end of childhood' arriving several years earlier than it has done in the past. David Buckingham argues the need for an understanding and recognition of the significance of this phenomenon:

> Over the past 20–30 years, the status of childhood and our assumptions about it have become more and more unstable. The distinctions between children and other categories – 'youth' or 'adults' – have become ever more difficult to sustain; but they are also increasingly significant, both in terms of social policy and in terms of the economy.[7]

The case of *South Park* illustrates that the distinctions between 'children' and 'youth' or 'adults' as social categories are significant on both counts: in debates about social policy in relation to regulation and censorship, and in terms of markets and the economy.

In regard to social policy, debates about children, censorship and regulation become particularly heated in relation to texts like *South Park*. Concerns arose because the series quickly became popular with children aged between 10 and 14, as well as with older audiences. This happened even though *South Park* does not fit in with the 'normal' scheduling of children's programming, and the insistence of its creators that it was not intended for and is not marketed to children and teenage viewers. However, this does not mean that children were not exposed to *South Park* either by directly viewing the programme – with or without parental knowledge – or by way of the other media and popular cultural forms they consume. As research shows, 'children have always preferred "adult" media, at least in so far as they could gain access to them'.[8] Today's children in places like North America, Britain and Australia have relatively easy access to 'adult' material because many have televisions and video recorders in their bedrooms. Moreover, research shows that even when they are technically forbidden to watch certain programmes, or forbidden to watch at certain times of the evening, children will often get access to VCR recordings of their favourite programmes with the assistance of friends, siblings and parents.[9] This seems to be as true of *South Park* as of other programmes. Where I live, the second series of *South Park* was moved from its established cult cartoon slot of 8 p.m. on Saturday nights to a later 9.30 slot on a weeknight because some of the episodes were classified 'M' for 'mature' viewers of 15 years and older. Subsequent market research showed that although the number of people tuning in to *South Park* dropped – especially in the children and teen group – the number of households watching it increased by 30,000. This was interpreted positively by the broadcaster as meaning that once the programme screened in a later slot, more VCR record- ings were made. The implication was that eventual viewing by children and teens could finally result in slightly higher viewing levels for *South Park* because of the availability of VCR copies that were swapped among friends and family. Hence, despite attempts to regulate children's viewing with a late night time slot, children's access to *South Park* actually became less and less possible to monitor the more the programme was repeated and videotaped.

In regard to the economy, the child and teenage markets for global media culture are large and growing, and purportedly 'adult' programmes like *South Park* also satisfy the desire for media texts and other products that service such markets. In the contemporary context of global media culture, however, it is not only through television that children come to know about and engage with texts like *South Park*. The economic importance of the children's market means that, as Kinder has pointed out, children are in the vanguard of 'trans-media intertextuality'. In such a context, 'distinctions between videos, computer games, movies, TV shows, advertisements and print texts have become increasingly irrelevant'.[10] Thus, since the programme began in 1997, *South Park* viewers and non-viewers alike have been

Helen Nixon

increasingly exposed to intertextual references to the television series and to 'information' about it in both traditional and 'new' media. A *South Park* computer game designed for the Nintendo 64 and for personal computers using Windows 95/98 has been released, followed by the film *South Park: Bigger, Longer and Uncut.* Stories about the creators, location and characters of *South Park* have appeared in popular entertainment and gossip magazines as well as youth-directed style and music magazines. By 1999 *South Park* merchandise was outselling all other comparable products in Australia, including those associated with *The Simpsons*, by a ratio of 10:1. In the same year, Comedy Central reported sales of merchandise to the value of over US$300 million.[11] Some of this merchandise obviously reached children, whether or not they were the target audience.

South Park has also maintained a very strong web presence ever since the release of the Parker and Stone *South Park* 'Christmas card' video that first brought their work to the attention of Comedy Central. This is part of a global phenomenon in which the world wide web has become an increasingly important 'information' source for young people who want to learn more about and engage with their favourite television and other popular culture texts (see Julian Sefton-Green's chapter in this volume). Where I live, by the time series one and two had screened on television, the Australian Yahoo! web guide reported that *South Park* ranked fourth in the list of most frequently searched terms and topics on the world wide web.[12] With such high sales of merchandise, and the high proportions of children having access to televisions, video recorders and computers in their bedrooms,[13] it is not surprising that many young viewers demonstrated some knowledge of *South Park.*

Indeed, the fact that *South Park* is considered 'adults only viewing' may well be part of its appeal for young viewers. Research shows that children are keen to keen to present themselves as successfully evading attempts at regulation of their viewing habits and are keen to assert their rights to have access to material of their choice.[14] It is possible that viewing programmes like *South Park* provides some children's and teenagers' enjoyment with a transgressive edge. It may signify their subscription to a particular anti-authoritarian and contemporary 'attitude' that operates as a shared code between peers and effectively marks them out against parents and other adults. For some children at least, demonstration of knowledge about *South Park* – possibly gained from sources other than direct viewing of it – may bring with it the reward of showing that they are familiar with a socially 'disapproved' text.

'Cool, dude!': The appeal for children of 'socially disapproved' texts

In Australia at least, it was the release in 1999 of *South Park: Bigger, Longer and Uncut*, a feature-length film based on the television series, that raised the level of public awareness about the 'controversial' nature of *South Park*. In my local media, journalists reported the shocked reaction of some parents to the film's language and content. Parents were concerned that they had had 'no warning about the swearing and violence [the film] contains'.[15] This was despite the film's MA15+ rating which required children under the age of 15 years to be accompanied by an adult. In addition, it became clear that many parents knew very little about *South Park* – and therefore what to expect of the film – despite its popularity with their children. Parents also seemed concerned that their children wanted to watch such material and uncomfortable at having to watch it with them. For parents, it seems that the whole experience of watching a film with their children that contained such controversial content blurred the distinctions often made between childhood and adulthood.

Newspaper reports about public response to *South Park: Bigger, Longer and Uncut* had some common features. Beginning with reports of reactions to the film by local parents and teenagers, they went on to discuss the results of a US-based study of the film by the company Media Index.[16] Media Index attempts to quantify the use of adult language in films as well as the number of violent acts, sexual situations and nude scenes they depict. The 'newsworthiness' of such media reports about *South Park: Bigger, Longer and Uncut* therefore related to 'local' events and concerns, but also focused more generally on questions of media morality and childhood. Much of the force of these reports lies in the quantitative methods used by the Media Index researchers. The 'findings' provide the kind of 'hard' data that is easy to report and difficult to refute. Examples include such attention-grabbing results as the tally of '399 examples of adult language, with 128 of those involving accompanying crude gestures'. The tally of words coded as 'obscene/profane' totalled 228 and the conclusion was made that with 'about five curse words a minute' the film 'almost doubled the rate of *Pulp Fiction*'.[17] The difficulty with such quantitative measures is the assumption of a causal relationship between the on-screen use of words and depiction of acts and their take-up by actual child-viewers in daily life. An additional difficulty is that such measures are unable to take account of the ironic, parodic and satirical contexts in which the language and actions are embedded. Given the creators' insistence that their work has been profoundly influenced by the work of *Monty Python's Flying Circus*,[18] this lack of attention to context, tone and style is a serious oversight on the part of *South Park* critics. The Monty Python style of comedy rests heavily on silly and senseless wordplay and actions and the humour largely arises from a combination of such absurdism and the exaggerated gestures and actions of slapstick. Some critics fail to register the futility of applying standards of 'realism' to such comic style.

It is a deliberate irony on the part of *South Park* creators Stone and Parker that the text of the film deals satirically and absurdly with precisely the questions raised by such media reports. Key themes in both include the supposedly simple carry-over of violence and other socially undesirable behaviours from the screen to actual children's lives, and the supposed social irresponsibility of producers of 'adult' cartoons that prove to be popular with children and teenage audiences. These are recurring themes of the television programme, which also frequently addresses the sensationalism and irresponsibility of the US news media and the hypocrisy of adults in relation to questions of morality and children's well-being. In this respect, both the film and television series of 'South Park' anticipate and speak to the critiques likely to be made of them.

'It's off to the movies we shall go, where we learn everything that we know': Learning lessons from the media

The most common critique of the texts of *South Park* is that they teach undesirable lessons to young viewers. This criticism rests on the argument that children and teenage viewers learn inappropriate language, behaviours and lessons from watching *South Park* and that this carries over into their daily lives. Adults, on the other hand, are assumed to be able to appreciate the texts for what they are – satirical and subversive comedies. However, *South Park*'s creators confound their critics by incorporating such criticisms into the very fabric of their work. The suggestion that children learn socially and morally undesirable lessons from the media is raised head-on in both the television series and the film of *South Park* and becomes the starting point of much of the satire.

South Park: Bigger, Longer and Uncut opens with 8-year-old Stan Marsh asking his mother Shirley whether he can 'go to see a movie that's supposed to be the best movie in town'. This question is a part of a long musical number that concludes with a chorus consisting of Stan and his playmates Kenny, Kyle and Cartman singing:

It's off to the movies we shall go
Where we learn everything that we know
'Cos the movies teach us
What our parents don't have time to say.

On this particular Sunday morning Stan and his friends plan to see *Asses of Fire*, a film-length version of their favourite television cartoon *The Terrance and Phillip Show*. In circumstances that parallel the history of the *South Park* texts, the children's favourite television cartoon has shifted from the small screen to the large screen. Unfortunately for them, the boys find that the film is rated R because it contains 'naughty language'. This requires that children be accompanied by a parent or guardian in order to gain entrance. By bribing a local street drunk to buy their tickets, the boys enact exactly the kind of 'undesirable behaviour' cited in my local press as likely to follow in real life from the *South Park* film's MA15+ rating:

The executive officer of television watchdog Young Media Australia, Ms. Barbara Biggins, said it would be easy for children under 15 to sneak in to see *South Park*.

'At some of these large theatre complexes, all a person has to do is buy a ticket and they have access to any movie theatre they like', she said.[19]

Once they are in the cinema and the film begins, Stan and his friends are at first shocked and then delighted at the rude words they hear being uttered by Terrance and Phillip. When adult viewers walk out of the film and criticize it for being garbage, the children take this as a further positive recommendation. By the time they get to school the following day, the film's unsavoury language has been seamlessly integrated into their normal speech. When their classmates hear the boys using swear words featured in *Asses of Fire*, they too are eager to see the film, gasping 'Oooh, we've got to see that movie, dude.' It is a humorous testament to the social importance of popular culture in the boys' lives that those who have seen the movie immediately assume a higher social status than those who have not. They are aware of their power and taunt their peers, saying: 'I saw the Terrance and Phillip movie. Who wants to touch me?' However, as Stone and Parker are no doubt well aware, this is exactly what lies at the heart of many adult concerns about *South Park*. Young people want to be 'in the know' about 'adult' forms of popular culture precisely because of the cachet among their peers such knowledge bestows on them.[20] This cachet in turn may well be associated with the child viewer's 'symbolic entry into adult time and space',[21] as they watch non-sanctioned films and television. Some adults feel threatened by the incursion of children into that symbolic space that they would prefer to keep separate from children.

In the classroom at South Park Elementary, the children's teacher Mr. Garrison finds that the behaviour of those who have seen the film has begun to deteriorate. When challenged by the teacher about his disobedience and use of unacceptable language, Cartman confirms adult fears about the effects of *Asses of Fire* when he answers: 'I can't help myself. That movie has warped my fragile little mind.' Soon, in what is intended to be a disciplinary measure, students wearing Terrance and Phillip T-shirts are happily sent home from school. Television news features targeting parents appear on such topics as 'Is the film destroying American youth?' and 'Kids are out of control'. And, according to Kyle's activist mother Sheila Broflovski as she addresses the South Park PTA, 'this is what happens when toilet humour is allowed to run rampant'.

As the Canadian-produced film based on *The Terrance and Phillip Show* assumes number one position at the box office, Sheila Broflovski mobilizes parents to find ways to 'cure' their children and find and stop the source of their foul language. As befits the musical genre parodied in *South Park: Bigger, Longer and Uncut*, a chorus of parents laments:

> Times have changed
> Our kids are getting worse
> They won't obey their parents
> They just want to fart and curse
> Should we blame the government?
> Or blame society?
> Or should we blame the images on TV?
> No, blame Canada! Blame Canada!

In an attempt to counter the supposed negative effects of the Terrance and Phillip movie on their children, South Park parents adopt two main courses of action. In one move, the Broflovski-formed organization Mothers Against Canada places Canadians Terrance and Phillip under citizen's arrest and encourages the outbreak of war between Canada and the USA. In a second move, a plan is formed to insert V-chips under the skin of South Park children. Before this plan is carried out, Eric Cartman is chosen to demonstrate the V-chip to parents and to wear it for a trial period. The V-chip inserted under his skin gives Cartman an electric shock whenever he utters what are considered to be 'dirty' or 'potty-mouthed' words. Both courses of action are designed to provide a 'smut-free' environment in which to bring up South Park children. Ironically enough, as the V-chip was invented in Canada, that country provides both the source of and the 'solution' for the adult concerns raised in the film.

As is often the case in *South Park* television episodes, in the film it is left to the children of South Park to save the day and show adults a more reasonable way forward. This is one of many occasions in *South Park* texts that confound social expectations that children are not interested in or capable of taking 'political' action. It is the children who attempt to save Terrance and Phillip from execution in order to avert the wholesale destruction of the world. And it is young Kyle who finally points out to his mother that she would be better off helping him to solve his problems rather than fighting causes in the abstract. Finally, in a typically subversive plot twist, complete global devastation is averted when Cartman utters the foulest language that he can muster in order to activate the full electric power of his V-chip to vanquish Saddam Hussein. In a complete turnabout from the original pre-mise of Mothers Against Canada, a child's imitation of Terrance and Phillip's swear words has consequences of the utmost benefit for young and old alike. On this point Kyle Broflovski is given the last word: 'You see, Mom? After all that, it was Cartman's filthy f***ing mouth that saved us all!' If the South Park environment had remained smut-free as parents had intended, the world would have been completely destroyed.

South Park: Bigger, Longer and Uncut continues a theme first introduced in 'Death', an early episode of *South Park* in which Mrs. Broflovski convenes a meeting of the PTA to discuss the negative effects on children of *The Terrance and Phillip Show*. In the fictional community of South Park the *Terrance and Phillip* cartoon stirs up as much controversy as the *South Park* texts have stirred up in real life. Incensed by the foul language and poor behaviour she believes the children have learned from *The Terrance and Phillip Show*, Mrs. Broflovski leads the South Park PTA in a campaign against the Cartoon Central network for the pro-vision of better TV for South Park's children. However, while the parents carry placards that read 'We want quality television' and 'Hearts not farts', the network responds with the 'prepared' statement of 'F**k you!', thus implying that no matter what parents want, ratings rather than 'quality' are what count for the network.

Meanwhile, in one of many displays of adult hypocrisy in the *South Park* texts, Mr. Garrison cautions his students that: 'Shows like *Terrance and Phillip* are what we call toilet humour. They don't expand your minds. You see, children, these kinds of shows are senseless, vile trash.' Further, he is 'concerned that you all seem to enjoy the show even if it isn't based on reality'. Hilar-iously, of course, regular viewers of the programme know that showing episodes of the TV series *Barnaby Jones* is a staple of Mr. Garrison's teaching method. Moreover, when challenged by his students about how much class time is given over to this pursuit,

Mr. Garrison's defence has been that they won't get very far in life unless they pay attention to the lessons learned from TV. Hence the children are at once criticized for learning lessons from TV and chastized for not taking enough notice of the lessons it teaches.

Finally, in the same episode, while their parents protest successfully and have *Terrance and Phillip* taken off air – only to be replaced by an adult programme which is similarly riddled with crude language – the South Park boys get into some serious trouble when Death comes to town. Despite several frantic phone calls to their parents, the children fail to convince their demonstrating elders that they need help. The refusal of the distracted South Park parents to heed the boys' urgent requests for practical assistance leads Stan to conclude: 'You know, I think if parents spent less time worrying about what their kids are watching on TV, and more time worrying about what's going on in kids' lives, the world would be a better place.' Such platitudes uttered from 'the mouths of babes' – often prefaced by 'You know, I/we've learned something today' – are a recurring feature of *South Park* texts.[22] While they serve to keep viewers delicately balanced between laughter and seriousness, the humour of the situation often turns on the displacement of conventional boundaries between childhood and adulthood. In the end, despite their occasional ignorance, selfishness and silliness, South Park children often speak and behave 'like adults' whereas the adults behave as stupidly and irresponsibly as children are generally assumed to do.

'What the hell was that?': Tensions between children's and adults' perspectives on the world

Because their protagonists are children, the texts of *South Park* necessarily depict children and childhood. However, as the writer E. L. Doctorow has pointed out, a central element of the condition of childhood is the experience of not knowing exactly what is going on. This provides those who write from the perspective of children with a technical advantage, in that child narrators and protagonists can be intimate with the story without knowing exactly what the truth is. In such cases writers, readers and viewers share a fuller knowledge of the situation than do the children. This certainly accounts for some of the humour that adult viewers find in the *South Park* texts, especially when the story-lines concern such topics as sex, war and the shady practices of businessmen and politicians. On these occasions, unlike Cartman and his friends – who are often heard to exclaim 'What the hell was that?' – older viewers can recognize what is going on and appreciate the humorous side of the children's naivety and ignorance.

This device, however, can tread a fine line between comedy and bad taste when it deals with sensitive social and moral issues. In the episode 'Cartman joins NAMBLA', for example, Cartman fails to understand the moral and physical danger he could be in when he decides he wants to 'start hanging out with more mature people' and decides to use the internet to meet 'men who like young boys'. In another episode, 'Starvin' Marvin', the children use a parent's credit card to sponsor a starving child in order to win a free sports watch, but fail to consider the attendant responsibilities and possible consequences for the child. However, on many occasions the events depicted are so bizarre that there is no possible answer to the question 'What the hell was that?' – as the residents of South Park are visited by aliens, pets from a parallel evil universe and rampant mutant vicious Thanksgiving turkeys. This is nonsensical humour just for the hell of it.

South Park scripts also focus on situations that adults and children alike will recognize as being integral to the condition of childhood. These situations include peer rivalries, boring or silly school assignments, schoolyard fights and birthday parties. In addition, children are shown caught up in power relations with adults. They are depicted being asked to do things that are difficult, distasteful or unfair – often absurdly so – by adults who either fail to recognize the possible effects of their requests or else do not care. *South Park* thus conveys a strong sense of the child's predicament as being 'subject' to adults. Paradoxically such situations are at times accompanied by directives to the 8-year-old children that they stop 'acting like kids' and stop being so 'immature' and 'juvenile'. Rather, they are told that they should 'grow up' and 'act like 8-year-olds'. In some cases, however, the boys turn the tables on such dictums, as when Stan decides to defy his parents and run away from home, declaring: 'You can't tell me what to do. I'm 8 years old!'

Memorable incidents when South Park's children are asked to do distasteful things include Kyle being asked to hold Cartman's grandma's catheter bag during dinner, and Stan being relegated to the basement to entertain himself with 'the geekiest kids in school' while his parents enjoy themselves at an upstairs adult party. Cartman is pressured to donate a kidney to save a friend, and Kenny is often asked to undertake physically dangerous challenges that result in his death. Even their beloved Chef ignores their pleas and makes the boys play in the international final of the extremely violent sport of dodgeball, against their express wishes. One of the most extended instances of cruelty towards the children occurs in the episode 'Chicken Pox' in which the children are unknowingly exposed by their parents to the chicken pox virus. When Kyle fails to contract the virus after having spent the night at the infected Kenny's house, his mother goes so far as to instruct him to play a game in which he swallows Kenny's infected saliva. Once Kyle realizes the extent of the plot that has been hatched, he leads the others in a revenge plot against their parents. In this case the children successfully fight back using the herpes-infected prostitute Freda to infect their parents' toothbrushes and other domestic utensils. This is one episode that concludes with the boys being offered full apologies from their parents, with Sheila Broflovski admitting that 'we were wrong for deceiving you'. On most other occasions, however, adult deception of children is taken for granted and viewers can recognize this even if the child protagonists cannot.

'Oh my God! They killed Kenny!': Using stories of children's lives to address controversial topics

Thus far I have grouped together Stan, Cartman, Kyle and Kenny and suggested that they somehow stand in for 'the children' of South Park. I have also suggested that the four boys are depicted having 'typical' childhood experiences. However, as I said at the outset, the boys are also depicted as four different stereotypes that provide amusing counterpoints to the range of stereotypes that regularly appear in *South Park*. The use of stereotypes also allows the creators to tap into some more controversial aspects and images of childhood as they play with, contest and critique stereotypical representations of children. My own favourite example of this is when the substitute teacher Miss Ellen learns the hard way that she should not 'f**k with' the apparently 'sweet' and mild-mannered Wendy Testaburger by competing with her for the affections of Stan Marsh.

The four main characters are stereotypical, although not consistently so across all episodes. Eric Cartman is fat, foul-mouthed and usually impossibly selfish. Stan Marsh is a naive and sensitive thinker who is sometimes something of a leader among the boys. Kyle Broflovski is the son of a Jewish lawyer father and a stereotypical Jewish mother with a New York accent. He is often to be seen grappling with some of the existential dilemmas associated with the apparent fixities of his Jewish identity. Kenny McCormick is the street-wise son of a drunken, unemployed and very poor father. In series four these four boys are joined as foci of the programme by Timmy, their intellectually and physically challenged new Grade Four classmate. Timmy's adventures add outrageous new dimensions to the political incorrectness of *South Park*. Meanwhile, the programme also regularly holds up for scrutiny the views of mainstream America on these same issues, including poverty, celebrity, war, gun laws, abortion, assisted suicide, sexual harassment, homosexuality, organized religion and attitudes towards the disabled. The texts of *South Park* satirize the kind of political correctness that destroys children's pleasures in the Christmas season for fear of offending non-Christians and minority groups, while they simultaneously continue to make offensive remarks about women, homosexuals, Mexicans, the Japanese and others.

Whereas Stan, Cartman and Kyle are by-and-large 'typical' 8-year-olds, Kenny McCormick is different in several respects. The most obvious of these is his voice, since what he says is mostly inaudible to the viewer. His dialogue is always muffled and only partially audible, largely because of the orange parka hood that closely circles his face leaving only his eyes exposed. However, although viewers can rarely hear the exact words Kenny speaks, other characters register that they clearly understand him. Thus the depiction of the Kenny character reverses the device discussed earlier in which the viewer 'understands' more than the boys. In the case of Kenny, the joke is on the viewers. Moreover, because the 'content' of what Kenny says is often clearly registered by his playmates as being either sexually knowledgeable or hilariously crude, viewers are implicated in attempting to decipher the sexual content or innuendo in his comments. Viewers are allowed just enough opportunity to use Kenny's tone, inflection and other contextual cues to infer that what he is saying is suggestive of an 'adult' rather than a child's knowledge of sexual matters. He is, for example, able to explain to the boys the *vas deferens*, and he knows the purpose of a dildo. Thus the Kenny character, unlike the other child characters, is not excluded from the domain of sexuality, and his sexual precociousness adds to the way the *South Park* texts blur the boundaries between childhood and adulthood.

A second obvious difference between Kenny and the other three boys is that Kenny is subjected to a weekly death. A predictable pattern as well as fantasy element of the *South Park* series story-line is that although Kenny is killed in every episode but one – the Christmas episode in series one – he reappears in the following episode as if nothing had happened. This provides viewers with an age-old narrative pleasure. In every episode they experience the delightful anticipation of the inevitable, and the gradual revelation (or withholding) of details about when and how Kenny's demise will happen. Nonetheless, as the critics point out, Kenny often dies in a very violent or gruesome, albeit cartoon-like, fashion. He is speared on the end of a flag pole, run over by cars and trucks, beheaded and shot. These deaths are attended by lots of blood and gore and sometimes followed by the appearance of scavenging rats. However, Kenny's dispatch can also be a very low-key event, such as the time he is killed by a falling cart of underpants or overcome by the chicken-pox virus and flat-lined in Hell's Pass hospital just as the other three boys celebrate their recovery. Clearly these incidents would be coded as 'violent' in the measures used by Media Index. On the other hand, they are obviously not meant to be taken seriously or measured against any index of 'realism'. What the critics of *South Park* seem to forget is that, as for 'action' and 'horror' movie fans, viewing pleasure is related to familiarity with conventions of narrative, characterization and dialogue. Such familiarity enables the writers to treat the use of 'violence' with a level of irony and sardonic humour that is recognized and appreciated by fans.[23]

An additional source of pleasure for the viewer when Kenny dies is the anticipation of how his death will be registered by the other boys. More often than not, each death elicits from Stan and Kyle the predictable cry of 'Oh my God! They killed Kenny. You bastards!' The occasional variations on this response, designed to match an episode's particular narrative line, provide moments of bathos or high points of dramatic and humorous contrast. Hence the cry sometimes changes to 'Oh my God! I found a penny' (as a stampeding crowd kills Kenny), 'Oh my God! They videotaped killing Kenny', or 'Oh my God! They killed the little orange coat kid'. Once this pattern has been established it can be varied to great effect – or, in the case of the episode titled 'A South Park Christmas', made the butt of a Christmas goodwill joke, as Kenny survives a series of situations that would in any other episode herald his demise. In the final scene Cartman, Kyle and Stan ponder why it feels that 'something's still not right' and feels 'unfinished'. As the credits roll, the still-living Kenny chuckles heartily. By series four of *South Park* the pattern of Kenny's death and resurrection is so predictable that it too can be parodied. In one episode the creators allow the 'reborn' Kenny to return in the same episode in which he dies. In the final scene of this episode the characters comment that 'God! This must be the fiftieth time this has happened!', only to be corrected with the news that it is indeed the fifty-second time that Kenny has 'died' and then returned to South Park.

A third point of difference between Kenny and the other boys is that his family's poverty is made the butt of many jokes that would by most standards be considered tasteless or politically incorrect. The chicken pox episode is illustrative of this process in action. When Kenny contracts the chicken pox virus the parents of the other three boys decide to send their children to a slumber party at the McCormicks' house. Their aim is to help the boys avoid the more serious consequences of contracting the virus when they are older. As they set out for Kenny's house, the boys' prejudices towards and intolerance of the McCormicks' poverty is obvious. Kyle's response is that 'he'd [Kenny] better have Nintendo', while Cartman approaches the house singing the refrain from a popular song, 'In the Ghetto'. The stereotypical depiction of a household living in poverty is evidenced by Kenny's father's unemployment, the colourful language spoken by the family, the low level of cleanliness of the McCormicks and their rat-infested house.

It is typical of Cartman that his response to what he sees at

Kenny's house is to threaten Kenny: 'Seriously, you'd better stop being so poor or I'm gonna start chucking rocks at you.' Kyle's response, on the other hand, is less predictable. While Kyle at first complains that Kenny does not have the kind of material possessions he's used to, he gradually begins to wonder how such inequities between poor and well-off families have come about. He decides to pursue this topic for his homework assignment on the theme of 'How I would make America better'. In the course of his 'research', he asks his father why it is that, if he and Kenny's father were childhood friends, the Broflovskis now live in a big house and have lots of food while Kenny's family eats frozen waffles for dinner and has rats on the floor. In a completely deadpan manner, his lawyer father 'explains' that it's 'because we have more money than they do'. He laughs at Kyle's suggestion that the Broflovskis could give the McCormicks some of their excess resources and assures Kyle that 'making America better' is not simply a matter of balancing economic inequities. Instead, Kyle's father points out the functional value of people 'keeping their place' in society. He argues: 'We humans live in a society, and in order for society to thrive, we need gods and clods.' He concludes his 'lesson' in economics and social justice by assuring Kyle that 'America needs both rich and poor to survive' and suggests that Kyle take heart because 'Kenny's family is happy just the way they are, and we're all a functioning part of America'. Older viewers at least will register the heavy irony, sarcasm and political satire in such episodes.

The characterization of Kenny McCormick and the story-lines with which he is associated thus tap into many of the domains of social life from which children have traditionally been excluded: the domains of violence and sexuality, of the economy, and of politics.[24] This may serve to explain some of the discomfort felt by many adults in relation to the texts of *South Park* and children's desire to watch them. Kenny's displays of sexually 'precocious' behaviour are examples of a range of manifestations of precociousness in children that 'threaten the separation between adults and children, and hence represent a challenge to adult power'.[25] When Kenny and the other three main child characters in the *South Park* display such forms of precociousness, they not only embody disturbing ideas about childhood but also act as vehicles for the expression of 'adults' ambivalent feelings about children, and about their own childhoods'.[26]

Helen Nixon

Is *South Park* a children's or an adults' television programme?

South Park is not programmed as 'children's television'. Nor would it normally be thought of as a 'children's programme', largely due to its language and its sexual and violent content. On the other hand, because of its focus on the lives of 8-year-old children, and because of its status as an animated cartoon, it would not normally be thought of as 'adult' viewing either. So is it a children's programme or an adult's programme – or is it both?

To debate this question is already to have made at least three assumptions. First, there is the assumption that television programmes can be neatly divided according to such categories as 'child' and 'adult'. Thus the question takes it for granted that television texts for children contain certain recognizable features against which *South Park* can be measured, and that the same is true of television texts for adults. Yet even if this may once have been the case, the situation is almost certainly changing.

A second and related assumption is that because a programme is intended for adults, it will therefore appeal to adults and not to children. However, as I have shown, this has not been the case for *South Park*. Indeed, many contemporary television texts – especially cartoons and comedies – have dual forms of address and crossover appeal to younger and older viewers. Although it often remains unstated, this second assumption is associated with a broader set of moral assumptions about the kind of material that is regarded as 'suitable' for adult viewers and 'unsuitable' for children. However, it is clear that children's viewing is not, and rarely has been, constrained by such views.

A third assumption that lies behind the question 'Who is *South Park* for?' is that people's viewing choices are made on the basis of their preferences for certain kinds of 'content' or genre. However, audience research points to the fact that people's viewing choices are more broadly socially motivated, and that this might especially be the case for child and teenage viewers.[27] For these audiences there are social benefits to be gained by being 'in the know' about media cultural texts that are currently popular, even where such knowledge has obviously been gleaned second hand from peers or other media sources. Moreover, research with children suggests that knowledge of and talk about television play a significant part in defining and negotiating identities in terms of age and gender.[28] Children's responses to *South Park*'s controversial content and to the definition of it as an 'adult' programme are therefore likely to be complex and differentiated according to a number of social variables.

Furthermore, the nature of the viewing audience for any particular television programme is likely to change over time. So, for example, a programme such as *Teletubbies* that was designed to appeal to children later gained cult appeal with older viewers and particular social groups who responded to its 'camp' elements (see David Buckingham's chapter in this volume). Conversely, I have suggested that the fact that *South Park* was from the first considered 'adults-only viewing' may well explain part of the appeal it later came to hold for young viewers. Yet the fact that *South Park* eventually became popular with child viewers may well explain why it appears to have lost popularity among some older teenagers and young adults. Perhaps it became more difficult for the programme to sustain its level of 'cool' cachet among young adult viewers once 9- and 10-year-old children started wanting *South Park* products and wearing *South Park* T-shirts to school. As is so often the case in its treatment of other matters, *South Park* shows a degree of self-consciousness and reflexivity in relation to the fads and fashions of popular culture. One episode deals with the desirability of the '*Dawson's Creek* Trapper Keeper', a high-tech personal organizer that provides access to radio and television signals as well as connectivity with computers and computer peripherals; while another episode, 'ChinPoko Mon', directly addresses the phenomenon of viewer fluidity, exploring the way popular culture fads decline among one audience once they gain popularity with a different age group or when the adult generation begins to show an interest.

Ultimately, there is much more at stake here than settling the question of whether *South Park* is or is not a children's programme. The texts of *South Park* are among the range of sites in which the social construction of contemporary childhood is played out. In their contestation and critique of accepted social expectations of childhood they can be at times shocking and funny and poignant. However, they may also provide some contemporary children and teenagers with material against which they can define and assert their identities, and with which they are able to negotiate changing social relations with their peers and with adults. Whether they do in fact serve such functions is a question that remains to be explored through audience research.

Notes

1. *Time*, 18 August 1997, p. 74.
2. R. Marin, ' "Peanuts" gone wrong. Review of *South Park*, *Newsweek*, 21 July 1997, vol. 130, p. 69.
3. *Going Down to South Park*, Channel 4 television/Warner Vision, 1999.
4. *The Adelaide Advertiser*, South Australia, 24 December 1997, p. 34.
5. D. Buckingham, 'Television and the definition of childhood', in B. Mayall (ed.), *Children's Childhoods: Observed and Experienced* (London: Falmer, 1994), pp. 79–96.
6. Market research for Australian public broadcaster SBS conducted by A. C. Nielsen showed that by the second series *South Park* had attracted the channel's largest audience since SBS was established in 1980. 60 per cent of these viewers were teens (13–17) and young adults (18–24), and 30 per cent had never previously tuned in to the minority multicultural and multilingual broadcaster.
7. David Buckingham, *After the Death of Childhood: Growing up in the Age of Electronic Media* (Cambridge: Polity, 2000), p. 77.
8. Buckingham, *After the Death of Childhood*, pp. 94–5.
9. P. Kelley, D. Buckingham and H. Davies, 'Talking dirty: children, sexual knowledge and television', *Childhood*, 6 (2), 221–42, 1999.
10. Kinder quoted in Buckingham, 'After the Death of Childhood', p. 90.
11. *Going Down to South Park*.
12. N. Manktelow, 'Three-letter word still Net's preoccupation', *The Australian*, 12 February 1999, p. 3.
13. Buckingham, 'Television and the definition of childhood', reports that half of 7–10-year-olds in the UK have TVs in their bedrooms and a significant proportion of these have VCRs (p. 83).
14. *Ibid.*', p. 85.
15. A. Gavin, 'Kenny and a little gang of shockers', *The Advertiser*, 17 July 1999, p. 39.
16. For example, see *ibid.* and W. Epstein and E. Tahaney, 'Right off the dirt meter', *The Advertiser*, 15 July 1999, pp. 44–5.
17. *Ibid.*, p. 44.
18. *Going Down to South Park*.
19. Gavin, 'Kenny'.
20. See Buckingham, 'Television and the definition of childhood'.
21. Kelley, Buckingham, and Davies, *Talking Dirty*, p. 239.
22. These 'lessons' learned by the children are frequently about the

media, although they can also be absurdly comical. For example, after they respond to a television advertisement asking them to sponsor a starving African child, Stan describes what he's learned about television and real life.

Stan: 'You know. I think I've learned something today. It's really easy not to think of images on TV as real people. But they are. That's why it's easy to ignore those commercials. But people on TV are just as real as you or I.'
Kyle: 'Yeah. And that means that McGyver is a real person too.'

23. Buckingham, *After the Death of Childhood*, p. 137.
24. *Ibid*.
25. *Ibid*., p. 14.
26. *Ibid*., p. 35. In interviews Parker and Stone admit that many of the scripts of 'South Park' begin with broad-ranging discussions of memories from their own childhoods.
27. *Ibid*., Chapter 6.
28. Kelley, Buckingham and Davies, 'Talking dirty'.

CHAPTER 6

Classics with Clout

Costume Drama in British and American Children's Television

MÁIRE MESSENGER DAVIES

As Robin Nelson has recently pointed out,[1] costume drama has traditionally found a home in children's television schedules. Buckingham *et al.*, in a discussion about classic TV adaptations for children, propose that British children's television is seen as 'the cornerstone of public service, an embodiment of "quality" and of a distinctively British cultural identity'[2] – which provides a possible explanation for why the genre has been so recurrent in children's slots. Nelson is writing primarily about British television's recent revivals of *adult* costume drama, such as the BBC's 1995 *Pride and Prejudice*, and does not explore further why children's schedules should appear to be a 'natural home' for the genre. In this chapter, I want to suggest a number of reasons why children's schedules are hospitable to costume drama and why child audiences are responsive to the genre (as they are). This chapter reviews some of the differences between costume drama on children's television and adult forms, and looks specifically at two examples of the genre: one, *Anne of Green Gables*, produced in North America, and thus, geographically at least, outside the paradigm of British high-quality 'heritage' programming; the other, *The Prince and the Pauper*, produced for the BBC in the UK, which also both conforms to, and challenges, this paradigm. Both were shown on each side of the Atlantic.

Children's television schedules

Children's schedules, whether on the BBC or within the British commercial system, have traditionally attempted to provide a microcosm of adult schedules. Children's drama, like adult drama, could be said to reflect, in John Caughie's terms, the dual emphases of realistic authenticity, based on TV's origins in live studio production, and prestigious literary 'heritage' drama, as in adaptations of classic literature. These twin traditions of realism and heritage are, for Caughie, the characteristic signifiers of British television drama:

> The effect of immediacy, of a directness which signifies authenticity, is one of the characteristics which gives British television drama its specific form – still at the beginning of the 90s, distinguishing it from cinema or from the American telefilm.[3]

Children's costume drama, especially the adaptations of literary classics, could further be said to fit the paradigm identified by Charlotte Brunsdon,[4] of British 'quality' television. For Brunsdon, the main components of this kind of 'quality' are: first, literary sources; second, what she calls 'the best of British acting', borrowing the prestige of classical theatrical performers, such as Dame Peggy Ashcroft in Granada's *The Jewel in the Crown* (1984); thirdly, money 'on screen', reflected in expensive location shooting and careful attention to period design; and fourth, 'heritage export', conforming to a popular theme-park notion of British culture which is expected to sell abroad, especially in the USA.

A primary market for heritage exports is the US Public Broadcasting Service's *Masterpiece Theatre*, sponsored by Mobil Oil, which showcases British classic TV adaptations. On the American side of the Atlantic, different configurations of money, taste, power and institutional influence determine definitions of 'quality'. These transatlantic definitions affect the international co-production of British children's television too. Lawrence Jarvik, an American critic, following, and extending, Bourdieu,[5] describes British costume drama as:

> a trading commodity valued in the markets of economic, social and cultural capital, with an exchange value determined by negotiation between Mobil, the British, the middlemen of PBS and the press,

and the highly educated and affluent audience of public television.[6]

Jarvik invokes Stuart Hall's concepts of 'negotiated readings' to point out that a phenomenon like *Masterpiece Theatre* cannot be fully understood unless interpreted from an American perspective:

> French and English scholarly traditions, while valuable, cannot unproblematically provide the specificity needed for analysis of *Masterpiece Theatre* ... American traditions, rooted in sociology, history and the study of communications, might provide some theoretical context ...[7]

Jarvik usefully draws attention to the point – which I will develop later on – that there can be no unitary categorizing of costume drama as a particular kind of genre, based on assumptions about audience readings. Certainly in the case of children's costume drama, American examples of the genre, as discussed below, are different from British examples in a number of ways, and have often been more successful with audiences than British ones. Further, academic analyses of the genre, based on adult class-oriented readings, do not always take account of the fact that children, as an audience, cross all social classes and all socially based demographic categories. Children have to read texts from the perspective of being children, as well as from the perspective of 'middle class' or 'working class' or 'ethnic minority' demographic groupings, and this will inform their interpretations in ways not shared by adult audiences. For example, children may find it easier to identify with American child characters than with British characters from environments similar to their own, as a 1996 study by Hannah Davies for Channel 4 found out.[8] I want to suggest that 'being a child' may be a more central aspect of identity for child readers and audiences than other demographic aspects – a point developed further in my study of children and television drama, carried out for the BBC.[9]

Quality, in Brunsdon's typology, like much British writing on television drama, *is* primarily related to concerns about social class. Such concerns have prompted academic uneasiness about the extent to which working-class cultural traditions have been economically appropriated by 'civic programmes' and private commercial redevelopments, and re-packaged back to their originators as 'heritage', as in the case of the mining museums which have replaced the South Wales coal industry. For John Corner and Sylvia Harvey:

> remodelled versions of 'identity' and 'belonging' have been ... offered as *compensatory* in relation to the undertones of destabi- lization and fragmentation carried by the enterprise imperative, along with its official melodies of opportunity and progress.[10]

In the same vein, 'quality' as Brunsdon defines it has connotations of '*the* quality' – the upper-class elite of British society – although she is careful to point out that more pragmatic definitions of the term are needed, especially in teaching and evaluating students' creative work.[11] For Jarvik, writing in the USA, the guarantors of quality have more market-oriented connotations, deriving from the financial muscle of 'trade' (Mobil). In Britain, argues Bruns- don, lavishly produced costume dramas, based on classic texts whose place in the literary canon has been secured, become automatically associated with upper-middle class, or aristocratic, tastes and values, and the origins of wealth in low commerce (even where these origins are acknowledged in the original novels) are hidden. In British classic dramas, given the association of 'costume' with 'upper class', even the low-life horrors of Dickens, no matter how realistically portrayed (as in ITV's 1999 production of *Oliver Twist*), become overlaid with the sheer taste- ful expertise of high-quality, costume-design research – 'designer rags'. These traditions also persist in children's programming but, because children's productions have less money, the temptation on the part of producers to dress up the sets with expensive- looking antiques is easier to resist. On the other hand, costume drama has the same economic advantages for children's televi- sion, as it does for adults'. As Lewis Rudd, formerly head of children's programming at Carlton, pointed out in a 1996 inter- view: 'Period drama has an enormous advantage because it doesn't date.'[12]

I want to argue that the apparent similarity between children's and adults' televised costume dramas is in many respects super- ficial. In the first place, with smaller budgets, less favourable scheduling, but similar requirements for 'quality' production values as for adult drama, children's television drama has always been the poor relation in the prestigious British tradition. This has, to some extent, worked in its favour, since innovative writers and producers could experiment, secure in the knowledge that the powers-that-be were not taking much notice of them, as Sandra Hastie, producer of ITV's ground-breaking *Press Gang* (1988–92), found out when she came to Britain from the USA.[13] Children's drama remains hidden from critical scrutiny. There is no tradition of press reviewing of children's drama (although I was allowed to write the occasional column about it in *The Listener* in the 1970s and 1980s) and academic writers on British 'quality' broadcasting, such as Brunsdon, Corner, Harvey and Caughie, make only passing reference to children's programmes. While there is an increasing amount of attention in Media and Cultural Studies scholarship to more 'down-market' children's forms such as cartoons, comic strips and crazes like *Pokémon*,[14] the television texts which cost the most money and, as their producers would argue, require the most intense and complex human creative efforts in terms of research, script, design, choreography, musicianship, craftsmanship, performance, cinematography, human organisation, planning, rehearsal, direction and general production values – that is, live-action drama – are hardly ever analytically discussed. This is all the more surprising given their prestige value, as proudly proclaimed by the BBC.

This lack of recognition of children's drama as part of the 'great tradition'[15] of British television, reflects a more general critical neglect of fictional material specifically labelled as 'children's'. Similarly, Peter Hunt has pointed out how literature for children written by otherwise venerated authors – Thomas Hardy, Graham Greene, Leo Tolstoy – becomes something other than literature once it is labelled 'for children' and becomes invisible to critical attention.[16] Children's television drama has suffered very much from this invisibility; much of it, even from as recently as the 1980s, does not survive at all, in video or any other form – a major drawback for the scholar, and another reason for lack of critical attention. Unless you happened to catch the broadcasts, you will not have seen, or perhaps even have heard of, many of the texts I am about to refer to. In this, children's television differs from children's literature: its supposed middle-class values have not been sufficient to guarantee its physical, and cultural, survival.

A further distinction between children's and adults' drama is that children's is explicitly, as distinct from only implicitly, required to be didactic. Thus, for example, Steven Andrew, former producer of *Grange Hill*, the BBC's contemporary series about a comprehensive school, stated: 'We have a responsibility within those stories to be informative and to have a clear moral guideline as to why we are doing the stories and the outcomes.'[17] Anna Home, former head of Children's Programming at the BBC, in her 1993 history of British children's television, defended the centrality of costume drama because 'It is important that children should get some element of historical perspective in their drama.'[18] One reason for the lack of prestige and seriousness allotted to children's television could thus be partly because, as with children's literature, it is, in Hunt's phrase, 'defined by use', not by standards of canonical cultural value. The common ground of most analyses of children's culture, including material like *Pokémon*, is that it is seen as having a socializing effect from which children either 'need' to be protected, as is implied in critiques of right-wing, unprogressive, nostalgic screen fiction,[19] or to which they 'need' to be exposed, as in the argument for giving them 'historical perspective'. Drama, even more than other sorts of children's programme, is expected to serve the discourse of 'need' and to help children in the task of growing up to be fully socialized citizens – 'programming for a liberal democracy', as David Oswell has called it.[20] Despite the public service discourse of 'quality' noted by Brunsdon, such socializing requirements are not laid to the same extent on adult programming.

The genres of children's costume drama

From the child audience point of view, 'need' is a less important component of the genre than spectacle, fantasy and diversity. Children's costume drama is more generically diverse than adults'. It cannot all be grouped under the single heading of 'literary heritage'. It does not rely primarily on classic literary adaptations, but has a number of forms. First, there are adaptations of children's classics written in the past, so 'historical' to us, but contemporary and 'modern', even 'daring', for their original readers when first published.[21] These are most similar to the adult genre in terms of their straight literary credentials and include Frances Hodgson Burnett's *Little Lord Fauntleroy* (BBC, 1995), *The Secret Garden* (BBC, 1950, 1962, 1975) and regular adaptations of E. Nesbit's stories set at the turn of the twentieth century, the most recent version of *The Treasure Seekers* being produced by Carlton for ITV in 1995.

These classics can be re-adapted to give different contemporary resonances every time they are produced. For instance, Agnieszka Holland's 1993 film of *The Secret Garden*, with its flamboyantly sexualized Gothic Romantic style and an opening sequence homaging *Pretty Woman*, made a marked contrast to Dorothea Brooking's 1975 BBC serialization, in which, typically for a British production, class was more central than sex: here (as in Burnett's original), it was the emotional and social rescue of two dysfunctional, neglected upper-class children by the local, earthy, Yorkshire working-class community, that was foregrounded. These dramas appear historical, and hence, perhaps, 'irrelevant' or 'unrealistic', to modern children, because of their costumes and settings, but they were not to their original readers, and they are not 'about' history. Unlike historical novels, in which real historical events serve as a backdrop for adventures featuring children and young people (as in the Roman Britain novels of Rosemary Sutcliff), costume dramas like *The Secret Garden* are not concerned with 'history' in its public sense. They are more accurately described as domestic dramas about the daily lives of children in the past.

The second category of costume drama is children's historical novels. Historical novels are those which are set in a time earlier than the author's own lifetime, and do feature real historical events. The author him or herself may also be a 'classic' to us; and this can give a doubly distancing effect, when produced with an awareness of both the social conditions contemporary to the author and the social conditions about which the author was writing (see comments by Julian Fellowes on p. 134). Examples – both written during the nineteenth century – are the American Mark Twain's *The Prince and the Pauper*, set in sixteenth-century Tudor England (BBC, 1996) and Captain Marryat's *Children of the New Forest* (BBC, 1998 and 2000), set during the English Civil War in the seventeenth century.

Children's historical novels are a less popular genre today than in the early days of broadcasting, reflecting a general nervousness in multicultural Britain about which versions of history should be offered, whether in the culture more broadly, or in the school curriculum. Anna Home refers to adaptations of *The Black Arrow* and *Treasure Island* in the 1950s and 1960s, Thames TV's serialization of *Warrior Queen*, starring Sian Phillips as Boudicca in 1978, and Catherine Cookson's *Our John Willie*, (BBC, 1980) about a mining disaster set in the industrial North East in the early 1900s.[22] Instead of historical novels like these, the currently most popular genre of children's drama is the 'wizard/witch' narrative, which does permit an element of 'costume', but is usually contemporary in setting. In these stories (for example, *The Magician's House*, BBC, 1999–2000, co-produced with the Canadian Broadcasting Corporation), magic is the agency whereby historical or geographical distance is provided, rather than imaginative transportation through time via an author's historical writing. The distancing effect is common to both genres, however: children are made aware of how events, circumstances and behaviours can become different from those they know, when historical or physical contexts are changed. In this, I would argue, the function and intended impact of historical and fantasy writing for children is different from the nostalgic escapism of the pure 'heritage' drama.

A sub-group of the historical novel category is children's 'historical' novels which are historical for children but not for adults because the events are in living memory, such as *Carrie's War* by Nina Bawden (BBC, 1974) and Michelle Magorian's *Goodnight Mr. Tom* (Carlton, 1998), set in the Second World War. In such productions, producers have to be aware that adult members of the audience have first-hand sources to verify the authenticity of the representations, and realism is a pronounced feature. Another example of this genre is the feature film, directed by Stephen Daldry, *Billy Elliott* (2000), about a 12-year-old boy who wants to be a dancer, set against the background of the 1984 miners' strike in North-eastern England – a classic children's story, unfortunately given a 15 certificate in the cinema in order to broaden adult appeal, because some of the characters occasionally swore.

In the BBC's *Just William* (1995), *The Chronicles of Narnia* (1988) and *The Box of Delights* (1984) the characters are all lovingly outfitted in the costumes of the 1930s and 1940s, with a period accuracy that no contemporary child would be capable of appreciating. The 'heritage' component in these cases – particularly for the Sunday teatime slot, when *Narnia* and *William* were scheduled – is aimed at adult audiences, in the way that the prep-school-uniformed five-year-old in the BBC's promotional film, *Future Generations* (1998), was aimed at adult audiences. In fact, there is no need for the William or Narnia characters to be clothed in anything other than present-day costume, nor would they be if they were being shown only to a child audience. For instance, in the 1960s, a young Denis Waterman played William as a 1960s contemporary child. However, now, the 'Sunday teatime' slot is seen as a time when adults are watching too, and it is to the adult licence payers that the period authenticity, with all its quality signifiers, is directed.

The fourth, and in many ways the most interesting, genre of children's costume drama, which is very common in children's storytelling, is the time-travelling fantasy. Examples include Helen Cresswell's *Moondial* (BBC, 1988), Lucy M. Boston's *The House at Green Knowe* (BBC, 1986) and Philippa Pearce's *Tom's Midnight Garden* (BBC, 1985). Time-travel stories are especially unsuited to a purely literary-heritage interpretation, because they do not permit the luxurious abandonment of the viewer into an apparently unchanging world of Heppelwhite furniture and Empire-line dresses for the duration of the episode. In time-travel stories, the characters are constantly moving between past and present, bearing insights and problems laid on them by the past into their contemporary lives. The desired sense of relaxation into the comfortably distant prettiness of 'heritage' cannot be achieved. The past is seen to be an unstable place, never to be relied on as a refuge. In no story, children's or adults', is the slipperiness of time, and the impossibility of memorializing the past intact, so brilliantly conveyed as in *Tom's Midnight Garden*, first published in 1958 and serialized by the BBC in 1985.

Time-travel stories are by their nature an alienating form, designed to demonstrate both similarities and disjunctions between contemporary children's lives and the lives of children in former times. This is often done through featuring children with rather unhappy and fractured lives, as with the orphaned Tolly in *Green Knowe*, or the disaffected teenagers in *The Magician's House*, who explore the conflicts in their own lives through similar experiences among children who are now dead. These past children, as in the *Green Knowe* stories, may be ancestors of the contemporary characters; as such they function as '*alter egos*', enabling the contemporary child to explore hidden aspects of his or her own identity and inheritance. They work particularly well in televised serial form. In stories like *Green Knowe* and *Tom's Midnight Garden*, the past serves as a parallel commentary on the present, linking themes of personal development with historical continuity and change. Far from providing a romanticized version of earlier eras of gracious living, the goal here is often to dwell on the social injustices and cruelties which befell children in the past, and which frequently parallel the problems of children in the present.

Gender and girls' fiction

Costume drama has sometimes been seen as a girls' or women's medium, and certainly many classic adaptations deal with girls' lives and feminist issues – another reason for not taking them seriously, as writers on adult women's literary tastes, such as Janice Radway,[23] have pointed out. Girls' lives and concerns have been much more prominent in classic North American children's writing than in British writing, which further distinguishes children's 'costume' fiction from adults'. Nearly all the nineteenth- and early twentieth-century classic girls' books which have been serialized for TV – *Little Women, What Katy Did, Pollyanna, Rebecca of Sunnybrook Farm, Little House on the Prairie*, and what is seen as a quintessentially English classic, *The Secret Garden* – are by American, or in the case of Hodgson Burnett, Americanized, authors. Alison Lurie, talking of *Little Women*, by Louisa May Alcott, published in 1868 and most recently filmed in 1994, draws attention to its feminist inspiration: 'For at least five generations of American girls, Jo was a rebel and an ideal and Louisa May Alcott's understanding of their own impatience with contemporary models of female behavior ... nothing less than miraculous.'[24] As Lurie acknowledges, *Little Women* is not seen by girls as a particularly liberationist story nowadays. However, in the 1994 film, with Winona Ryder as co-producer and star, Gillian Armstrong (*My Brilliant Career*) as director, Claire Danes (*My So-called Life; Romeo + Juliet*) as Beth, Kirsten Duntz (*The Virgin Suicides*) as Amy and Susan Sarandon (*Thelma and Louise*) as the central matriarch 'Marmee', the combination of so many female talents with a reputation for feistiness was able to draw attention to Alcott's original radical feminist message, using the crinolines and aspidistras as a foregrounding mechanism. Like Canadian Patricia Rozema's daring rescue in 1999 of Jane Austen's sombre tale of child neglect, exploitation, corruption, adultery and patriarchal failure, *Mansfield Park*, from the kind of conventional elegance of the BBC's 1986 production, Armstrong's *Little Women* used the costume-drama form, allied with unconventional casting and direction, to highlight feminist issues in ways which would have been less possible in a straightforward contemporary setting. Such bold re-readings seem to be more forthcoming from North American adapters than they are from British ones.

TV dramatizations, contemporary ideological 'spin' notwithstanding, are usually fairly faithful to the plots of the original texts. In contrast, *Little House on the Prairie* formed the basis of a long-running series on both American and British network television in the 1980s, in which the characters from Laura Ingalls Wilder's novels featured in stories which did not derive from the books at all. The same fate has recently (summer 2000) befallen one of the best-loved of all North American girls' books – *Anne of Green Gables*, by Lucy Maud Montgomery, first published in 1908, and set on Prince Edward Island in the Maritime States of Canada. Kevin Sullivan's *Anne of Green Gables: The Continuing Story* (shown in North America on PBS and CBC in 2000, but not shown yet in Europe), following his earlier more faithful adaptations of *Anne of Green Gables* (1985) and *Anne of Green Gables: the Sequel* (1987), illustrates the difference between reinterpreting a classic text by exposing authorial themes and motives obscured by canonization (as with Rozema's *Mansfield Park*) and plundering the text for its characters, in order to introduce themes and story-lines which, in their contemporary modishness, could never have been produced by the original writer. *Anne of Green Gables: The Continuing Story*, like *Little House*, bears little resemblance to its original author's novels, nor to the earlier Anne films.

By contrast, Kevin Sullivan's first two Anne films, shown in the UK on Channel 4 in 1986 and 1987, and repeated a number of times since, have been successful primarily because they are widely recognized as satisfying interpretations of Montgomery's radical original. They had all the markers of Brunsdonian quality in terms of their production values, their literary origins, and even a British acting Dame, Wendy Hiller, in the second movie, *The Sequel*. However, the films were not British but Canadian, and like the original book, have characteristics and qualities which do not conform neatly to quality definitions of costume drama based on class-bound British critical criteria. In particular their feminist qualities are much more typical of North American children's fiction than of anything written or produced in the UK.

Anne Shirley, of Green Gables, like Jo March in *Little Women*, is a misfit, and, as fans' contributions to the unofficial web site for the TV 'Anne' films illustrate, she functions as a symbol of unconventionality and freedom for girls, similar to the function of Scarlett O'Hara for the wartime women interviewed in Helen Taylor's study *Scarlett's Women*.[25] Anne is an unloved orphan who is adopted at the age of 11 by a middle-aged brother and sister in a nineteenth century-farming community, Avonlea, on Prince Edward Island. The opening of Sullivan's film, dramatizing the book's harsh backstory, reveals Anne (played by Megan Fol-lows) farmed out by her orphanage as a mother's help to an overworked, slatternly mother of three pairs of twins. Anne's only escape is fantasy; she walks through her daily chores reciting poetry and making up absurdly romantic stories. In a striking image of loneliness (taken from the book), we see Anne confiding in 'Katy Maurice', a little girl reflected in the glass door of a bookcase – her own reflection. This prefigures the way in which Anne (like her author, like Jo March and like Alcott) will find liberation; she will end up writing her own story. Anne is even-tually adopted by Marilla and Matthew Cuthbert of Green Gables and her adventures begin. Unusually, and satisfyingly, these adventures, deriving both from her incorrigible fantasizing and her streetwise commonsense, are primarily comic, and all are ultimately triumphant for the heroine.

Anne, like other North American girl protagonists of the period, is satisfying as a heroine in ways which heroines of British nineteenth- and early twentieth-century children's books seldom are (even the independent Edith Nesbit made her girl characters feeble). Like Jo/Alcott, Anne lives through the imagination, and finds fulfilment, first through a circle of girl friends with whom she plays fantasy games based on *The Lady of Shalott*, then by becoming a bright college student, vying with her long-time rival, Gilbert Blythe, for first place in the class, then a teacher of lit-erature, and finally a writer. Like Jo March, she also finds emo-tional fulfilment in marriage and motherhood in later sequels of her story (there are eight books altogether, the last, *Rilla of Ingleside*, dealing mainly with her grown-up children), and also like Jo, becomes singularly uninteresting as a heroine when this happens. Marriage and motherhood were required destinies for fictional heroines in Montgomery's and Alcott's day – but neither author was able to make these destinies as convincing as their heroines' adventures in childhood. This would clearly have been a problem for Sullivan had he tried to faithfully adapt the later Anne books, which all represent Anne as a wife and mother, supporting other people's adventures, rather than having any of her own, and – most significantly of all – no longer reading or telling stories.

The real tragedy for heroines like Anne is that they have to grow up at all (which perhaps says something about the necessity of remaining in childhood if you want to be a creative writer). Only in childhood can girls (as Anne does) fall into rivers; walk along ridge-poles of houses; rescue lost children; hit boys over the head with their slates; accuse respectably pious neighbours of being hateful; and get their friends inadvertently drunk on blackcurrant wine. It is these aspects of Anne's life that made the book a classic, and which rescue Sullivan's original Green Gables film from being primarily a picturesque travelogue romanticizing the pre-motorized beauties of the Island, where even a poor orphan was able to look 'perfectly elegant', to use an Anne phrase, in handknitted cardigans and calico pinafores. Sullivan's films edit out the poverty, death and resultant family break-up which feature so prominently in Montgomery's originals, but they faithfully foreground Anne's career as a student, a schoolteacher, and writer, and the centrality of her professional and financial independence. Equally reassuringly, the Anne books (and the films) never deny the centrality of love and nurturing for the healthy development of children – Anne's devotion to Marilla (Colleen Dewhurst in a last, career-crowning performance) and Matthew (the late Richard Farnsworth, of *The Straight Story*), her unconventional foster parents, is unwavering. In return, Marilla supports Anne's ambitions, but also teaches her not to ignore the emotional reality of her attachment to her truest 'kindred spirit', Gilbert Blythe, the spurned childhood lover and academic rival who encourages her to write her first book. The desired moment of Anne's first kiss with Gilbert is satisfyingly deferred until the very final shot of the second film. Anne's independence of character and intellect provide her with a career which no heroines of British girls' novels of the time would even contemplate, except as something shameful.

The filming and updating of 'classics' in such cases is thus not just a way of enforcing traditional bourgeois values from the past;

on the contrary, it is one of the ways in which popular media, such as film and broadcasting, can continue to fulfil what Lurie calls their 'subversive' functions for young audiences – especially, as in the Anne series, for girls. As the comparative failure of *The Continuing Story*, in contrast to *Anne of Green Gables*, indicates, such programmes are most successful with audiences when they reinforce the adventurousness and radicalism which made the original books classics in the first place.

'The Prince and the Pauper': teatime heritage drama

A serialization of *The Prince and the Pauper*, based on Mark Twain's fantasy story about Prince Edward, later King Edward VI, the 14-year-old son of Henry VIII, who changed places with a poor boy who looked exactly like him, was broadcast by the BBC in the Sunday teatime slot in winter 1996. As with *Anne*, Twain's *The Prince and the Pauper*, first published in the United States in 1882, does not fit comfortably into the British critical stereotype of 'quality' heritage drama, with its nostalgically reassuring visions of a supposedly stable past. The book is a 'fantasy with a republican edge', in Peter Hunt's words.[26] Like *Little Lord Fauntleroy*, another children's book 'with a republican edge', published in 1886, it offers a naïf's-eye critique of the offensively autocratic behaviour of kings and dukes, and the social injustices arising from such behaviour; although, when the child protagonists are restored to their rightful places, as they have to be in children's stories (another didactic requirement, as Peter Hunt points out), there is inevitably a conservative reinforcement of the status quo, which can belie the radicalism of the early chapters. The book has been televised in the UK twice before, the last time twenty years ago. As such, the 1996 production could be seen as an example of conservatism, and of returning to the suspect 'great tradition' of British children's television. The casting of Keith Michell, star of the BBC's 1970 series, *The Six Wives of Henry VIII*, as the dying king Henry VIII in *The Prince and the Pauper*, invoked this great tradition even more deliberately.

Buckingham *et al.* tend to disapprove of the characterization of children's drama as 'the cornerstone of public service ... and of a distinctively British cultural identity.'[27] However, as I have argued, whenever a historical classic is reinterpreted, as much can be revealed about contemporary ideological preoccupations as about the actual history represented in the story; and it is a mistake to assume that producers are not consciously aware of the opportunities offered by classic texts to challenge their audiences ideologically. In an interview on the set of *The Prince and the Pauper* – a full-scale 'quality' location in a Sussex country house – Julian Fellowes, the adaptor and producer, explained the difference between his production and previous ones. For him, the production had to balance his own sense of responsibility to historical verisimilitude, with the need to recognize the ideological perspectives of a contemporary audience, which are bound to differ from those of twenty years ago, when an earlier version was produced:

> I'm terribly conscious of the fact that it is the 1990s ... now, because we have a rather different attitude to politics and royalty ... and we have a rather degagé, disentangled vision of it at the moment – although I'm not in the least a republican – I think that does allow one to examine the predicament of the prince, and particularly the pauper who is living the life of the prince, in a different way ... I think that twenty years ago that wouldn't have been the case.[28]

Fellowes defended the representation of a scene showing non-conformists being burnt at the stake for 'teatime viewing' as being a morally necessary lesson in cultural relativism and tolerance, which would not have been acceptable in a children's drama twenty years ago. He also expressed an awareness of his own contribution to posterity:

> This was a cruel time and ours is not the only generation that have done brutal things ... We all remember in *Bambi* when the mother is shot. I cannot believe that some Disney executive wasn't sitting there saying, gee fellers, I dunno if we should let this guy's mother be shot, but the truth is that was one of the great moments of one's childhood. I'm not pretending that I think I'm making the great moments of someone's childhood, but nothing would give me more pleasure than if someone were to say to me when they were an old man, I remember the moment I got into history was when I saw the burning scene in *The Prince and the Pauper*. Then one would feel one's life had been well lived.[29]

Costume drama's appeal for children

The challenge for producers of children's costume drama is different from that of adult productions, partly because children lack historical knowledge, and are unlikely to notice, or care about, any failure of authenticity. Children's producers, as in Fellowes's case, will obviously want to defend themselves against charges of anachronism, but their main task is to take aspects of the past which by definition are unfamiliar to children, and make them familiar in ways that child audiences can understand, and learn from. Series like *The Prince and the Pauper*, set against the background of real historical events, which need to be portrayed accurately enough to satisfy educated adult audiences, can use the strangeness of the past, and its alienating aspects, to bring into relief aspects of children's lives that are especially relevant for them – identity, separation, independence, injustice and power-lessness. They can also be used, as Fellowes's production of Hodgson Burnett's *Little Lord Fauntleroy* in 1995 was used, to adopt a foreign perspective on British history and its class arrangements, which may be less flattering than homegrown interpretations.

Children's drama producers always have to be aware that this may be the first time an eight- or nine-year-old child has ever heard of the Tudor period: the historical detail has to be given straightforwardly, without intertextual references to other representations of the Tudors, of the kind so liberally scattered through, for example, the film *Shakespeare in Love* (1997). Irony and *double entendre* not only do not work for children, they undermine the point of historical costume drama, in which the adult generation is able to say to children: 'Here is a story you haven't heard, about some children whose predicaments you might recognize, set in a period of time where people did things differently from how we do them now.' The importance of historical context in the interpretations of classic texts – one of the central lessons of Cultural Studies – is an indispensable ingredient in producing credible historical dramas for children.

Another major source of appeal of costume drama for children is not just its historicity, but the sheer pleasure of costume itself – the enjoyability of spectacle and 'dressing up', as in children's own play. Costume is more than clothes, as children well know; it represents character and permits transformation. In 'quality' heritage drama, it may be merely an external signifier of expense, lavishness and prestige, in which 'money on screen' confers status and cultural centrality. However, when such prestigious sources of cultural capital are made available to children, transformation is possible: the child audience – for a change – is placed in the mainstream of the culture. Children are reminded that they are part of history too. For children, setting stories in the past also serves psychological functions – the same functions as 'long ago and far away' in fairy tale. Paradoxically, by exoticizing, the costume drama is able to generalize. The past, like the dark forest, is another country, in which problems of love, hate, sibling rivalry, power and reconciliation can appear in clear relief, unencumbered by realist distraction.

Given the association of costume drama with elitist middle-class values, one of the most surprising findings of a study with over 1300 5–13-year-olds in England and Wales, which colleagues and I carried out for the BBC in 1996–7,[30] concerned this genre. A quantitative analysis of children's responses according to a 'special needs index', based on the schools' own statistical information about the proportions of their children having free meals, living in council housing and needing special teaching or help with English, yielded the unexpected finding that children from high 'special needs' schools were very significantly more likely to want 'more stories from books' and 'more stories about children a long time ago' than children from lower special needs schools.

This reinforces the case for specialized children's programming made by the original producers of *Sesame Street* – that it is the most disadvantaged children who are most reliant on television, and television should thus serve such children above all others.[31] This is not a popular point of view in a fragmented, market-driven television environment and a culture where children are seen primarily as sophisticated consumers of a postmodern plethora of identity-conferring brands. Although increasing numbers of children in Britain have access to satellite/cable and computers, the UK is still a society in which around a quarter of all children are officially poor. In Britain, too, one of the remits of public service broadcasting has been to compensate for this state of affairs by offering to economically, and in many cases, culturally, deprived[32] children, similar cultural experiences to those of children whose parents can buy them, or transport them to, such experiences. The finding that traditional forms of children's dramatic storytelling were favoured by some of the most disadvantaged children in the study suggests that costume drama – perhaps by its very alien-ness – is able to detach children's dilemmas from contemporary realist settings, where particular groups of children, whether 'posh' or 'common', are going to feel excluded, and to universalize these dilemmas in ways which can be meaningful to all. For disadvantaged children, too, the spectacular aspects of television costume drama – the dressing up, the exotic period detail, the time-travel – as with fantasy drama and surrealist comedy, offer aesthetic experiences which other, more culturally capitalized children can gain from theatre trips, foreign holidays, visits to museums and trips to stately homes provided by their parents.

I will give the last word to two of these children, one from Oxfordshire, the other from an inner-city primary school in Cardiff. As their comments indicate, their enthusiasm for 'stories set in the past' does not preclude – nor is there any reason why it should – an enjoyment of contemporary realism and other dramatic genres:

INTERVIEWER: If there was a story that you would like to see on the telly, could you think of anything good that you could make into a television programme?

BOY: In our English group, I have written a story about Greece, and all the heroes and gods are in it ... There is a book called *The Giant Under the Snow* and that would make a good one. (Boy, 10 years, Oxfordshire primary school)

GIRL: I would like more about Tudor times and other history programmes. I would also like more dramas about *Byker Grove*. (Girl, 8 years, Cardiff inner-city primary school)

Acknowledgement

I would particularly like to thank Steven Cameron of Farleigh Dickinson University, New Jersey, for his help in researching North American video versions of classic children's literature, and his general advice and information on those adaptations.

Notes

1. In a chapter on costume drama, in G. Creeber, (ed.), *Television Genres* (London: BFI, 1991).

2. See David Buckingham, Hannah Davies, Ken Jones and Peter Kelley, *Children's Television in Britain* (London: BFI, 1999), p. 49.

3. From John Caughie's discussion of 'The golden age: Early television drama', in John Corner (ed.), *Popular Television in Britain: Studies in Cultural History* (London: BFI, 1991), p. 23.

4. Charlotte Brunsdon, *Screen Tastes* (London: Routledge, 1997), p. 142.

5. Pierre Bourdieu, *Distinction: A Social Critique of the Judgement of Taste* (Cambridge, MA: Harvard University Press, 1984).

6. Lawrence Jarvik, 1999, p. 3. Jarvik, a critic for the *New York Times*, has written widely on quality in American television. The title of his book, *Masterpiece Theatre and the Politics of Quality* (Lanham, MD: Scarecrow Press), speaks for itself.

7. *Ibid.*, p. 5.

8. Hannah Davies, 'How children see themselves on television: children's identification with people on screen', report for Channel 4, 1996.

9. Máire Messenger Davies, *'Dear BBC': Children, Television-Storytelling and the Public Sphere* (Cambridge: Cambridge University Press, 2001).

10. John Corner and Sylvia Harvey, 'Mediating tradition and modernity: the heritage/enterprise couplet', in John Corner and Sylvia Harvey (eds), *Enterprise and Heritage: Cross Currents of National Culture* (London: Routledge, 1991), p. 46. Elsewhere in the same book, Tana Wollen, in a chapter entitled 'Nostalgic screen fictions', further argues that nostalgia can be an agent of unprogressive and reactionary approaches to history: in [some] 'mainstream British screen fictions ... their nostalgia yearns for a nation in which social status is known and kept and where difference constitutes, rather than fragments, national unity' (p. 181). However, I am suggesting that nostalgia, while a compelling ingredient of the heritage/enterprise nexus, is unlikely to be a component of how children read historical dramas.

11. I discuss quality in terms of criteria for evaluating and examining broadcasting students' creative work in 'Making media literate: Educating future media workers at undergraduate level', in R. Kubey (ed.), *Media Literacy in the Information Age*, Current Perspectives on Information and Behavior, vol. 6 (New Brunswick, NJ: Transaction, 1997), pp 263–84.

12. Interview with Lewis Rudd in Máire Messenger Davies and Kate O'Malley, 'Children and Television Drama: A Review of the Litera-

ture', unpublished report to the BBC (London: London College of Printing 1996), p. 162.

13. Sandra Hastie, interviewed in Máire Messenger Davies, Kate O'Malley and Beth Corbett, 'Children and television drama: an Empirical Study with Children Aged 5–13 Years in England and Wales', unpublished report to the BBC (London: London College of Printing 1997).

14. See, for example, Marsha Kinder, *Playing with Power in Movies, Television and Video Games: From Muppet Babies to Teenage Mutant Ninja Turtles* (Berkeley, CA: University of California Press, 1991) and Marsha Kinder (ed.), *Kids' Media Culture* (Durham, NC: Duke University Press, 1999).

15. Jay Blumler's report, *The Future of Children's Television in Britain: An Enquiry for the Broadcasting Standards Council* (London: BSC, 1992), promotes this notion of the 'great tradition', and has stimulated much discussion about children's provision and public service values in the UK.

16. Peter Hunt, *An Introduction to Children's Literature* (Oxford: Oxford University Press, 1994).

17. Steven Andrew, interviewed in Davies, *'Dear BBC'*.

18. Anna Home, *Into the Box of Delights* (London: BBC, 1993), p 93.

19. See Wollen, 'Nostalgic screen fictions'.

20. David Oswell, 'Early children's broadcasting in Britain, 1922–1964: programming for a liberal democracy', *Historical Journal of Film, Radio and Television* 18 (3), 375–93, 1997.

21. To emphasize the difference between 'set in the past' and 'written in the past': *The Secret Garden* was 'modern' and 'up-to-date' both to its author, who incorporated contemporary psychological theories of child-rearing into it, and to its readers. However, for children in 2001, it is 'historical', because of its setting and (when seen on TV) its costume. Because of their association with the 'costume drama' genre, Edwardian settings and clothing carry un-modern, and un-progressive signifiers, despite Mrs Burnett's original radical intentions. To understand this distinction, one might suggest that 'media-literate' children (and adults) are those who are able to separate ideology from clothing.

22. Home, *Into the Box of Delights*.

23. Janice Radway, *Reading the Romance: Women, Patriarchy and Popular Literature* (Chapel Hill, NC: University of North Carolina Press), 1984.

24. Alison Lurie, *Don't Tell the Grown-ups: Subversive Children's Fiction* (London: Bloomsbury, 1990), p. 13. Lurie argues the case for classic children's fiction being 'subversive' rather than supportive of a conservative status quo.

25. Helen Taylor, *Scarlett's Women: Gone with the Wind and its Female Fans* (London: Virago, 1989).
26. Hunt, *An Introduction to Children Literature*, p. 85.
27. Buckingham *et al.*, *Children's Television*, p. 49.
28. In Davies, *'Dear BBC'*.
29. *Ibid.*
30. Davies, *et al.*, 'Children and television drama', *'Dear BBC'*.
31. See Edward Palmer, *Television and America's Children: A Crisis of Neglect* (Oxford: Oxford University Press, 1988).
32. 'Culturally deprived' could be seen as a value-laden term, but is not intended to be. It is not necessarily synonymous with 'economically deprived'; and in this case, the relationship between children in schools with high special needs and cultural consumption was clearly complex. However, the majority of children in the study, including the economically deprived groups, mostly lived outside metropolitan areas and had limited access to public cultural institutions, such as museums, cinemas, galleries, concert halls, theatres, libraries, bookshops, sports arenas and good public transport in order to visit these and other places of interest. This phrase does not imply the children were *intentionally* deprived of these things.

CHAPTER 7

Keeping It Real

Grange Hill and the Representation of 'the Child's World' in Children's Television Drama

KEN JONES AND HANNAH DAVIES

Grange Hill is ... amateurish and sub-standard [and lacks] ... the element of fantasy and romanticism so important to children's stories. In its obsessive attempt to be realistic *Grange Hill* abandons both these elements; yet surely children don't want to see bad portrayals of themselves at school, but want a story which can entice, amuse, grip and delight them.[1]

There were all these bought in film series like 'Robin Hood' and 'William Tell', American cartoons and the BBC cultural auntie thing – *The Secret Garden* and Enid Blyton. And you know, you didn't see many horses or spies on our council estate. So I just wanted to make a series that reflected life for the majority of kids as they grow up.[2]

The moment of *Grange Hill*

Writing about the 'converging histories' of broadcasting and cinema, John Caughie argues that important elements in British film and television have a common origin and reference point in the idea of 'public service'.[3] Public service, as elaborated by the documentarist John Grierson and John Reith, first Director-General of the BBC, had several characteristics. It was defined in opposition to commercial interests, claiming to service the nation, not private business; and its overriding mission was to raise levels of culture and understanding. Its output was frequently focused on 'social problems', for which it sought amelioration and reform; and to do this, it was inclined to use the representational forms of social realism. However, public service was not a completely settled or homogenous concept. Although the culture which public service film and broadcasting sought to promulgate was often no more than an unproblematized version of middle-class preferences, public service ideology was also open to more controversial inflections of the 'public interest'. Broadcasting and cinema were hospitable to radical professionals, and in certain periods public service involved critical as well as consensual projects.

At least until the changes of the 1980s, public service ideas were fairly well rooted in the BBC, where they informed a range of practices relating to subject-matter, programme mix and the ways in which audiences were addressed. As we shall see, even in the deregulated milieu of the 1990s and beyond, they retain an influence on sectors of television practice. But the particular inflections given to public service have varied considerably from one period to the next, and nowhere are these shifts made clearer than in the history of children's television.[4]

The BBC Children's Television Department was established in the late 1940s. From the beginning, its producers took their public service responsibilities with great seriousness. The department operated at first with a protectionist idea of childhood: children should not watch too much television; and they should watch only programmes made for their particular age group. It also saw its role as developmental: children should be educated, especially through watching TV adaptations of classic literary texts, to become sensitive and discriminating viewers. Neither protectionist nor developmental approaches allowed scope for engagement with popular cultures of childhood, and the establishment of a rival, commercial channel in 1955 dealt them an almost fatal blow. Put simply, ITV gave children what they wanted, rather than what it was thought they needed. Within a couple of years, four out of five children with TV sets were watching ITV's programmes – a mix of American cartoons and Anglo-American adventure stories. The BBC Children's Department was unable to recover a large share of this audience and was closed down in 1964, with the Director of Television's verdict ringing in its ears – it was 'too bloody middle-class'. However, the BBC's new strategy – of making programmes aimed at a wider 'family' audience – was not successful either, and by the late 1960s a separate Children's Department was re-established.

The reformed Department retained strong elements of an agenda of cultural improvement, envisaged in class-related terms. As its new Head, Monica Sims, explained:

> All education is middle-class – has to be – because to learn and realise your potential is actually a middle-class aspiration. I think there was always a realisation that the people with whom the children identified had to accept their responsibility as role models. They would ... not be allowed to be very thuggish or eat chocolate and chips ... There was always this belief in behaving well and considerately to other people.[5]

But at the same time, the failures of the 1950s had taught the BBC a lesson: it had to be 'popular' as well as 'good'. The great successes of the 1960s – especially in adult television drama (*Z Cars, The Wednesday Play*) – were based on the learning of this lesson. In the case of the Children's Department, achieving success meant engaging with new, post-1960s forms of children's culture, and in the process calling into question its own established cultural preferences. The progressive educational ideologies of the 1960s and 1970s offered important support to this new approach. In relation to programming for young children, they encouraged an emphasis on 'play', and a move away from too overtly didactic an approach to content. As far as older sections of the child audience were concerned, progressivism helped legitimize an emphasis on the 'social'. Internal BBC memoranda of the period frequently allude to the ideas of educators like Bernstein, who argued that schools needed to be much more closely attuned to the home cultures of children, and to take account of the differences between the formal, organized knowledge of the school and the everyday experiences of learners. Progressivism's influence was reinforced by other kinds of change. Programme-makers could hardly overlook the flourishing youth cultures of the later 1960s and the 1970s. Magazine shows relying heavily on pop music came to depict a somewhat sexualized version of children's culture, while at the same time they acknowledged the generational separateness of children and youth. Also influential was the new tone of fiction either written for a child audience, or thought suitable by teachers for inclusion in the school syllabus. English authors such as John Rowe Townsend, Bill Naughton, Joan Lingard and Stan Barstow and Americans like Betsy Byars and Judy Blume located their narratives in urban settings, made their stories out of 'difficult' experiences of bullying, divorce and racism, and (at least for a time) established realism, rather than fantasy, as the dominant mode of child-orientated writing. In doing so, they helped create an aesthetic climate to which the Children's Department could not but be sensitive.

Thus, a variety of pressures – social, educational and aesthetic – was pushing the Children's Department towards change; and without fully departing from an overall cultural protectionism, it expanded the cultural range of its programmes so as to address what was understood as youth-specific or working-class experience. As we've suggested, music-centred magazine shows such as *Swapshop* (first screened in 1976) were an important part of this shift. But more significant – and certainly in some respects more immediately contentious – was the Department's expanding drama output. Central to this expansion was drama of a new kind – the school-based series *Grange Hill*, first screened in 1978, and the Department's most controversial product.

Courting controversy

Partly because its high cost lends it a certain status, and partly because of the dominance of traditional, literary criteria of value, drama has always been at the centre of the Children's Department's work, and has provided the means to make a broader statement about its social and aesthetic purposes. As Edward Barnes, Head of the Children's Department during the late 1970s and early 1980s, acknowledged, *Grange Hill* was a programme 'about working-class children'.[6] As such, and in the context of changes in broadcasting, education and the meaning of childhood, it was bound to take on a wider significance, even if its origins lay in accident rather than the design.

Anna Home, the executive producer who commissioned *Grange Hill*, was looking for a generic school-based drama series, rather than demanding the kinds of social, and political, orientation that *Grange Hill* came to embody. The writer she commissioned was Phil Redmond, who later wrote the soap *Brookside* and founded the production company Mersey Television. Redmond saw himself as someone writing in reaction to the 'middle-class type of drama that was getting pushed down kids' throats'. His intention, he claimed nearly 20 years later, was 'to do something from my own background, in which people (were) speaking in working-class accents about working-class issues'.[7] Working on this basis, he broke the conventional mould, and took the Department, often reluctantly, with him. In doing so, it produced what Home described as the first programme to represent what by the 1970s was the majority form of secondary education – the comprehensive school.[8]

The comprehensive was in itself, of course, a controversial institution. In 1965, the Wilson government had urged all local authorities to establish non-selective secondary education. By the mid-1970s, most authorities had done so, and in Scotland and Wales, state secondary education was almost entirely comprehensive. In England, however, there were many authorities which still retained selective education. For them, and their defenders in the media, the comprehensive school was an institution which threatened academic standards and destroyed the established 'high culture' of state secondary education, embodied in the grammar school. Increasingly, these concerns came to be shared even by those who advocated reform. On the one hand, the Labour Government of 1974–9 produced legislation that required LEAs to develop – albeit not necessarily to implement – plans for a non-selective system. On the other hand, it began to nurture doubts about the educational culture created by comprehensivation. As one government advisor, Bernard Donoghue, explained:

> I felt that some of the dogmatists around in the 1970s were really discrediting comprehensive education. I also felt that the permissiveness was meaning that people were simply not working hard enough . . . liberalism was becoming a fig-leaf for idleness. It made it so easy for teachers to do very little on the basis that it was unfair to make the students do very much . . . There had become a tragic transformation from a relatively small group of dedicated teachers in a small profession to a mass industry of teachers, many of whom viewed teaching as just one job like any other.[9]

The first act of Mrs Thatcher's government in 1979 was to repeal Labour's 1976 legislation. The motivations for repeal were many. In part, they reflected the desire of middle-class social groups to preserve enclaves of privilege. But they also related to a much wider cluster of meanings and values, in which the threatened grammar school came to stand for civilization itself. From this point of view, the danger of reorganization was not only its threat to academic standards. Donoghue's perception of comprehensives as places dominated by dogma, permissiveness and sloth was developed and magnified on the political right. Here, the comprehensive seemed to be an institution in which established culture and authoritative knowledge were being continuously undermined. Truancy, indiscipline, teacher militancy and curricular experiment were different faces of an assault on traditional educational order through which the tried-and-tested curriculum of the grammar school was being ousted by one which depended on negotiation with the interests and experiences of students.[10] What from a conservative perspective was even more serious, was the intersection of these educational problems with a wider social crisis of youth, especially in the cities. Punk music, Notting Hill Carnival riots, fascism and antifascism, and school-student participation in teacher-led protest were all read as signs of breakdown.[11] To make a programme based in a largely working-class London comprehensive school was thus from the beginning to court controversy.

Moreover, it took BBC children's drama into a troubling new area. Almost since the dawn of television, there had been academic and popular concern about its physiological, intellectual and moral effects. This concern drew from, and overlapped with, a wider set of fears about representations of violence and 'delinquent' behaviour, and the development of deviant and hedonistic youth sub-cultures, during the post-war period.[12] *Grange Hill* was seen as a programme that took not just children's television, but public service children's television, into this area of danger. 'Realism', in this context, threatened to become scandalous – it provided representational means by which potentially corrupting subject-matter could appear before a young audience. To conservative opinion especially, it presented evidence not just of overall cultural decline, but of a betrayal by public service professionals of their original mandate and responsibilities. Producers, it was argued, were failing to interpose a screen of selection, interpretation and judgment between the child audience and television's representation of their experience.

The first, 16-episode series of the programme was received fairly mildly. But the second and third series – which Redmond described as 'all about student militancy and behind the bike shed and horrendous things like periods and first bras' – were met with hostility. In Home's account, adults, who had little experience of the new schooling, 'didn't like the programme: they thought it was much too raw'. It was common for children to be forbidden to watch it. As our epigraph suggests, at least one television critic lamented its lack of the 'fantasy and romanticism so important to children's television'. The National Viewers and Listeners Association of Mary Whitehouse thought that it encouraged bad behaviour.[13] Some Members of Parliament commented unfavourably and teachers, according to Redmond, 'didn't like it because they thought it was undermining their authority'. These 'extreme reactions', as Redmond calls them, led to the programme being put under close surveillance within the BBC:

> ... it became one of those things that never happens in television
> – we were told what we could and couldn't have in it. We'd get in a
> room and everyone in BBC suits and we'd be told we could do this
> but we couldn't do that.[14]

Paradoxes

Yet for all that it provoked more public controversy than any children's programme that had preceded it, *Grange Hill* was in many ways a re-telling of familiar tales. It had affinities with other school stories, set in other times and at very different levels of the private/public hierarchy – Billy Bunter, Malory Towers, St Trinians. It used and re-used characters and story-lines that owed a lot to these forebears and featured such recognizable character types as the school swot, the cheeky rebel and the 'good girl' tempted by romance. It was, moreover, a cautiously constructed programme, nowhere more clearly than in the ways its plots were resolved through the intervention of wise and teacherly authority; and it relied much more heavily than its critics recognized on resolutions and closures that affirmed conventional values. Its teachers, for the most part, were not the permissive militants who featured in media accounts. Here, in the feature-length video produced in 1981, Mr Mitchell, the embodiment of such authority,

urges two truants (Tricia Yates and Benny Green) back to school
– the non-speaking Benny is black:

MITCHELL: Shall we sit down and talk about this? Come on. Right, sit
over here. Who's gonna start? Right, what about you Tricia? I think
I know why you're here – that letter? Do you think running away
has solved anything?

TRICIA: Probably made matters worse.

MITCHELL: And all because you wouldn't obey a few simple rules.

TRICIA: But why do we have to, sir?

MITCHELL: It's a question of discipline ... Look, I wish I could offer
you easy answers, but I can't. It seems to me that to some extent
you're both suffering from the same problem: you both feel you're
being picked on. You (Benny), by Doyle and his friends and you
(Tricia) by the school. Right? Now you, Benny, are being singled
out because through circumstances you are different. Whereas
with you, Tricia, it's for wanting to be different. And of the two, I'd
say Benny has the greater problem because he has no choice in the
matter. Whereas you, young lady, have. And if you disagree with
school uniform so strongly why not do the thing properly and join
the existing campaign for its abolition.

TRICIA: I suppose so, sir. What's Benny gonna do?

MITCHELL: That's very much up to him, Tricia. Look, Benny, you are
always going to run into people like Doyle but hopefully they'll be
far outnumbered by people who are prepared to accept you just
for yourself.

Mr Mitchell here has to carry what might be called the burden of
children's television, as it evolved within the BBC Children's
Department of the 1970s. He has to engage with children's cultures and quickly resolve the problems that arise from doing so.
He has to insist on the complexity of life, and at the same time
obscure questions of power and desire. He must be both radical
and responsible. He has to listen to children and to ventriloquize
their responses. He must acknowledge their dissenting viewpoints
and secure their agreement to his. It is a difficult role, yet one
which goes for the most part unchallenged by characters who
might speak from other positions. Indeed, parents and students
for the most part concede to the school the role of arbiter of moral
and behavioural questions. 'The fault lies not with the school,'

says the mother of one wrongdoer to the headmaster who is about to cane him, 'but with Peter ... I don't know ... But I do know he's old enough to know the difference between right and wrong.'

Exchanges like these provide powerful evidence to support critics like David Lusted, who in 1981 argued that the programme worked to endorse rather than challenge the power relations of schooling.[15] But to leave things at that point, and to claim to have thus identified the hidden conservative core of *Grange Hill*, is clearly inadequate, if only because it renders the furore that surrounded the series explicable only as some kind of essentially groundless moral panic. Formal analysis is unlikely, alone, to explain why *Grange Hill* appeared so scandalously radical. We can find better starting-points by looking, again, at audience response.

Texts and audiences

No detailed contemporary record exists of audience responses to the series, though we can guess at its impact from the frequent appearances of its stars as pin-ups in teenage magazines. Our attempt to describe and account for the programme's relationship to its audience therefore relies on retrospective material of two kinds. The first is drawn from fanzine web sites.[16] These tend to celebrate what are seen as the anarchistic 'glory days' of *Grange Hill* and mourn what is claimed as its decline. The following lament, by Graham Kibble-White, is fairly typical:

> There was to be never more an ugly kid, a bad kid or a mad kid. No more acne, sunken eyes, grimy shirts and Roland Browning girth. Instead it was to be crisp clothes, wedge hair-cuts, skinny ties and lots of liberal minded sixth formers drinking coffee ... It was as though the *Grange Hill* production team had embarked on a mission of rectification, making amends for all the bogeymen they had unleashed since 1978. It was like ... the Chess Club and all the sensible girls were now calling the shots ... *Grange Hill* now. Middle-aged, dare I say it, middle-class? Middle of the road.

Our second source is our interviews with those who, 15–20 years ago, were its fans. The difficulties of such recourse to oral and informal-retrospective history are self-evident; but even so, the consistency of the stories told by one-time viewers is striking.

The web sites enthuse over the programme's perceived unruliness. Interviewees stress the programme's personal significance, as well as its function in playground conversation. 'No television programme has been as important for me,' recalled one interviewee. 'I saw for the first time things that made complete sense to me, like adults being irrational and horrible to children. It made other stuff look like lies.' 'It was always on a Tuesday and a Friday,' said another. 'My mum re-arranged our piano lessons to a Tuesday and I was devastated because it meant I'd miss *Grange Hill* and I wouldn't know what people were talking about.' 'I was not allowed to watch it,' another viewer told us. 'I remember being able to get away with watching it if my mum was about, but my dad did not like it! To some extent, I felt left out, because all the children were talking about it at school and what happened.'

How was it that *Grange Hill*, notwithstanding its conservatism at the level of plot resolution and closure, was able to evoke such emotions and to serve such a central function in playground life? The beginnings of an answer can be can be found in its serial construction. The 16-episode structure of the early series made it something very different from the single play or the six-part series which were the more usual forms for socially realist television drama. The serial structure brought with it elements of soap opera: *Grange Hill* followed the lives of a group of characters, and represented 'public' issues and conflicts from the perspective of their personal meaning for members of the group. This familiar device could be read as a way of diminishing the social, by relegating it to the status of a background for personal dramas; but in the context of contemporary debates about schooling and culture, the programme's foregrounding of the personal had an importance that took it beyond the reach of customary criticisms of soap. This was largely because it showed or alluded to that which usually went unrepresented in children's television – namely, the lives lived by *children* in the margins or interstices of institutions designed by adults. *Grange Hill's* students inhabited an everyday generational culture which went on, intensely and only half-noticed, in the secret places of the school (toilets, boiler rooms) or under the imperceptive gaze of teachers. Children's spaces such as the cloakroom, the walk to and from school, or the local shopping centre provided the site of the drama alongside the more familiar teacher-dominated school spaces such as the classroom.

Moreover, the programme 'dignified' the lives of children by connecting their experiences, interests and commitments to wider social currents. Thus, it depicted conflicts around 'race' and around different conceptions of the feminine, bringing out the school's censorious attitude to images of femininity that circulated in commercial popular culture. Likewise, it insisted on representing children as 'classed': representations of class conflict, lived out through culture and style as much as through economic difference, were central to the early series, and the number of references, often made in asides, to the connection between intra-school events and extra-school conditions, is too high to be coincidental. In these ways, the programme's stress on the personal and the experiential involved not so much a dilution or displacement of the social, as a means of entry to it; and by 'entry', we mean not simply the raising or flagging of a social issue, but also the offering to the audience of an opportunity for passionate identification with the characters involved in it, as people who, as it were, shared a collective institutional life with the characters in the programme.

Two examples from the second, controversial series can illustrate and develop this argument.

Free dinners

It was common in the secondary schools of the 1970s and 1980s for the organization of school meals at lunchtime to make explicit the distinction between students who paid for their meals, and those whose parents' low level of income entitled them, on production of a ticket and at cost of social stigma, to a free dinner. (A short story of the time, Farrukh Dhondy's 'Free Dinners', also turns upon this distinction.[17]) In *Grange Hill*, Benny Green, best friend of Tucker Jenkins, is not allowed to sit at the same table as the rest of his friends at lunchtime because children like him who receive free meals have to sit at a dedicated table. Benny, as we've seen, is black and earlier story-lines have established that there are financial worries at home. Tucker decides to sit with Benny but is told to move by one of the canteen staff. Tucker refuses – arguing that it is discriminating and unfair to single out those on free meals. At this point his response connects to a wider politics, that of the 'Student Action Group', whose militant campaigns around issues of school uniform and students' rights have provided an on-going story-line throughout the second series. In keeping with their previous tactics – pickets of governors' meetings, boycotts of sporting events – SAG members decide that if they can't sit where they want then they won't sit at all. They will, instead, stand on the dining tables; and in a moment of defiance and in solidarity with his friend, Tucker too stands on the table. The camera, colluding with his protest, moves back, and a wide-angle shot shows us that his example is being followed across the canteen.

For one of us (Hannah Davies), who as a young viewer, familiar with the petty tyrannies of school canteen regulations, watched the episode, the dramatic force of this moment was exhilarating. It offered her identification with a fight against injustice, and legitimized her solidaristic responses by placing her in the midst of the collective action of her contemporaries and peers, the canteen's inhabitants. The programme thus constructed for its audience a momentary perspective which was radically different from the 'official' position established by the plot and its resolution. In these latter terms, solidarity, rebellion and 'empowerment' are qualified by the fact that the issue is resolved quietly and off-camera by the headteacher, who changes the mealtime regulations. But neither for Hannah Davies, nor for others to whom we talked, was this the salient point of the story-line. They responded not to the thread in the programme that encouraged assent to the legitimate, consensual authority of the school, but rather to the moment of resistance. To put it another way, their viewing of the programme focused in these instances not so much on narrative as upon spectacle. This preference of viewers for a 'momentary' rather than a 'linear' reading' can tell us much about what *Grange Hill* offered its audience – opportunities for intense gratification that were both 'psychological' in the way that they allowed immediate investment and identification, and 'social' in that they enabled participation in playground or class-room discussion.[18]

Racists out

The late 1970s and early 1980s were a period of intense confrontation between anti-racists and racist organizations, not least within education. These were years in which fascist movements produced newspapers – such as the National Front's *Bulldog* – for sale in schools, and made a point of renting schools for public meetings. The period was the heyday, also, of the Anti-Nazi League (and its offshoot, Schoolkids against the Nazis), of Rock against Racism, of the All-London Teachers Against Racism and Fascism, and of numerous street protests by black and Asian youth against policing strategies.[19] It was in this context, in which the reception of particular plot-lines would be over-determined by wider political events and experiences, that *Grange Hill* evolved a 'racism' story-line. Over the course of the second series, the racist bully, Gripper Stebson, and his gang have been bullying younger pupils. Their fairly low-level money-with-menaces tactics develop into fully fledged racially motivated attacks. A particular target is a Sikh pupil. The bullying becomes nastier and more systematic but the school authorities refuse to see that it is racially motivated and no action is taken against Gripper. Gripper's come-uppance is two-fold. First, and most memorably, a group of black pupils organize and wait for Gripper one evening – and Gripper's gang are revealed as cowardly as well as ignorant. Secondly, the true nature of Gripper's aggression is finally discovered by the teachers; and the firm-but-fair PE teacher 'Bullet' Baxter condemns Gripper in a speech about the cowardice of racism and then marches him out of the school forever.

The morning after this episode was broadcast, Gripper's expulsion was 'the' subject of conversation in school playgrounds across the UK – a kind of children's equivalent of 'who shot JR?', or 'who shot Phil Mitchell?', except that it focused less on individual than on collective issues. Once again, the programme had succeeded in addressing its viewers as if they were inhabitants of a parallel, cognate world to that of *Grange Hill*. Once again, it offered them a point of identification with student self-organization, although this time, it was aligned with the official position of the school. The collective feeling of disgust at Gripper and the relief that he'd finally been recognized and punished was immense.

The *Grange Hill* tradition

There is thus a convergence between the responses of the programme's critics and the readings of its fans. Both focus less on questions of narrative development and plot resolution than on issues of topic, incident, spectacle and momentary confrontation. It was not what happened to particular characters – the inevitable consequences, for instance, of their transgressive behaviour – that moved or disturbed, but the very fact of such behaviour being represented. The representation of character and action had, moreover, a continual political and social significance. It evoked an unsettling world, in which established values were being turned on their head, and in which protest and individual rebellion were transvalued, to become qualities that were subject to condemnation or reconciliation at the 'official' level of closure, while remaining thrillingly and invitingly 'open' at the level of moment, event and episode. It was these qualities in *Grange Hill* that troubled its critics, and it is about the programme's incapacity now to deliver such transgressive spectacle that the web sites complain.

Yet while some mourn what they see as the programme's descent into respectability, others offer a different evaluation. Advocates of the public service tradition have been concerned for some time about the effects on children's television of globalization and deregulation. For them, this opens wide the door to a commercially driven determination of content, in which global economies of scale and American domination of the market lead to the creation of culturally homogenous schedules, dominated by cartoons or by easily marketable programme brands. Against these trends, they have attempted to make explicit the values of public service children's television: they cite the example of dramas like *Grange Hill*. 'Children should hear, see and express themselves, their culture, their languages and their life experiences, through television programmes which affirm their sense of community and place,' reads the 1995 Children's Television Charter.[20] In this context, *Grange Hill* comes to be viewed as an epitome of all that globalization threatens – locally produced, culturally specific television that in some sense voices children's 'life experiences'. It thereby achieves a canonical status, not now as a vanguard and troubling programme, but as the representative of an embattled tradition. The fact of such a further transvaluation can tell us much, not only about the development of children's television over the last two decades, but also about much wider trajectories of cultural and political change.

How, then, have such battles over the purpose and significance of children's television affected the subject-matter, mode of address and story-lines of *Grange Hill* 2001? In some respects, the programme has changed considerably, in ways that are strongly influenced by adult soaps. The number of plot-lines per episode has multiplied, and the pace of scenes and of cutting between scenes has increased. In terms of content, the family now assumes a more central role, and – as in soaps – conflict between family members, and the accompanying problematization of issues of parenting, has become an important generator of character and story-line development. Yet, unlike the generality of soaps, *Grange Hill* has maintained a strong connection to the public sphere. Concentrated into its 25 minutes is an attempt, strikingly more strongly made than in the 1980s, to represent the 'condition of Britain'; and to this condensed extent a radical version of public service television lives on. Questions of social class may occupy a less central role, but other kinds of social issue, especially ones concerned with race and sexuality, have become prominent.

In the Spring 2001 series, for instance, asylum seekers, the commercialization of schooling, lesbian sexuality, and date rape all figure among the story-lines. In each of them, the agency of the student protagonists is presented as a central feature. Commercialization is opposed by a student who, objecting to the vandalizing of his design for a school tracksuit by a sponsor's logo, carries a billboard around the school that states, playing with performative contradictions, 'I am not an advert'. Students' responses to asylum-seekers involve participation in efforts to hide them from immigration authorities. Continuing the insistence on agency, an 'out' lesbian insists to her friend that 'your sexuality isn't something that happens to you'; it, too, is a matter of choice. Even in the classroom, teachers maintain that issues of standpoint, perspective and commitment are central to knowledge. 'One person's freedom fighter is another person's terrorist,' the history teacher tells her class. 'The way we define events throughout history depends on whose side we're on.' Conversely, while the agency of students is emphasized, when the programme focuses on adult life it is to focus on questions of vulnerability and constraint. Parents need help to recover from separations or worry over the extravagant political commitments of their children. Teachers, outside the classroom, are subject to envy, jealousy and fear. They are as likely to be the victims of student aggression as to be aggressors themselves. In its treatment of both students and adults, the *Grange Hill* of 2001 is thus more emphatic than its predecessor.

It is difficult not to see something reflexive in all this, as the programme lives up to the role defined for public service television by its embattled defenders, and in the process speaks about its own significance. There is a self-conscious adherence to a *Grange Hill* tradition, as the programme comes to accentuate those features which first marked it out from other kinds of children's television. Thus, faced with the billboard campaign, the headteacher responds with the tolerant claim that 'free speech is a principle which Grange Hill has always sought to encourage among students'. It is difficult to resist here the conclusion that what he is celebrating is less a strongly rooted feature of state secondary education than a culture that is peculiar to 'Grange Hill' itself.

Indeed, the gap between the culture of *Grange Hill* and that of the system which provides its real-life referent is now considerable. The English school system of the early twenty-first century is marked by policies which emphasize centrally monitored delivery of a uniform curriculum. *Grange Hill*, by contrast, emphasizes student self-activity, and insists on the cultural diversity, and conflict-ridden nature, of schooling. As such, one might expect it to have generated as much, if not more, controversy than it did in the late 1970s and 1980s. What prevents it from doing so is perhaps less its own subject-matter than the changing position of public service television itself, and of the dwindling connections between television culture and social movements. Twenty years ago, in a regulated context of broadcasting in which only three channels existed, the public meanings of particular, mould-breaking television programmes assumed an immediate importance. In 2001, by contrast, *Grange Hill* is broadcast in a multi-channelled environment, where the diversity and sometimes transgressive character of children's culture has become a norm. Moreover, what is missed by the more nostalgic fans of the programme – its depiction of anti-authoritarian, excessive youth cultures – is missing also, now, from the public sphere as a whole. Or, at least, it is present only in a diminished form, there being no equivalents to punk as a cultural movement, or to campaigns against youth training schemes as forms of mass protest. In such a situation, *Grange Hill* cannot but be less troubling.

Acknowledgement

The research for this chapter was part of an ESRC-funded project on 'Children's Media Culture' (L126251026), based at the Institute of Education, University of London.

Notes

1. W. Campbell, *Television Today*, 25 January 1979.
2. Phil Redmond, interview with the authors, 1996.
3. John Caughie, 'Broadcasting and cinema: converging histories', in C. Barr (ed.), *All our Yesterdays: 90 Years of British Cinema* (London: British Film Institute, 1986), pp. 189–205.
4. In what follows, we draw particularly from D. Buckingham, H. Davies, K. Jones and P. Kelley, *Children's Television in Britain: History, Discourse and Politics* (London: British Film Institute, 1999), Chapter 2; and from K. Jones and H. Davies, 'Representing education 1969–1980', *History of Education* 30 (2), 141–51, 2001.
5. Interview with the authors, 1997.
6. Interview with the authors, 1997.
7. Interview with the authors, 1996.
8. Interview with the authors, 1997.
9. Donoghue, quoted in C. Chitty, *Towards a New Education System: The victory of the new right?* (Lewes: Falmer Press, 1989), p. 67.
10. The most influential assertion of these arguments was contained in the 'Black Papers': B. Cox and R. Boyson, *Black Paper 1977* (London: Temple Smith, 1977).
11. For further details, see K. Jones, *Right Turn: The Conservative Revolution in Education* (London: Hutchinson Radius, 1989); and C. Richards, 'Teaching popular culture', in K. Jones (ed.), *English and the National Curriculum: Cox's Revolution?* (London: Kogan Page, 1992).
12. This concern was expressed, for example, in the Newsom Report of 1963: *Half Our Future: a Report of the Central Advisory Council for Education [England]* (London: HMSO). For further discussion, see also M. Barker, *A Haunt of Fears* (London: Verso, 1984).
13. See M. Tracey and D. Morrison, *Whitehouse* (London: Macmillan, 1979).
14. Interview with the authors, 1996.
15. D. Lusted, 'The school and the street: Grange Hill', *The English Magazine* 6, 1981.

16. See the websites http://web.ukonline.co.uk/ott/grangehill.htm and www.tv.cream.org
17. F. Dhondy, 'Free dinners', in *Come to Mecca and Other Stories* (London: Fontana, 1978).
18. Andrew Burn provides a complex and illuminating discussion of these different types of reading – centred on school-students' responses to Neil Jordan's film *The Company of Wolves* – in his unpublished PhD thesis, *Pleasures of the Spectatorium: Young People, Classrooms and Horror Films* (Institute of Education, University of London, 1998).
19. Richards ('Teaching popular culture', p. 93) offers the following (incomplete) list of school-students' actions in the 1970s and 1980s:

    1976–80: participation in protests against ILEA's programme of secondary school closures and amalgamations; 1976–1980: anti-racism; 1979: protests against the effects of teachers' industrial action (the closing of schools at lunchtimes); 1981–88: participation in protests against successive proposals to abolish ILEA; 1984/5: action in Newham and Tower Hamlets against racist attacks; 1986: walkouts in support of Militant-organised strike against the Youth Training Scheme; 1985–87: sporadic support for teachers' industrial action over pay and conditions.

20. The Charter is reproduced in Buckingham *et al.*, *Children's Television in Britain*, p. 172.

CHAPTER 8

Pink Worlds and Blue Worlds

A Portrait of Intimate Polarity

MERRIS GRIFFITHS

Young children in Western societies are now born into commercial environments where anything and everything can be
viewed as a saleable commodity. Advertising is so pervasive as to
be largely taken for granted. Of course, there has been a long
history of concern about the so-called 'effects' of advertising on
young children, largely focusing on the risks of commercial
'exploitation'. Indeed, there has recently been considerable
debate about the possibility that the European Union might ban
advertisements targeted at young children for this reason.[1] Yet
there has been rather less discussion about the potential contribution of advertising to the formation of children's identities.
This chapter will focus specifically on the issue of gender identity,
and its role in children's televised toy advertisements.

Although the intersection between toys and gender has often
been identified as having 'much to do with identity',[2] there has
been little research into the nature of this interrelationship. Likewise, while much research has been conducted on children's
advertising in general, many investigators have omitted toy
advertisements from their samples on the basis that they are too
infrequent and seasonally dependent. However, the assumption
here is that the sheer concentration of toy ads in the two-month
period leading up to Christmas is particularly significant in terms
of channelling children's thoughts towards procuring certain
(gender specific) goods. These goods then invariably occupy the

159

child's space (home and bedroom) for lengths of time far longer than the actual sales period, perhaps perpetuating the (gender-specific) play-patterns demonstrated in the ads.

One of the reasons toys were selected as a basis for investigating gender identity is the fact that toy products tend to be highly prescriptive in terms of their intended user, while play is seen as an integral part of the maturation process.[3] Toy-play is frequently hinged on the concept of 'gender appropriateness', where it has traditionally been seen as 'inappropriate' for boys to play with dolls or for girls to play with cars. Numerous studies suggest that children's play is a reflection of gender stereotyped socialization patterns and that toys are important in their ideological formation.[4]

One of the most obvious ways that gender manifests itself is through observable behaviour patterns. In the context of advertisements, gender models are presented as 'naturalized' in terms of exhibiting so-called 'appropriate gender behaviour'. Such gendered portraits have endured over time and can be found cross-culturally. Ruble *et al*.[5] suggest that children actively seek information about gender behaviour and, using play styles and sex-typed toys as their experimental equipment, learn how to behave in a manner that society deems acceptable. Indeed, young children may actually be very comfortable with their re-enactments of predictable gender behaviours because of the social acceptance attached to being conformist.[6] Likewise, television is often seen as a major influence on both children's and adults' perceptions of their own and others' sex roles;[7] and there is empirical evidence to indicate a positive relationship between exposure to gender-stereotyped media content and stereotyped perceptions, attitudes and behaviours.

There is a kind of circularity to these arguments. Advertisements lean heavily on socially generated notions of gender as a means of targeting products at appropriate consumer sectors, appealing to the individual and casting the product in the image of the user. Toy advertisements promote goods that arguably contribute to a gender-based construction of the self and the adoption of so-called 'appropriate gender behaviour'. Thus, one could argue that the gender models seen in toy ads form a base for modelling and imitative behaviour, contributing to the ways that children learn the characteristics of their own sex,[8] whilst also providing examples of the 'props' available to enhance role-playing. Both the cognitive and social learning approaches to sex-role development attach considerable importance to this kind of imitation of same-sex models.

However much one may dispute the apparent determinism of this approach, there are undeniable cultural pressures on boys to be 'manly', while girls are expected to be 'ladylike'.[9] Dyer,[10] writing at length about gender stereotypes, describes them as simple, easily grasped forms of representation, which condense a great deal of complex information and have many potential connotations.[11] Yet while the structural theory of stereotypes has been contested and problematized by feminist critics, who place greater stress on the notion of 'gender performativity',[12] traditional conceptions of gender are still clearly applicable to toy ads. Indeed, there has been little or no change in the content and composition of toy ads in the last 25 years.[13] Children may either reject or accept such portrayals, but they offer an easily available 'yard-stick' against which to measure social reality.

Traditional theories of gender stereotyping tend to rely on a basic set of binary oppositions, which can be summarized as follows:

'Male' gender traits	*'Female' gender traits*
Independent	Dependent
Rational	Irrational
Rough	Gentle
Nasty	Nice
Brave	Cowardly
Insensitive	Sensitive
Aggressive	Placid
Competitive	Co-operative
Physical	Emotional
Disobedient	Obedient
Active	Passive
Unhappy	Happy
Assertive	Unassertive
Confident	Unconfident
Uncaring	Caring

As a process, stereotyping may be a positive necessity for advertising, to a much greater extent than for other media forms or genres. Advertisers must strongly prescribe a 'preferred meaning' within their advertisement texts, so that the intended message is conveyed to the audience as effectively and effortlessly as possible, restricting the process of meaning making.[14] To build a 'preferred meaning' into an advertising campaign requires an over-determination of the process of encoding, making the desired conclusion about the product more obvious than any other reading.[15] This involves careful structuring and formatting in order to instruct the viewer in how to interpret the meaning of the advertisement;[16] and one could argue that such practices could also be applied to the construction of models of 'appropriate gender behaviour'. Ideologically, such 'closed' texts are thought to have greater impact because they offer fewer interpretational possibilities.[17] Therefore, one could argue that if a child accepts the way in which s/he is defined as either a 'boy' or a 'girl' in toy ads, then the advertisement would be more influential.

Stereotyping is most obviously manifested in the overt themes and representations of advertisements, but it also occurs in their technical or formal features. While those working in the advertising industry vehemently deny that technical features are (consciously) used to appeal to certain genders,[18] it is clear that most ad campaigns, especially those targeted at children, are structured with specific target audiences in mind. The consistency with which certain technical features are used when appealing to these audience sectors makes it possible to argue that they are 'gendered'.

The aim of this chapter, therefore, is to analyse the ways in which gender stereotyping operates on the most subtle and unobtrusive levels within toy advertisement texts, and thereby to describe and explain how the 'gendering' of both product and purchaser operates. An analysis of this kind demands that one look below the more obvious surface meanings of texts to the underlying structure of their 'hidden' (or unconscious) appeals. I intend to clarify how toy ads create a gender-polarized world for children, whilst demonstrating that the situation is a little more complex than simple divisions between 'blue' and 'pink'.

Of course, it should also be noted at the outset that textual analysis only identifies the parameters within which audience readings occur. *How* these readings occur is a matter for further research. The social worlds of boys and girls may in fact be much less polarized than the famously constructed worlds of *Barbie* and *Action Man*. Yet when faced with a 'packaged world',[19] it may well be that children have no option but to learn their place within it, seeing the patterns of behaviour that are represented there as unalterable fact.

Content analysis

The primary aim of this chapter is to apply semiotic concepts to analyse a selection of children's televised toy advertisements. However, the initial starting point was a detailed content analysis of 117 toy ads broadcast on British television in the period leading up to Christmas 1996. While the methods and results of this analysis are reported elsewhere,[20] the major findings will be used here as a way to frame the current focus on semiotics.

The content analysis comprised the coding and counting of two major elements in the advertisement sample: camerawork features (shot sizes and angles, and camera and lens movements), and editing and other post-production features (transitions, shot duration and voice-overs). In the main sample, 43 ads were classified (by a number of independent adult coders) as being targeted at boys, with 43 targeted at girls and 31 aimed at a mixed audience.

A number of emergent content patterns were evident. In terms of camerawork features, the dominant shot size and angle by far were the mid-shot and the level angle. The boys' ads employed greater use of long shots and fewer close-ups, and also contained more low angle shots than the girls' ads. Similarly, the boys' ads used more overhead and canted (tilted) shots, while the girls' ads demonstrated greater use of peds (up and down). In terms of editing and post-production features, the boys' advertisements used more cuts while the girls' advertisements used more dissolves. The boys' ads had the shortest shot duration, when measured against the average for the sample as a whole, while the girls' ads were consistently above average. The length of the shot was directly proportional to the overall sense of pacing in each ad, where boys' ads appeared to be faster moving than the girls' ads. Overall, the sex of the voice-over corresponded with the target gender for the advertisement, but there was a predominance of male voice-overs across the sample as a whole, since they were more frequently used in mixed appeal ads.

Using these more obvious and quantifiable content features as a framework, the next stage was to determine whether such 'gendered' patterns were also reflected in the more subtle features of specific toy ads. The application of semiotic principles was considered the most appropriate and effective approach here. Gendering in children's ads is not as self-evident as one might first think, and immediate impressions can obscure what is happening under the surface. Semiotics can be used to show how formal features work in a given context to create specific meanings, offering a necessary progression from frequency-based content analysis.

The foundation for selecting the ads analysed in this chapter is the (linguistic-based) concept of 'markedness', discussed in detail elsewhere.[21] For the purpose of this chapter it is sufficient to state that, in the content analysis of the main sample, the mixed appeal ads emerged as being more closely aligned to the boys' ads than to the girls' ads in terms of both production and post-production features. The boys' and the mixed ads can consequently be described as 'unmarked', in that certain technical features are so often used that they become naturalized, invisible, unquestioned and perceived as the norm, simultaneously privileging the 'male'. A 'marked' technical feature, on the other hand, is something that it not used as often and subsequently appears different or unusual. This certainly applies to the features noted in the girls' ads, where the 'female' elements seemed 'unnatural' and 'un-masculine'.

Using the idea of 'marked' and 'unmarked' categorizations of technical features, the content analysis findings can be summarized in tabular form. Using the mixed ads as the so-called 'norm' or neutral category, the following table clearly illustrates that the girls' ads contained significantly more marked features than the boys' ads:

Marked features: *girls' vs. mixed ads*	*Marked features:* *boys' vs. mixed ads*
More level shots	Fewer close-ups
More peds (up and down)	Fewer high angles
More dissolves	
Use of female voice-overs	
Greater shot duration	

It is therefore arguable that, even though there were clear-cut paradigms available to advertisers offering many alternative possibilities in terms of production and post-production techniques, more often than not they employed techniques specifically attuned to the target gender for the advertisement.

Methods

Toy ads are characteristically complex, carefully crafted mini-narratives with powerful structures, appeals and meanings, framing the child audience as either 'boy' or 'girl'. The ads analysed in this chapter were selected using 'markedness' as a way to judge how closely individual texts might be deemed typical of their type. That is to say, typical girls' ads needed to exhibit more level shots, peds and dissolves than mixed advertisements, together with greater shot duration and the use of female voice-overs. Typical boys' ads, on the other hand, needed to exhibit fewer close-ups and high angles than mixed advertisements, together with the identifiable 'masculine' features of shorter shot duration, male voice-overs, use of cuts and use of 'dramatic' camera angles.

The 86 boy- and girl-targeted ads from the main sample were carefully sorted with the aim of selecting examples that illustrated these key features most strongly. Interestingly, very few individual advertisements in the sample exhibited *all* these key features. This further emphasizes a point made in the content analysis study, in that gendered production patterns are not immediately apparent in individual advertisements but become strikingly obvious across a large sample. The aim here was to select a number of advertisements that could be described as being *as closely aligned as possible* to the overall framework, and hence representing the so-called archetypal structures on which all other advertisements are based.

Through a process of elimination, six advertisements were identified as exhibiting a significant number of the key content features. The chosen boys' advertisements were Meccano Junior, Tomy R/C Turbo Sports Car, and Hot Wheels Criss Cross Crash, while the girls' advertisements were Pattie, Baby Born Accessories, and Amy's Pony Tales. The following table provides brief descriptions of the selected ads:

Product name	Brief description of the advertisement
Meccano Junior	This is a construction-based product. Two boys demonstrate the creative possibilities of the product by building vehicles and bridges, using the components and tools included in a Meccano set. They race and crash the vehicles in an environment that looks rather industrial.
Tomy R/C Turbo Sports Car	The advertisement is set in a bedroom. A young boy sits on the floor, wearing a large crash helmet and clutching a plastic car steering wheel. He is shown driving a 'turbo sports car' around the room, negotiating obstacles. Before the end of the advertisement the boy's 'father' appears on the screen and helps to steer the car. They both cheer as they cross the finish line.
Hot Wheels Criss Cross Crash	The product is a complicated racetrack based on two figures-of-eight that cross at a centre point. The aim is to send Hot Wheels cars around the track at high speed, enjoying many near misses before the inevitable crash. Two young boys are shown excitedly using the product, displaying exaggerated reactions when the cars crash.
Pattie	The advertisement features a talking doll designed to recite the nursery rhyme 'Pat-a cake, pat-a cake, baker's man' every time her hands are clapped together. She has rosy cheeks, long hair and wears a mop-hat. Two girls interact with the doll and recite the nursery rhyme with her. The advertisement is set in a rather hazy, flower-filled garden.
Baby Born Accessories	This advertisement features a group of girls who descend on a boutique selling nothing but baby clothes and accessories for their favourite dolls. They each hold up items of clothing in wonder, talking amongst themselves and nursing their dolls as they shop.
Amy's Pony Tales	This advertisement intersperses shots of actual stables with shots of the product. It illustrates all the various activities and chores required in the running of a stable and the upkeep of horses, based on the character of Amy.

Each of the boys' advertisements contained all but one of the key content features identified above, whilst the girls' ads contained *all* the key content features. It is therefore arguable that the chosen sample convincingly adheres to the established content patterns in 'typical' ads of this type, and in children's toy ads as a whole.

A semiotic approach to the texts

While the content analysis revealed strong patterns, it should be stressed that the frequency with which given elements or factors appear is not necessarily proportional to or synonymous with their level of significance. Hence, a number of issues will be considered in this analysis. A semiotic framework will be used to focus on the specific and often different ways in which the techniques were used to appeal to certain audience sectors, as well as considering how the features can be formalized in terms of the specific codes that operate across toy ads. This will include identifying any overriding features or techniques that can be applied to the genre as a whole, considering both specific thematic codes and more general advertising codes. The aim is to construct a semiotic framework in which *all* children's toy ads can arguably be located.

Since the advertisements aimed at boys and those aimed at girls have already been clearly identified as different from one another, this chapter will focus on a comparison of the ways in which the key content features are (differentially) used to appeal to each target audience sector. This semiotic analysis will retain a strong gender focus, with the aim of illustrating that both the overt content and the more subtle techniques and connotations in toy advertisements are specifically gendered.

This analysis will utilize a number of key semiotic concepts, focusing on the key camerawork features – shot size, shot angle and camera movement – and post-production features – transitions, shot duration and voice-over. Each feature will be considered in turn, followed by a consideration of the thematic and advertising codes.

Camerawork features

The most prominent and frequently used shot sizes and shot angles were the mid-shot and the level angle. Since these features occurred in *every* sampled ad, it is arguable that they represent the norm within the genre. The level shot represents the 'conventional' gaze of an individual looking directly ahead towards a scene, while the mid-shot represents the 'middle ground' or optimum distance from which a scene can be viewed. Indeed, a level shot might connote some form of stability and equilibrium, while the mid-shot might offer a comfortable compromise between the apparent detachment of a long shot and the intense involvement of a close-up.[22]

Of all the shot sizes, the close-up shot was most intriguing in terms of its differential use across the two groups of ads. Arguably, the close-up shot is stereotypically associated with connotations of emotional (female) involvement in a scene. The close-up appeared most frequently in the ads aimed at girls, but this is not to say that it *never* appeared in the ads targeted at boys. It is therefore interesting to compare how the technique is (differentially) used in each type of advertisement to achieve specific effects.

In fact, the close-ups in the girls' ads focus on details such as facial features or some aspect of the product (accessories and/or decorations). In the advertisement for Pattie, for example, there are numerous close-ups of the doll, specifically focusing on her eyes, mouth and hands. Each of these features is important in terms of the overall appeal of the product. Her mouth and hands are vested with considerable power because it is only through the action of clapping that the doll actually recites the nursery rhyme 'Pat-a-cake'. In a sense, the use of close-ups in the girls' ads guides the (female) viewers from one specific product feature to another, denoting the importance of these details in the context of product use and indicating where attention should be focused. Where a close-up of both the product and the product-user occurred in the girls' ads, a sense of intimacy and interrelationship between the two is connoted. This technique is very apparent in the ad for Baby Born Accessories, since the product and product-user are frequently shown in the same shot, connoting a sense of mother–baby interaction and intimate 'connection'.

The use of close-ups in the boys' ads differs slightly from the girls' ads, not simply because there are fewer examples of them but also because they tend to frame the various technical details of the product rather than focusing on faces (either of people or doll-products). In the Tomy R/C Turbo Sports Car ad, for example, there are a number of close-ups of the 'magic steering wheel'. This feature includes a number of special components such as a turbo button and lots of dials, emphasizing the importance of the wheel to the product, and connoting a sense of power and control to whoever might be holding it. The use of close-ups to show product detail in the boys' ads thus emphasizes the authenticity and attention to detail inherent in the products, enhancing their desirability.

Hence, while the girls' ads focus on 'human' aspects, the ads targeted at boys focus on 'non-human' or technical aspects. Each of these concerns might, in turn, be associated with classic gender stereotypes of 'personal' and 'professional' concerns respectively. It is arguable that the differential points of focus employed in the advertisements set a precedent for behaviour patterns (particularly when interacting with the products) amongst boys and girls. While the girls seem to be encouraged to focus on 'people', the boys seem to be encouraged to focus on 'things', making a clear distinction between emotions and material objects.

The use of shot angles is interesting and varied, particularly in the ads aimed at boys. A very basic pattern emerges when considering the use of shot angles in the girls' ads, since there tend to be only two types – the level angle and the high angle. The level angle is most often employed, as the 'conventional' angle or viewpoint, connoting a sense of being even-tempered, calm and methodical. There is nothing exciting about such an angle, and it seems predominantly unobtrusive in its 'naturalness' and predictability. The high angle offers a slightly different perspective in the girls' ads, but again does not seem to suggest anything particularly dynamic or exciting. In the Baby Born ad, for example, the high-angle shot represents the 'user-gaze', looking down on Baby Born as she sits on her changing mat, connoting an adult–child relationship and a sense of guardianship, care-giving and protection. The camera adopts the perspective of the 'eyes of the child' during product interaction, with sensory implications regarding how it might feel to be in a play scenario.

The use of shot angles in the boys' ads is more varied and open to interpretation. In this small sample, *all* the 'dramatic' camera angles are identifiable, including overhead, low and skewed/canted shots. Taking each of these in turn, it is possible to illustrate how angles are used to create particular effects.

In the Criss Cross Crash ad, for example, an overhead shot offers an extreme view of the 'crossroads' feature forming the main product focus. In addition to providing an obvious vantage-point over the most saleable characteristic, it also creates a sense of high drama. Yet there is also a sense of detachment in that the audience is placed in the position of uninvolved spectator. The fact that the shot angle is so extreme might even connote a sense of god-like superiority over the proceedings at ground level.[23]

The use of low-angle shots is also intriguing in the boys' ads, particularly given that there was no such example in the girls' ads. In the Tomy R/C Sports Car ad, for example, the camera is placed in a position that appears to be slightly below ground level, framing the car as it speeds around the young boy's bedroom before suddenly travelling towards the camera. The effect of using the low-angle shot means that the audience is faced with the front of the car from *below* the level of the bumper, so that the bonnet and roof of the car disappear from the field of vision. Consequently, the product appears oversized on the screen and dominates the shot. This technique effectively connotes a sense of product potency,[24] together with the implied inferiority of everything else within the shot. Such a rhetorical appeal is arguably more 'masculine' than 'feminine' in the sense that it implies power, superiority and impact.

The final dramatic camera angle that is used to great effect in the boys' ads is the skewed or canted shot. This particular angle frames a scene at 45 degrees, so that we are forced to tilt our heads to the side to view the scene as it would actually occur. While all three of the selected boys' ads contain examples of canted shots, the Criss Cross Crash ad contains a total of five examples – a quarter of the shot angles used in the ad as a whole. One of the main effects of the canted shot is to create a sense of dynamism, movement and drama. Since the shot is 'unhinged' from the norm of the level shot, there is a sense of unpredictability and danger. The Criss Cross Crash ad makes use of this shot angle to follow the Hot Wheels cars as they career around the racetrack at high speed, connoting the risk of imminent disaster. This ad even goes as far as to use a combination of dramatic shot angles, since high and canted shots are used together in a single frame, increasing the sense of drama and tension.

The only other notable production feature identified in the content analysis is the camera movement known as the pedestal or ped where the camera moves up and down its own 'spine' to show a level shot from different heights. The girls' ads employ this technique more frequently than the boys' ads. The advertisement for Amy's Pony Tales shows how peds can be used to create a certain visual impact and an overall 'feel'. The ad opens with a shot of a hedgerow, green and idyllic, featuring an 'Appletree Stables' wooden sign. The labelling of the location in such a way makes it explicit and 'bounded'. At this stage, there is little or no view of anything beyond the hedge and the sign. Gradually, however, the camera begins to ped up so that the audience sees over the hedge, connoting a motion similar to rising up onto 'tip-toes'. Rather than being voyeuristic, it creates a sense of being drawn into a new world of stables and horses. A sense of symmetry is achieved when we return to the hedgerow at the end of the ad. This time, the camera peds down so that the stable yard is once again obscured. The syntagmatic structure creates the impression that we have spent a pleasant day with Amy and her friends, where the ped up marked a sense of beginning and the ped down marked a sense of ending or closure.

Interpretations of the camerawork features can be summarized in tabular form, demonstrating some of the possible connotations of each feature depending on textual content, advertising intentions, product image and target audience:

Camerawork feature	*Function and/or connotation(s)*
Long shot	Detachment, scene-setting
Mid shot	Middle-ground 'norm'
Close-up	Involvement, focus, intimacy, interrelation ship, emphasizing detail
Level angle	Conventional gaze, stability, equilibrium, calm
High angle	User gaze, superiority, hierarchy
Low angle	Potency, power, impact
Overhead	Detachment, drama
Skewed/canted	Dynamism, movement, drama, danger, unpredictability
Peds	Tracking, guiding, spying

Post-production features

One of the most important post-production features is the use of editing transitions. Transitions can be divided into the two main types: the cut, a clean break between one scene and another, and the dissolve, where one frame is faded out as another is simultaneously faded in. Gender patterns in the use of these different transitions are apparent across the main ad sample.

The use of cuts is rather straightforward in comparison to the use of dissolves. The cut provides a clear division between one scene and another, where a scene can either follow on from the one before it or show a completely new perspective. The boys' ads use nothing but cuts to jump from one scene to another. Both the Tomy R/C Sports Car and the Criss Cross Crash ads contain numerous examples of this technique. Since both these ads show car-related products, it is arguable that cuts effectively connote a sense of unpredictability, dynamism and action. The scenes follow on so rapidly from one another that a sense of speed and danger is created, making it difficult to focus on any single aspect of the product. In this way, cutting acts as an attention-grabbing mechanism.[25] The abrupt changes of scene 'demand' higher levels of attention from the audience than the slow, gradual effects created by the dissolve transitions. This more forceful and disjointed style could be seen as more stereotypically masculine in its appeal.

Dissolves were only seen in the sample of ads aimed at girls. Dissolves are gentle and gradual, facilitating a smooth shift in perspective from one scene to another, and have therefore been seen to create a stereotypically feminine ambience.[26] The use of dissolves in the selected girls' ads suggests many interpretational possibilities.

One of the most conventional uses for a dissolve is to connote the passage of time, and this is effectively employed in the ad for Amy's Pony Tales. One scene focuses on Amy, saddling up her horse to go 'off for a ride' (as the voice-over explains). This then dissolves to a scene in which Amy has returned from her ride. Whilst emphasizing the apparent passage of time, there is also a sense of safety. The protective environment of the stables is not obviously breached because the audience is never privy to any activity outside the perimeter (white picket) fence.

The second conventional function of a dissolve is to connote a sense of moving between 'reality' and 'fantasy', or vice-versa. Short of including 'squiggly dream lines', dissolves provide the misty fuzziness that so effectively connotes the crossing from one 'universe' to another. This is again seen in Amy's Pony Tales. Once the horses have been returned to the paddock the scene dissolves into a 'real footage' shot of the actual stables, connoting that we have somehow snapped out of the 'fantasy' (play) situation and into 'reality'. The fact that the dissolve fuses the 'unreal' and the 'real' together strengthens the feelings of wish-fulfilment associated with the product.

Dissolves can also provide linkage between one scene and another. The simplest example of this linkage can be seen in the ad for Pattie, where a dissolve fuses the penultimate and final shots together. In the penultimate shot, Pattie appears in the play context in a picturesque garden. Once the girls reach the end of the 'Pat-a-cake' rhyme with the words 'for baby and me', the garden scene dissolves into a conventional product still in which all the different types of Pattie doll are displayed in rows, together with the product logo and other (small print) information. With the fusion of these two scenes, the linkage or connection between the product-in-play and product-in-retail contexts is made clear and obvious, facilitating recognition within the market-place.

Transitions are directly proportional to the number of shots and the duration of the advertisement. In the main sample of toy ads, the boys' ads contained a greater number of shots within a shorter space of time, resulting in a very rapid cutting rate. The cutting rate has a direct impact on the overall pacing and ambience of the advertisement, where a fast rate connotes a sense of speed, energy and excitement, showing life as little more than a blur. The faster cutting rate was characteristic of ads targeted at boys and can therefore be described as 'masculine'. While the boys' ads were consistently below average shot duration, the shot duration in the girls' ads was consistently above average due to their greater use of dissolves (because a certain amount of time must be taken to fade one scene out whilst fading another in). The use of dissolves therefore makes the pacing of the advertisement seem more leisurely and relaxed, and hence more 'feminine'.

The various functions and connotations associated with cuts and dissolves can be summarized as follows:

Post-production feature	Function and/or connotation(s)
Cut	Abrupt, dynamic, divisive, action-packed, attention-grabbing, jumpy, 'fast'
Dissolve	Gentle, gradual, smooth, relaxed, 'slow', passage of time, daydreams, linkage

The other noteworthy post-production feature here is that of voice-over. There is a clear pattern in terms of the types of voice-overs used to appeal to certain audience sectors, in that only male voice-overs were heard in ads aimed at boys, while the majority of voice-overs in the girls' ads were female. The overriding rule is that advertisers match the sex of the voice-over with that of the most likely product user, so that the advertisement 'speaks' to its target.[27] Advertisers frequently acknowledge that girls are more flexible than boys when it comes to accepting opposite-sex appeals, be it in terms of interacting with products or listening to opposite-sex recommendations.[28] This might therefore account for the fact that the occasional girl-targeted ad used a male voice-over, while the equivalent crossover never occurred in ads aimed at boys. The predominance of male voice-overs in the ad sample was made more obvious by the fact that the mixed audience ads employed more male than female voice-overs, again privileging the 'masculine', making the 'feminine' a 'marked' category, and following established gender-stereotyped conventions.

When seen in the context of the sample ads, it is clear how and why voice-overs are used in certain ways. In the Tomy R/C Sports Car ad, for example, a deep-voiced man with a Cockney accent narrates throughout. This produces an interesting juxtaposition with the screen images. While the voice-over speaks in the first person, conveying the 'inner thoughts' of the screen character, the voice is quite inappropriate for the frail-looking blond-haired boy on screen. The voice-over emphasizes the aspirational qualities of the advertisement, in that it represents what the boy will eventually become – a man. A similar technique is used in the advertisement for Amy's Pony Tales, where a female voice-over narrates the activities on the screen, speaking in the first person. In this case, however, the voice-quality of the narrator is closer to how one might expect 'Amy' to sound, since the narrator is a young girl.

Thematic codes

As well as analysing the key production features it is also possible to identify a number of general thematic codes running though the ad sample. A thematic code may be defined as the underlying narrative structure within a (media) text, forming the basis of the story being recounted on screen or, in the context of advertisements, the product image or philosophy. A number of themes were identified in this sample and the table below summarizes how they were distributed in the ads. (The reader should note that most of the ads contained multiple thematic codes.)

Product Name	Sense of order	Sense of chaos	Gendered role-play	Gendered interests	Friendship	Rivalry	Action starts slowly	Ad opens mid-action	Passive characters	Active characters	Destructive play	Constructive play	Toy empowers	Maintain status quo
Meccano Junior	✓		✓	✓	✓	✓				✓	✓	✓		
Tomy R/C Turbo Sports Car		✓	✓	✓	✓			✓		✓		✓	✓	✓
Criss Cross Crash		✓				✓		✓	✓	✓		✓		
Amy's Pony Tales	✓		✓	✓		✓			✓			✓		✓
Pattie	✓	✓	✓	✓		✓			✓			✓		✓
Baby Born Accessories	✓		✓	✓	✓				✓			✓		✓

Many of the terms used to classify the thematic codes are self-explanatory, but others require brief clarification here. *Gendered interests* was used to classify those ads which showed boy and girl characters pursuing (product-related) activities that were traditionally regarded as 'male' (e.g. vehicles) or 'female' (e.g. babies, animals).[29] A product may be portrayed as *constructive* (having the positive connotations of producing something) or *destructive* (having negative connotations of eliminating something). A product may be shown to *empower* the user by making him/her more popular, successful or socially accepted. The on-screen characters might appear *passive* (in the sense that the product governs and constrains their actions) or *active* (in that they have the freedom to control the product). Finally, the action on the screen might *start slowly* so that the audience is gently coaxed into the situation, or open *mid-action* to throw the audience in at the 'deep end'.

The most obvious thematic code shared by the ads in the sample is of gendered role-play activities. The three girls' ads are based on stereotypical 'feminine' activities, including nurturing, shopping, singing and domestic chores. The three boys' ads, in contrast, are based on stereotypical 'masculine' activities, including driving cars, construction, competition and technical tasks. It is arguable that the activities depicted in the girls' ads would be just as unappealing to a group of boys as vice-versa. For maximum effectiveness, advertisers and toy manufacturers aim to appeal to the perceived likes and dislikes of boys and girls as quickly and efficiently as possible, so by restricting the thematic codes to gendered role-play activities it is arguable that they can communicate more immediately with their desired target audience.

The spread of other thematic codes sets up a number of distinct contrasts. In the first instance, it is apparent that the girls' ads are thematized around the idea of order and routine, while the boys' ads depict more chaotic activities. The integral rhythmic rhyming of 'Pat-a-cake' in the Pattie advertisement, for example, sets an ordered beat around which all the activity takes place. The physical movements of the on-screen characters therefore appear measured and specific, establishing order. The boys' ads, in contrast, consistently spiral into an out-of-control, unpredictable and volatile world. In the Tomy R/C Sports Car ad, for example, it is doubtful whether the on-screen boy character actually understands how to control his car, because there are a number of potential accident situations and near-misses. Similarly, there is a sense of imminent disaster in the Criss Cross Crash ad, particularly when the momentum begins to build to a climax.

Further contrasts emerge in terms of the interrelationships between the on-screen characters. The girls' ads are generally dominated by a sense of friendship and co-operation. The girls appearing in the Pattie ad, for example, take turns to interact with the doll-product, gleaning much enjoyment from the shared experience. While the idea of friendship and co-operation is also discernible in the boys' ads, there is a more notable atmosphere of rivalry and competition between the screen characters. The Meccano Junior ad starts off positively as the boys share tools, building up a kind of co-operative buddy narrative. However, this congenial atmosphere soon degenerates as they start to compete against one another by racing their vehicles. The underlying implication is that only experts can triumph during head-to-head competition, and a great deal of prestige is attached to victory in this context.[30]

Another contrast between the boys' and girls' ads is in terms of constructive and destructive activities. Perhaps predictably, the girls' ads contain many more examples of constructive behaviour patterns than the boys' ads. These kinds of activities may be described as having positive connotations because something 'good' is achieved. The boys' ads, however, seem to exhibit more destructive behaviour patterns, where things are ultimately destroyed. One of the highlights of the Meccano Junior ad, for example, is when the cars collide and smash into pieces.

The gendered audiences are also differentially addressed. The girls' ads open by introducing the action quite gradually, allowing the text to take on a specific narrative structure with a beginning, middle and end. In Amy's Pony Tales, for example, we arrive at the stables in the morning and then follow the key activities throughout the day before finally leaving in the evening. The boys' ads, in contrast, launch straight into the action without warning, wasting no time setting the scene, and creating a more frantic and fragmented atmosphere.

A final thematic contrast involves the way the on-screen characters behave as they interact (or not) with the product. Once again following the established gender patterns, the girls are passive while the boys tend to be active. In the passive scenario, the product user is not in control of the product performance but is a spectator whose chief role is to appear 'impressed'. In the Baby Born ad, for example, the girls do little more than say 'wow' every time a new accessory materializes in front of them. In contrast, the boys seem able to take on a more active role by actually having input into the product. In the Meccano Junior ad, for example, the boys are only restricted by their own imaginations in terms of the kinds of things they can create.

Out of these thematic codes come a series of identifiable binary oppositions. At the most basic level, binary oppositions are a way of formalizing the polar ends of a spectrum, by listing a series of opposites that are related to one another, such as 'good' and 'bad' or 'pretty' and 'ugly'. The binary oppositions in this sample consistently tend to equate with notions of gender-appropriate product targeting. That is to say, the 'oppositions' are either in line with the male stereotype or the female stereotype, and link directly to the nature of the product and to the intended target audience. Broadly speaking, the thematic codes translate into gendered binary oppositions in the following way, which can be likened to the earlier table identifying 'gendered traits':

'Masculine' connotations	*'Feminine' connotations*
Destructive	Constructive
Unco-operative	Co-operative
Rivalry	Friendship
Fast	Slow
Excited	Calm
Active	Passive
Detached	Intimate

Clearly, there is a strong sense of alignment within the sample of ads. The culturally generated gender stereotypes are acknowledged and promoted, and consistently follow established patterns. It is also important to note that these patterns are an integral part of children's advertising texts, observable and sustained over a larger sample and not just within individual ads.

The codes of kids' advertising

So far, I have identified the semiotic patterns specific to the gendered target audience for each ad. However, it is also possible to identify certain general semiotic patterns that are applicable to children's toy advertisements as a whole. These patterns are essentially the main conventions of the genre and set up a series of similarities between the ads that are irrespective of the target gender for the product. Some of these are related to the use of production features in certain standard ways, while others are grounded in the general function of ads.

A very simple pattern of production features emerged across

the sample of toy ads, indicating that certain camerawork conventions are used in a stock way. These features include the use of level-angle mid-length shots to provide a 'normal' or 'naturalized' view of the scene. Furthermore, advertisers use either mid- or long shots when framing the closing product-still, to increase the likelihood of a lasting impression of the product. Long shots are also conventionally used as establishing shots to set the scene. Finally, an interesting pattern emerges when considering how angles are used to create a certain 'feel'. A level angle is conventionally used to show the product. If, however, advertisers wish to imply that the product is being interacted with, a high angle is adopted to mimic the user's gaze.

Wherever possible, the ads in the sample included some form of product demonstration. This technique does not necessarily imply that the child audience is guided through product-use in a step-by-step way, but simply shows a number of possible ways in which the product can be interacted with, or what the key features are. The necessity of showing some form of product demonstration is closely aligned with the composition of a scene in which user and product appear in the same shot. Conventionally, the product will be foregrounded and placed in the centre of the screen while the user will appear in the background, slightly out of focus (and therefore less important by implication). What tends to dominate is hands-on interaction with the product, and advertisers will often favour a (gender non-specific) shot of hands to connote the play situation. The Tomy R/C Sports Car ad, for example, features a significant number of hands-around-steering-wheel shots to emphasize the centrality of the wheel to the product.

The appearance of product and user within the same frame arguably functions to strengthen the association between the two, emphasizing that they are interrelated and mutually significant within a play scenario. An interesting pattern also emerges when more than one on-screen character appears in a shot. Rather than being shown as two independent individuals, a premise is generally established in which they form some kind of interrelationship. In the Pattie ad, for example, the two girls gradually become friends as they share in the experience of product interaction. In contrast, the relationship between the boys in the Meccano Junior ad becomes progressively more competitive as they race against one another. In both instances, the advertisers are seeking to show some kind of interpersonal interaction, signifying that the play experience is social whilst simultaneously alluding to gendered behaviour patterns.

The only other notable pattern to emerge across the ad sample as a whole is the way in which all the toy ads end with a product-still. Such a shot basically functions as a way to show off a range of accessories associated with the product, together with the product logo and any other small-print information or disclaimers. A closing shot of this nature occurs in *every* toy ad in the sample, providing a neat form of closure. Up to the point of the product still, it is likely that the audience will have seen only brief glimpses of the product (especially in the ads aimed at boys), but the product-still conventionally pauses a little longer to allow things to register properly. This kind of shot also serves to mark the boundary between one ad and the next.

Conclusion – an overriding pattern

One of the advantages of a semiotic analysis is that it is often possible to reduce a range of texts to a model of interrelations. Having analysed a contained sample of advertisements in detail, it is possible to generate a model that represents children's toy advertisement texts in general. In this case, it is possible to account for the emergent patterns in two ways. The *similarities* between the ads can be accounted for in terms of *genre*, while the major *differences* can be accounted for in terms of *gender*.

This idea can be incorporated into an established semiotic model suggested by the structuralist semiotician, Algirdas Greimas.[31] Greimas adapted his 'semiotic square' from the 'logical square' of scholastic philosophy in order to analyse paired concepts more fully. The main intention of the square was to map the conjunctions and disjunctions relating to key semantic features in a text, suggesting that the possibilities for signification are more complex than the either/or of a binary model. The square seems particularly appropriate in the context of this chapter, because the aim is to look beyond how the technical features might be interpreted as either 'masculine' or 'feminine' towards a framework which suggests that things are rather more complex in terms of gender and audience address.

Since the Greimasian 'square' is constructed on a four-part axis, it is arguable that the children's toy ads in this sample can be interpreted in terms of a complex interaction between the notions of genre and gender, and those of function and connotation. The distinctions between and intersections within these notions can be formalized in the style of a classic Greimasian square, as follows:

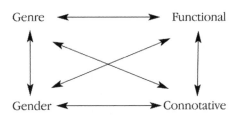

The key differences related to genre and gender can be further summarized in tabular form, based on the interrelationships between the components in the above square, to illustrate and explain why certain production features and techniques are used in the ways previously identified:

Similarities related to genre	*Differences related to gender*
Functional use	Connotative use
Show product	Subtle 'behaviour cues'
Enhance narrative sequence/story	Creating a 'suitable' atmosphere

What should also be apparent is that the genre-related components are generally what one could describe as 'surface' components. That is to say, the functional patterns within an advertisement might be easily identified and clearly apparent to an individual after glancing only casually at what is happening on the screen. Several of the gender-related components, however, are less obvious and apparent, tending to account for the subtle underlying features that might well be subconsciously internalized by the audience. It is exactly these subtle components that are drawn out and made explicit through the application of semiotic principles.

There is an intriguing contradiction here, which expands upon an observation made when analysing the content of the main sample of toy ads. There is a curious relationship between the 'big picture' of children's toy ads that utilize distinctly gendered features and the details of the individual ads that have 'relative autonomy' from the patterns generated across the larger sample. At first glance, this would suggest that the broader theoretical framework is too over-simplified and 'deterministic' to demonstrate the complexities and diversities evident in the texts. However, a close semiotic analysis of the construction of the texts indicates that the 'big picture' and the individual instances are in fact mutually dependent and interrelated, rather than independent and unrelated. It is exactly for this reason that the Greimasian square offers a useful interpretative tool.

The interrelationship between the 'big picture' revealed through content analysis and the relatively autonomous 'details' of individual texts is thus a complex one. It is arguable that the former imposes a gendered structure on the texts, ensuring 'appropriate' target audience recognition, while the latter creates the illusion that these gendered structures do not exist. This notion is well illustrated when one considers the notion of 'markedness' and the fact that 31 ads in the main sample were categorized as having mixed appeal. In fact, however, the mixed ads were consistently 'masculinized' in terms of their formal features, even though this was not obviously apparent to an audience (of both adults and children whom I interviewed as part of my research) who were effectively 'tricked' into thinking that the texts were gender neutral. This illustrates the notion of 'intimate polarity' alluded to in the title of this chapter: children's toys and toy ads seem initially polarized in terms of gendered binary oppositions (boy/girl, blue/pink), but they are simultaneously complex, contradictory, interrelated and inter-dependent. The marking of gender is more complex and less immediately visible than one might first assume; and some of this necessary 'indeterminacy' can only be revealed through a detailed semiotic analysis.

Notes

1. AEF (Advertising Education Forum): http://www.aeforum.org/
2. Dan Fleming, *Powerplay: Toys as Popular Culture* (Manchester: Manchester University Press, 1996), p. 7.

3. Janet R. Moyles, (ed.), *The Excellence of Play* (Buckingham: Open University Press, 1994), p. 16.
4. Dixon, 1990, in William A. Corsaro, *The Sociology of Childhood* (Thousand Oaks, California: Pine Forge Press, 1997), p. 151.
5. Cited in Judith Van Evra, *Television and Child Development* (New Jersey: Lawrence Erlbaum Associates, 1990), p. 120.
6. David Brown, 'Play, the playground and the culture of childhood', in Moyles (ed.), *The Excellence of Play*, p. 60.
7. Adrian Furnham and Nadine Bitar, 'The stereotyped portrayal of men and women in British television advertisements', *Sex Roles* 29 (3/4), 1993, 297–310.
8. See, for example, Alice E. Courtney and Thomas W. Whipple, *Sex Stereotyping in Advertising* (Lexington, MA: Lexington Books, 1983), p. 47
9. M. D. Shipman, *Childhood: A Sociological Perspective* (Windsor: NFER, 1972), p. 36.
10. Richard Dyer, *The Matter of Images – Essays on Representations* (London: Routledge, 1993), p. 12.
11. *Ibid.*, p. 14.
12. See, for example, Judith Butler, *Gender Trouble: Feminism and the Subversion of Identity* (London: Routledge, 1990).
13. Daniel Chandler and Merris Griffiths, 'Gender differentiated production features in toy commercials', *Journal of Broadcasting and Electronic Media* 44 (3), 2000, 503–20.
14. Denis McQuail, *Mass Communication Theory: An Introduction* Third Edition (London: Sage, 1994), pp. 239 and 242.
15. See, for example, Stuart Hall, Dorothy Hobson, Andrew Lowe and Paul Willis (eds), *Culture, Media, Language* (Working Papers 1972–9) (London: Hutchinson, 1980), pp. 128 ff.
16. See, for example, Jib Fowles, *Advertising and Popular Culture* (London: Sage, 1996) p. 83.
17. McQuail, *Mass Communication Theory*, pp. 239 and 242.
18. Roger Singleton-Turner, children-media-uk archive (October 1997): http://www/mailbase.ac.uk/lists/children-media-uk/
19. Shipman, *Childhood*, p. 28.
20. Chandler and Griffiths, 'Gender differentiated production features in toy commercials'.
21. *Ibid.*, p. 516.
22. See, for example, Tania Modleski, 'The rhythms of reception: daytime television and women's work', in H. Baehr and A. Gray (eds), *Turning it on: A Reader in Women and Media* (London: Arnold, 1996), pp. 104 ff.
23. See, for example, Erving Goffman, *Gender Advertisements* (London: Macmillan, 1979).

24. See, for example, Herbert Zettl, *Sight, Sound, Motion: Applied Media Aesthetics* (Belmont, CA: Wadsworth, 1999), p. 190.

25. Gerald Millerson, *The Technique of Television Production* (London: Focal, 1985), p. 111.

26. Renate Welch, Aletha Huston-Stein, John C. Wright and Robert Plehal, 'Subtle sex-role cues in children's commercials'. *Journal of Communication* 29 (3), 1979, 202–9.

27. Dan Acuff, *What Kids Buy and Why – The Psychology of Marketing to Kids* (New York: Free Press, 1997); Gene Del Vecchio, *Creating Ever-Cool – A Marketer's Guide to a Kid's Heart* (Gretna: Pelican, 1997).

28. Stephen Kline, *Out of the Garden: Toys, TV and Children's Culture in the Age of Marketing* (London: Verso, 1993) p. 192.

29. Acuff, *What Kids Buy and Why*, pp. 142–3.

30. Del Vecchio, *Creating Ever-Cool*, p. 45.

31. Daniel Chandler, 'Semiotics for beginners: http://www.aber.ac.uk/media/documents/S4B/semiotic.html

CHAPTER 9

Cementing the Virtual Relationship

Children's TV Goes Online

JULIAN SEFTON-GREEN

Children's TV has never been an isolated medium. Right from its earliest days, it has been surrounded by a range of other texts in other media – especially print. From the *Blue Peter Annuals* of the 1960s to the character merchandise of the 1980s, children's TV has always recognized that as an experience it competes and inter-sects with other media in children's lives. The spread of the home computer and especially the internet has had a particular impact on children's TV, which is evident from even the most casual of channel hopping today. All the main broadcasters of children's programmes in the UK, from the BBC and Children's ITV to the global multinationals like Nickelodeon, Disney and Cartoon Network, maintain extravagant and dynamic web sites. Not only are these sites frequently mentioned by continuity announcers and in adverts, but they figure centrally in design logos and other publicity material.

Such web sites are likely to act as a central space for advertising and promoting the channel or the company, beyond its part in broadcasting to children. The BBC's web site for example is one of the largest in the UK. It contains huge sections on sport, news and education in general as well as a specific area devoted to children's TV. Not only does the web site function independently of the TV station – acting as a gateway to the net in general – but it seeks to offer a range of experiences that complement straight-forward broadcasting. These will include shopping, information, links to other parts of the company's multi-media empire and so on. At the moment, most children claim to be aware of the internet from its TV presence; and certainly many sites developed for children derive from an interest in children's TV. The main exception to this is sites promoting or selling music – though even here, channels like the BBC or Nickelodeon try to incorporate this topic in their online presence.

In keeping with this book's broad focus on the textual structure of children's TV, the objective of this chapter is to analyse the kinds of web sites currently being developed by children's TV companies, as complements, supplements or substitutes for broadcast programming. I will select several indicative sites (Cartoon Network, *subzero* on CBBC and Noggin) and offer an analysis of their salient textual features, especially concentrating on what makes them distinctive as 'interactive' or online experiences. However, this chapter needs to be considered as work in progress – or, like all good web sites, as 'under construction' – for a number of reasons.

The nature of the online experience is clearly changing rapidly, both as a result of technological innovation and the penetration of the web into domestic spaces. Any account of the textual structure of web sites runs the risk of being out of date within a very short time. Certainly the lead-in time for an academic publication such as this might well render attempts to map an emerging field of study – the textual structure of web sites – redundant. On the other hand, appeals to the pace of change often stand as excuses, especially as many of the claims about the newness of online experiences are, in fact, somewhat over-hyped. Indeed, many online texts replicate the pre-wired world, reproducing some very familiar patterns and structures. Nevertheless, the transient, 'impermanent' nature of a web site as a constantly evolving kind of text[1] needs to be acknowledged and somehow built into the kind of analysis I am offering.

The relationship between TV broadcasting and the web is also part of this changing picture; and the second feature of online developments which needs to be considered is the changing nature of '–casting'. Here the prefix '–' stands both for 'broad' (as in broadcasting – the traditional form of the other texts described in this volume) and 'narrow' or 'web'–casting. It also covers the concept of online publishing or indeed any of the changing institutional relationships media producers might have with their audiences as a result of the new interactivity implicit in the online environment. Here, one key question is what role online '–casting' has within the gradual move towards fully integrated broadband interactive communication – which is promised to deliver audio-visual content into the home at the viewer's demand and to their specification. Although this model of communication does not yet exist, an idealized notion of two-way on-demand interaction between viewer and producer is now increasingly held up as a holy grail for the media industries. Indeed, there is an assumed inevitability that when the technological conditions are right, this is the desirable state of affairs to which we shall all be moving. This is in spite of all the historical evidence which suggests that many media forms are still valued alongside developments which may appear to have superseded them.[2] The online environments I shall be describing are frequently described as staging posts in this teleological trajectory.

From this point of view, these new texts might be seen to stand as an example of the changing nature of mass communications; and studying the text, which is where viewer and producer meet, can thus be seen to offer an insight into the evolving role of media institutions. An analogy might be made here with the music industry. Paul Brindley's discussion of the role of the web in changing the nature of music distribution identifies three models of distribution: a hybrid retail model; a digital download model; and an on-demand streaming model.[3] These models offer different ways of consuming music by contrast with the traditional model of simply purchasing a disc in a shop. All three options have significant implications for the organization and structure of the music business. Likewise, the role of online experiences and their relationship to broadcast TV have important implications for the kind of experience producers will create in other media – or what a BBC children's TV executive whom I interviewed called 'complementary media'.[4] Indeed, Brindley's modelling of different distribution scenarios is part of the same intellectual challenge facing all media producers: how to supplement, replace or invent in parallel to existing models of content creation.

As this implies, these online texts for children point towards significant re-configurations within the media industries. At least according to its producers, children's TV is at the cutting edge of change within the broadcast industries, as they develop in concert with the impact of the web. So, moving on from the simple capacity to email a programme when it is on-air, we can find assorted games, competitions, programme follow-ups, background information, and brand–supported holiday activities for young people. Some of these changes may not be as radical as some critics fear or suggest, but some do point towards a quiet shift in emphasis between consumer and producer. Children here are very much the testing ground for the future – or, as some cynics might say, are being educated to behave as the online consumers of the next generation. So to what extent do these online texts tell us about the future of childhood, or of the media in general? What kinds of experiences will be on offer to children? And how will they be expected to behave in the new digital dispensation?

The www text

Research into the web is to a great extent uncharted water for academic commentators.[5] There are no established models of textual analysis and very few examples of critical writing. There is some agreement about the methodological challenges facing analyses of web texts, one of the most obvious being that the www text itself is not clearly bounded. In particular, the distinction between a channel (Cartoon Network, BBC, etc.) and a programme (*Johnny Bravo, Blue Peter*, etc.) is blurred. The web sites established by children's TV companies in general promote the company or the channel; and although, as we shall see, there are specific pages or texts that might be seen to function like programmes, there is little comparable sense that web pages function *generically* in the same way as television. This is not to say that web pages are not generic, but that a magazine programme or a cartoon is constructed in a way which can to some extent be separated from the framework of the channel around it. Of course, critics of children's TV have pointed to the blurring of this distinction in respect of the programme/advert boundary, especially as regards action cartoons.[6] But web texts point to the way that the establishment of a 'relationship' between the TV channel and the viewer has become the key preoccupation of the entertainment text itself. Here the continuity announcer, the competition, the company brand logo and identity have become the very text of children's web TV itself.[7] The boundary between 'content' and 'context' has effectively evaporated.

Figure 9.1 Home page: www.cartoonnetwork.co.uk (1 June 2000)

An example of this might be the opening frame of the Cartoon Network site (Figure. 9.1). The viewer is being invited here to join a kind of club. The central frame – an advert for a game – contains the single command or request 'Play ... '. Experienced users of this site would recognize that this frame contains a game, and that it, in addition to the boxes surrounding it, are the 'doors' to further activities. There are a number of observations we can make at this stage. However, there is very little instructional data within this page. It is text free (or limited) and this is clearly deliberate, implying two key principles of web sites for children. First, they must be interactive, or at least offered as simple problems to be solved: if you don't know what to do, click to find out! Secondly, this site, which is intended for the full range of child audiences (from the very young to early adolescents) tries to avoid a reliance on print text in favour of visual cues. This is underpinned by a philosophy which seeks to make the web as 'intuitive' as possible. It is often suggested that visual cues are naturally communicated and transcend the need for formal education (as compared with learning to read print text). Neither of these suggestions is entirely true. Despite the apparent naturalness of this kind of text, it too follows a logic and a grammar which readers need to learn to read, in the same way we are all initiated into print literacy.[8] On the other hand, while new readers of this text might spend a bit more time than experienced users before choosing what to do, it would not be difficult to find your way around, given a little time.

The content of this site primarily involves participating in activities, for example playing 'Dexter's Bubble Juggle', looking at the toon-news (though whether very young children will appreciate the intertextual reference to the UK's prestigious *News at Ten* is debatable), or playing 'Smelly Telly' (a half-term holiday activity, involving using a scratch 'n' sniff card at specified points during the day's schedule and then filling in a competition entry to be submitted via email). Here, the web site seems to try to replicate the brand identity of the TV station – defined in terms of play or fun (Figure 9.2). The simple Shockwave or Flash games (see Figures 9.3 and 9.4) use the characters of the cartoon pro-gramming and borrow some of the humour and the cartoon-like sounds.[9] However, the activities at this point on the site are not in any way like the individual cartoon texts or programmes them-selves (in the sense of narrative or genre). The web site seems to be trying to extrapolate the essential nature of a Cartoon Network

Figure 9.2 www.cartoonnetwork/mystery machine (1 June 2000)

Figure 9.3 www.cartoonnetwork/play this (1 June 2000)

Figure 9.4 Screen shot of Powerpuff Girls Shockwave game

experience. This involves taking certain kinds of tropes (the
characters) and pleasures (fun or play) and then re-presenting this
'channel experience' in an online form. Whether the essence can
in fact be distilled in this manner or whether it is qualitatively
different in these kinds of online formats must remain open to
question.

The final point I want to make about these kinds of texts is that
viewers are alerted to them as part of their TV viewing experi-

ence. Although it is possible that children might come across the site as part of casual surfing, or indeed visit the site regularly as part of a menu of sites they might 'flick through' when (web-) channel hopping, the site is more orientated towards users who come to it for a purpose. The 'in-jokes' and intertextual references on the home page support this. The TV channel itself contains a significant amount of continuity announcements – often made by cartoon characters in funny voices – which urge viewers to go to the web site and play games or competitions, or advertise secondary TV channels like Boomerang (see bottom right-hand side of home page, Figure 9.1). There is an interesting marketing ploy in this gambit, as the TV channel is effectively suggesting to viewers that they leave the TV screen and go online to continue the Cartoon Network experience. (As we shall see below in my discussion of *subzero*, this apparent conflict has to be negotiated in some interesting ways.)

Although the actual web games and activities aren't like a cartoon programme in narrative terms, they do attempt to embody the essence of the particular cartoon's humour. For example, 'The Powerpuff Girls versus the Randy Ruff Boys' (Figure 9.4) begins with a hyperbolic piece of rhetoric in the form of a scrolling text written in the mock heroic style of the programme, giving a background story to the game. However, the activity of the game itself is a simple piece of Shockwave animation, which involves moving sprites around the screen (the Powerpuff Girls) and 'kicking' the Randy Ruff Boys by pressing the space bar. From this point of view, the site itself functions as an extension or supplement to the experience of viewing, as it brands what is in many ways a limited activity or experience with the distinctive tropes, humour and style of the channel. The user brings to their play with the web site a history of pleasures gleaned from the cartoons, which may give the interactivity some depth and 'added value'.

www texts as programme units

Noggin.com is an independent production company which was set up as a collaboration between Nickelodeon and Children's Television Workshop. The 'What's Noggin' button on the home page – www.noggin.com (Figure 9.5) – contains an account of

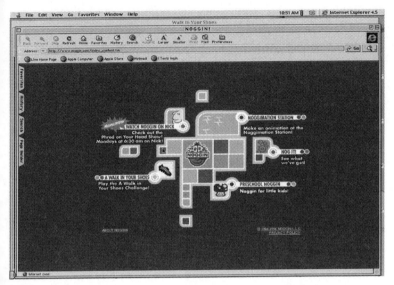

Figure 9.5 Home page: www.noggin.com (5 June 2000)

this history written in the kid-friendly lingo characteristic of most contemporary children's TV companies:

> The people who make *Blue's Clues*, *Doug* and *Nick News* thought that the stuff that Children's Television Workshop made was really cool.
> Meanwhile, at the VERY same time . . .
> Children's Television Workshop, the people who make *Sesame Street*, *3–2–1 Contact* and *The Electric Company* thought the stuff that Nickelodeon made was really cool.
> So . . .
> They decided to put their NOGGINS together to make a whole bunch of NEW and DIFFERENT COOL stuff . . . and they decided to call it . . . NOGGIN.
> The end.
> 'Um, that was a really nice story and all, but what exactly IS Noggin?'

This text is followed by yet more information, as seen in Figure 9.6.

Noggin is currently trying to position itself at the forefront of interactive online-casting. The convergence implied by being a 'TV channel, a website, a promise, a place and a platform' not

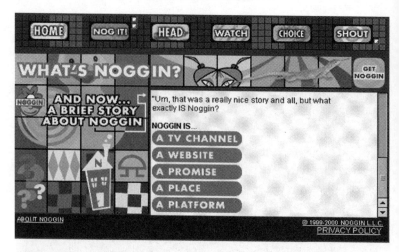

Figure 9.6 Part of 'What's Noggin': www.noggin.com/whatsnog/ (5 June 2000)

only blurs kid-friendly discourse with marketing hype – the promise – but promotes a hypothetical newness – being all of these different things at once. This is part of a larger pattern played out in the media more generally, where they not only promise to provide particular texts to readers, but at the same time offer the unique experience of the changing medium itself as part of a new entertainment future. I want to explore some of these claims in an analysis of one of Noggin's experiments, 'A Walk in Your Shoes' (bottom-left-hand quadrant of the home page, Fig. 9.5).

'A Walk in Your Shoes' is a familiar programme idea, taking people from one environment and swapping them with individuals from another. So for example, Jared, who is at summer camp, switches with Pat, who works in a candy store. The narrative derives from a (frequently comic) tension between difference and sameness. Thus, although individuals come from opposite backgrounds and places, they discover commonalities – although many of the narratives stress either a fondness for home comforts or the surprise at discovering how the strangeness of one's 'twin' is familiar. 'A Walk in Your Shoes' (WIYS) exists both as an independent piece of TV, broadcast on Nickelodeon, *and* as an independent piece of web content. Both the TV programme and the www text share film sequences. For example, the same

Figure 9.7 'A Walk in Your Shoes' 1: www.noggin.com/wiys/ (5 June 2000)

video diary segments are embedded in the web text and the broadcast. However, Noggin claim that the web experience is both independent of the TV (in that it offers a different range of experiences and texts) and complementary to the TV programmes (in that it offers a range of additional material building on the TV experience). Despite the tendency towards marketing hype, the programme (on both platforms) is clearly trying to define the boundaries of each medium, as well as how they might profitably complement each other – and such experimentation deserves serious scrutiny.

The web text begins with a screen which explains the programme (Figure 9.7). It loads the text slowly, spinning each word around. This has the effect of 'speaking' the text, and the pace of delivery (i.e. the time it takes for each word to arrive on the computer screen) suggests a rather dramatic, portentous voice-over. Once the user presses the 'star' button, the programme loads. It is scripted in the interactive programme Shockwave, so the user has to ensure that the appropriate plug-in (for the web browser) is present. While the screen moves to the next stage a series of time-filling questions are fired at the user like 'How's math class?', ' Watcha doing this weekend?', 'How's the family?' or even 'How's your computer these days?'. These aren't interactive (in the sense that a reader might be able to answer them), but are merely attempts not to lose the user during a rather dull screen moment. This kind of strategy may very well be a temporary kind of device as broadcasters become more secure about using the web. As I have already suggested in relation to Cartoon Network, it is likely that users will come to this site with a premeditated purpose. Certainly it is unlikely they would have got this far without being deliberate, and needing to hold onto them in this way seems redundant. On the other hand it could well be that the blandness of these questions merely underlines how much work TV channels put into constructing their 'ideal viewer' – in this instance, the 'Kid' constructed by a whole host of other Nickelodeon experiences.

In addition to these text-based actions, the screen design so far utilizes a number of graphics. There is the Noggin head/world (top right-hand quadrant of Figure 9.7), the walking shoes which accompany the words, moving across the screen until they turn into the text in Figure 9.7, and the stylized buttons at the top of each page, allowing the user to navigate both within the item and the Noggin site at large. This constant reminder of how a web site is framed is, of course, fairly standard, but it tends to work against the conventions associated with broadcast TV. We are all familiar with the channel logo super-imposed on a programme to help the channel surfer recognize where they are. By contrast, these buttons constantly offer the user an alternative, inciting him or her to switch around the site. In fact, the 'Walk in Your Shoes' text itself is rather linear, in that it takes the user through a series of screens. There is some choice but, on the whole, bits of the narrative have to be viewed in sequence. However, the constant reminder at the top of the screen acts as a warning: if you get bored, move on. (Here again, the use of graphic puns (the walking shoes, or even the Noggin head) serves to reinforce the slightly wacky kid-humour running through the whole experience.)

However, the next screen (Figure 9.8) offers the web user a different kind of control over the programme from that of the TV version. Here the paired images down the left-hand axis clearly show the user which characters are being contrasted with each other. The user can select a pair to view and, as in this screen, is offered a brief text summary of the programme: 'Jared, who goes to summer camp, SWITCHES lives with Pat who works in a Candy

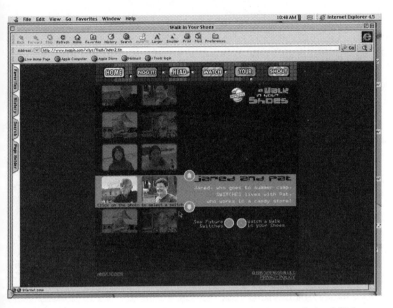

Figure 9.8 'A Walk in Your Shoes' 2: www.noggin.com/wiys/ (5 June 2000).

Store.' The user can either watch the pair he or she has high-lighted (in which case further options offer themselves) or catch a sneak preview of up-and-coming switches (which presupposes a user who has some familiarity with the show (on TV) or the site (through frequent use)). This choice is available through the buttons in the middle (slightly below the centre of the screen).

There are a number of observations to be made about this structure. First of all, it attempts to build in opportunities for new and frequent users at the same time. In fact, the notion of a frequent user (that is, someone who knows their way around the narratives but wants to do something different with this text) may be as much a fiction created for the benefit of the first-time user as a reflection of the actual usage of the site. It enables a first-time or infrequent user to get the impression that they are part of a community of readers (of varying experiences) and hence that this is a supportive environment. Secondly, it should be noted that interactivity at this stage is limited to choosing from a menu of narrative options (although later we shall see that other kinds of involvement with programmes are made possible). We will follow the screens from the point-of-view of a first-time user, and discuss

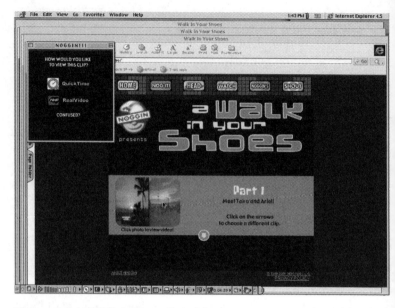

Figure 9.9 'A Walk in Your Shoes' 3: www.noggin.com/wiys/ (5 June 2000)

some of the more complex options in this structure.

Figure 9.9 is not untypical of the design dilemma facing web authors. In particular, it demonstrates a tension between our reliance on moving image and print grammars and how such grammars may be translated into the semi-moving, but symbol-based, screens of the web. In essence, the screen functions as a transitional title sequence. It acts as a kind of sub-heading; and in print we would probably represent its function in bold text or capitals. It signposts users to the swap between the two characters selected. However, in typical web style, it also offers yet more options or choices. The reader can either view a brief video (see the window already opened, top left-hand corner) or of course choose yet another pair of swaps. For the first-time viewer, choice in this instance will militate against narrative pleasure: until the reader has watched one 'Walk in Your Shoes' sequence or is 'into' its story, being given choices is not going to get one hooked onto the central narrative. Of course the fact that the video sub-window also offers technical choices (Quick Time/Real Video or download) is typical, demonstrating just how much textual

Figure 9.10 'A Walk in Your Shoes' 4: www.noggin.com/wiys/ (5 June 2000).

knowledge young web readers must learn to work with.

On one level, this screen is redundant; its essential information could be compressed into the next one. However, its signposting role is important, even if it seems a rather awkward translation from print to 'slide-show' grammar. We also have to account for the fact that all of these screens load quite slowly, so that the whole experience of this site is frequently accompanied by a feeling of frustration as well as a kind of deferral. It takes a long time to get to the 'heart' of the narrative and even then it is unclear that the reader has got to the point to the story, as yet more choices imply a continuous journey.[10] The next screen (Figure 9.10) appears to be yet another opportunity for further choice, although it is actually the compressed summary of the swap. This is qualitatively different from watching a TV sequence and, as with the Cartoon Network site discussed above, Noggin tries to replicate the 'essence' of the TV experience through supplementary activities, such as playing games and doing quizzes (Figure 9.11). In Figure 9.10 the viewer can read basic facts about the swap characters, supported by iconic images and expressed in kid-friendly text, for example about one of the characters who 'has never ever DREAMED of going to Alaska'. In keeping with

Julian Sefton-Green

Figure 9.11 'A Walk in Your Shoes' 5: www.noggin.com/wiys/ (5 June 2000).

the structure of the programme, these facts are expressed as parallel opposites. The viewer/reader is then invited to participate in a game to test their knowledge of the facts – a game which clearly emphasizes geographical and cultural differences, thus highlighting the implicitly worthy and 'educational' nature of the programme.

These substitutions, where narrative depth is replaced by summary (both visual images and key text-based phrases) and by activities (communication with the makers though quizzes, and competitions or games), are central to the difference between TV and the web. Together, they point to both the strengths and limitations of www.tv. On the one hand, the viewer might gain by participating in a game, and enjoy receiving responses from the company; although this participation merely emulates an experience of personal communication rather than creating 'authentic' inter-personal relationships. Nevertheless, this involvement – however we define the nature of the relationship – is not the same as an involvement in story and character – which is where TV can offer much greater depth. Noggin is obviously trying to move beyond a simple web site which merely gives background information; and, like Cartoon Network, seems to think that participation can both capture and replace the essence of the brand experience. Nevertheless, the textual possibilities offered by the web as a medium still seem to limit the potential here.

Subzero – towards the interactive programme

Subzero was an innovative magazine/competition programme broadcast on Children's BBC (CBBC) on Saturday mornings in 1999/2000. The programme was conceived as a way of integrating cyberculture in general, and the web in particular, into broadcasting. For a variety of institutional reasons, the Children's Department was in a strong position to exploit online developments in a coherent and integrated fashion. It wanted to develop a cutting-edge programme which reflected its perception of the importance of cyberculture in modern children's lives; although, in the context of the 'digital divide', it could be argued that webcasting contradicts the principle of universal access that is inscribed in the BBC's public service remit. According to its producers, '*subzero* was the first programme that we designed to grow out of its web activity, rather than the other way round'.

The programme incorporated a number of distinct uses of online media and was apparently very successful. Not only did the broadcast programme itself get acceptable ratings, but the web site took huge numbers of page hits both during and after the show. Indeed the producers were convinced that the first episode created such an intense amount of internet traffic that the BBC server came under almost unbearable pressure:

> So you have kids messaging in live to the programme, which was an intensely complicated thing to do, because Broadcast Online hadn't actually created the software to operate forums quickly so [when] the first programme actually went out ... we were processing emails, 4,000 emails in half an hour, and 55,000 web page requests and we needed those for British internet! There was actually a newspaper article which said that there was severe congestion on the internet at about 11 o'clock on Sunday morning, ... which is as yet unexplained.

In this instance, the use of the web points towards a variety of 'interactive' textual strategies that are now emerging in the age of www.tv. The first key issue relates to the tension, noted above,

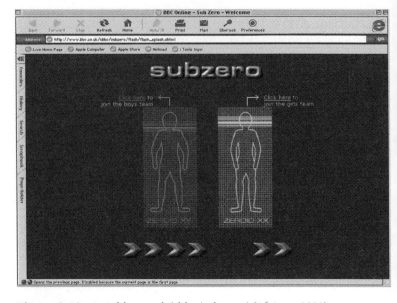

Figure 9.12 www.bbc.co.uk/cbbc/subzero/ (16 June 2000)

caused by the simultaneous use of both media, web and TV. The narrative of *subzero* establishes a competition between opposing same-sex teams, which involves finding and collecting 'bio-rats' (or plastic balls to the cynical adult observer) (see Figure 9.12).

There are a number of ways in which the teams are aided by audience input (online and by phone). However, viewers can not only join a team of their choice but also find bio-rats online; and this activity feeds into the competition between the male and female teams in the programme. Email comments are flashed in real time across the TV screen, which looks like a busy computer screen, with sub-windows, banner headlines and flashing 'buttons'. The site provides activity and participation when the programme is off-air, but it really comes into its own during transmission. On the one hand, this is at odds with the fact that the web is mainly geared to offering non-synchronous communication: it provides the illusion of direct and immediate communication, but in effect much of this is either automated or not actually transacted in real time. However, by contrast, *subzero* used audience participation through the web as a means of creating the illusion of a shared public experience. The producers were keen to create this notion of belonging to a community, of membership of a club, and fully accepted that the competition (with its traditional sex-differentiated teams) was a pretext to facilitate this. Indeed, they were absolutely clear that they were trying to create the distinctive aura of participation – even though there was no prior evidence that the technologies might be able to deliver this:

> We didn't think kids could go online and watch television simultaneously. We didn't think it was a UK phenomenon. We knew it was an American phenomenon, where kids on Saturday mornings were watching television, ringing their friends, and that had extended into the web. The process of Saturday morning television in America is frequently a community based one, where people actually talk their way through the Saturday morning show – the Saturday morning strand – but we had no evidence and we hadn't been able to find any evidence ... that kids had PCs ... or were sitting close enough to a television or would be prepared to sprint to a PC, save a message and come back. And the actual evidence came in, and Lorraine Heggessey, Head of Department, said her daughter missed five minutes of the show whilst sending an email. But she didn't mind – that was grand – because the chance that the email might have appeared on air was very important to her.

As this implies, working at the 'cutting edge' of web TV does mean that programme development is motivated by intuitive hunches and anecdotal evidence rather than research. Ironically, one of the producers tells a story that on the eve of the first episode he was rung up by a member of the BBC hierarchy who wanted to discuss the fact that the programme was intending to use forums (i.e. live online feedback) when the BBC as an institution hadn't yet established its corporate policy in this area.

As in the case of Cartoon Network, there is a gamble in encouraging viewers to go online at the expense of taking them away from the TV screen; but this can effectively work to support viewers' experience of the brand, by reinforcing the distinctive nature of the experience. Here, as in much children's TV, it is the experience of belonging and of participating which makes the difference. Of course, there is a long history of this in children's TV. From the early days of *Blue Peter* and *Crackerjack* in the 1950s and 1960s, children have been ceaselessly encouraged to write in to and (in some cases) to appear on programmes, and thereby to develop a 'personal' relationship with 'their' pro-

grammes or channels. This was very much sustained in the presenters' continuity sequences and in the Saturday morning
magazine shows developed during the 1970s and 1980s. For
example, the factual magazine programme *Blue Peter* still places a
central emphasis on developing relationships with its audience. In
the first quarter of 2000, the programme received around 27,000
competition entries; and emails (about 5000 over this period) are
slowly replacing letters as the dominant means of communication.
This kind of participation also partly accounts for the success of
some 'kidult' programmes like Channel 4's *The Big Breakfast*, and
most recently for 'reality shows' such as *Big Brother*[11] (which the
producers of *subzero* cited as an influence on their work). Indeed
the trend for adult programmes like *Big Brother* to replicate this
feature is frequently advanced as evidence of the infantilization of
TV in general.

The producers of *subzero* were happy to admit that the idea of
teams was a device to facilitate this sense of belonging; and they
recalled a wide of range of possibilities they had contemplated
using before settling on the very obvious boy/girl dichotomy. The
reasons for this decision relate clearly to the need to inspire
immediate identification, either through opposition or loyalty.
The aim, right from the beginning, was to exploit the new medium of the web, to see how it buttresses or replaces the use of
other devices (competitions, direct address) as means of developing viewers' personalized relationships with the TV company.
In the process, it had to be prepared to take the risk of excluding
some children. Although the huge number of page hits (up to
350,000 per week when the show was on air and even 2000–3000
off-air) is statistically opaque and difficult to interpret, it nevertheless suggests intense enthusiasm.

As this example suggests, online technologies do allow for
direct and immediate participation, albeit of a limited kind. If, for
example, a viewer sends in an email and it is selected to be on air,
the child is getting immediate feedback. Being a net detective and
finding the bio-rats or playing as part of your same-sex team
(technically cross-gender participation is possible but unmea-
sured) gives the viewer a sense of influencing the show's outcome. Of course, there is a law of diminishing returns here. If a
child is part of a relatively small community and can gain a sense
of its size, it is possible to estimate one's personal contribution.
However, the larger the community of viewers, the smaller one's

impact. What is interesting about *subzero* (and indeed adult participation shows) is how the interface appears to allow the viewer a sense of direct control, of intervening in public narratives, whilst of course one's actual contribution may be relatively insignificant. It would be interesting to discover how accurate participants' sense of their power actually is in these situations.

Ultimately, though, we need to assess whether this kind of interactivity is merely a matter of fashion, or whether it reflects deeper values. Was *subzero* successful simply because it was different and new, or does the capacity to join in a programme in this way suggest a more profound change in viewers' relationships with media? Recent research suggests that children may now be living more solitary existences, confined in their media-rich bedrooms;[12] and this might in turn suggest a growing need for media which seek to build community, as a form of compensation. Yet as I have indicated, this is by no means a new phenomenon – as the case of *Blue Peter* suggests. The need to belong to a community (or indeed a 'gang' or a 'club') could be a timeless need, or alternatively an ideal constructed through successive representations of childhood. More research about the pleasures and limitations of such forms of 'belonging' – not least in relation to virtual communities – is clearly needed.

Conclusion

One important feature of the community constructed by www.tv is that it addresses the child acting independently – although some TV adverts for the web do stress that the child should get an adult's permission to go online. (In the UK at least, this is to protect domestic phone bills as well as to appear responsible in the face of anxieties about the dangers of the web.) As has been noted elsewhere, one of the claims for new technologies is that they allow traditionally disempowered social groups (like the young) to become more equal participants in society;[13] and from this point of view, www.tv appears to construct the child as more 'grown up' than do some other aspects of children's TV.

In the mid-1990s, it appeared as if interactivity, almost the 'golden rule' of the digital age, was conceptualized in an absolute sense: as I suggested in the opening to this piece, it was seen as a matter of offering viewers complete control over their entertainment experiences. At present, however, interactivity seems to mean several rather more limited kinds of involvement. There is the idea that readers might affect narrative outcomes by selecting either endings or characters from a menu of choices – which lies behind the structure of sites like *www.itsyourmovie.com*, for example. Meanwhile, in the sites I have discussed here, interactivity seems to mean that the user or consumer can enter into a dialogue with the producer. So, the net makes it easier for children to write in or enter competitions, and even to do so in real time. Interactivity in this sense is best thought of as a *social relationship*, established by the producer, in which children are invited to participate. The relationship requires a series of exchanges, usually of information, creating the illusion of inter-personal communication. In this kind of www.tv the company is usually fronted or mediated by a cartoon character or, as in *subzero*, a youthful presenter, intended to be a surrogate 'friend' or older sibling. The competition structure, used in both *Noggin* or *subzero*, has the effect of time-limiting the communication, and this creates a sense of urgency; although it also prevents anybody having the opportunity to question the authenticity of the relationship.

The kinds of texts I have described in this chapter do undoubtedly create an atmosphere of participation and involvement; but we might have good reason to doubt whether this qualifies as genuine interactivity. They create a more direct relationship between the producer and the viewer, although there are significant limits in the extent to which this can be seen as equal or authentic. As I have indicated, the new forms of text being developed here have a considerable degree of continuity with the more familiar broadcast texts of children's television. In this respect, we might well ask whether they do in fact represent anything significantly new. When these kinds of texts become commonplace, when they stop being valued for their innovation and 'trendiness', will we really value their 'personalized inter-activity' as a distinctive pleasure? Or will they too become as repetitive and routine as the texts they have appeared to replace?

Notes

1. See A. Mitra and E. Cohen, 'Analysing the web; directions and challenges', in S. Jones (ed.), *Doing Internet Research: Critical Issues and Methods for Examining the Net* (London: Sage, 1999).
2. See B. Winston, *Media, Technology and Society: A History* (London: Routledge, 1995).
3. See P. Brindley, *New Musical Entrepreneurs* (London: IPPR, 2000).
4. Quotations here and elsewhere in the chapter are taken from my interviews with Greg Child, Annette Williams, Rebecca Shallcross, Simon Hall, Marc Goodchild, Clare Bradley, Adrian Johnson and Paul Tyler from BBC Children's TV (June 2000). Many thanks to them for their time and input.
5. See Jones, *Doing Internet Research*.
6. See T. Engelhardt, 'Children's television: the shortcake strategy', in T. Gitlin (ed.), *Watching Television* (New York: Pantheon Books, 1986).
7. See Chapter 3 of D. Buckingham, H. Davies, K. Jones and P. Kelley, *Children's Television in Britain: History Discourse and Policy* (London: British Film Institute, 1999).
8. See, for example, G. Kress and T. Van Leeuwen, *Reading Images* (Burwood, Victoria: Deakin University Press, 1990).
9. The BBC producers commented that Cartoon Network could obviously afford to use high-quality programming (both Flash and Shockwave are Macromedia products), and that the site demonstrated a high level of investment comparable to their own. They also pointed out that users need a reasonably good standard of computer and internet connection at home in order to use the site.
10. See I. Snyder, *Hypertext: The Electronic Labyrinth* (Melbourne: Melbourne University Press, 1996).
11. *Big Brother* was first broadcast in the UK on Channel 4 in August–September 2000.
12. See S. Livingstone and M. Bovill, *Young People, New Media*, report of the research project 'Children, Young People and the Changing Media Environment' (London School of Economics, 1999); and D. Buckingham, *After the Death of Childhood: Growing Up in the Age of Electronic Media* (Cambridge: Polity Press, 2000).
13. See J. Sefton-Green, *Digital Diversions: Youth Culture in the Age of Multimedia* (London: UCL Press, 1998).

CHAPTER 10

Pandora's Box or the Box of Delights?

Children's Television and the Power of Story

HELEN BROMLEY

The story teller is omniscient. (Gonzo, 'The Muppets Christmas Carol')

In this chapter I intend to explore the intricate relationship that exists between literary and media texts for children. Whilst it has long been recognized that children are not passive recipients of media texts, any more than they are passive recipients of so-called literary texts, much of the discussion in this field tends to assume that the role of literature is automatically positive, and that of the media automatically negative. This is true even within popular culture itself. In a recent series of the popular British sitcom *Men Behaving Badly*, for instance, the two male protagonists are pictured sitting on the sofa, mindlessly watching television, not even truly aware of the programme they are watching. Meanwhile, one of their female counterparts taunts them from the pages of her rather thick and serious-looking book. The message is clear: men + TV = bad and mindless; women + book = good and thoughtful.

I want to suggest that such a dichotomous view is not the most helpful way of understanding how these different types of texts work or interact. Indeed, the notion of 'effects' – that television has a necessarily negative impact on children's behaviour, that can only be redeemed if it results in increases in the sales of books – would seem positively misleading in this respect. By contrast, I wish to look at how television and literature co-exist, and indeed suggest the presence of a symbiotic relationship where both support and enhance the other. My central focus is not so much on questions of cultural value, as on the different kinds of 'literacy' that are required and developed by these different media, and specifically those which relate to the role of narrative. However, I also want to explore these issues from a personal perspective, drawing anecdotally on my own experience of childhood viewing and on my more recent experience as a teacher and a parent.

Watching with mother

As a British child of the late 1950s, my own television viewing began with the week that many 'forty somethings' will remember: *Picture Book, Andy Pandy, Rag, Tag and Bobtail, Bill and Ben (The Flowerpot Men)* and *The Woodentops*, collectively broadcast by the BBC under the title of *Watch With Mother*. As David Buckingham suggests in his introduction to this book, these programmes are the stuff of a collective national, as well as personal, nostalgia. I regularly watched these programmes (with my mother, needless to say), and took great pleasure from them. Each programme was different in nature, and thus over the period of a week provided for a range of 'readers'. For me as a child, part of the attraction of the programmes derived from the ritualistic openings and endings. These offered a sense of familiarity, like opening a known and well-loved book, with the added attraction that there would be something new each time. Watching the bricks turn to spell Andy Pandy's name, savouring the turning of the pages of *Picture Book* and joining in with the introduction to *The Woodentops*, were all valuable strategies for engaging the child viewer.

Ultimately, though, what kept the viewer involved was the calibre of the stories themselves. Story devices that would also be found in children's literature recurred throughout the programmes, offering models of narrative that were enticing and magical. Many British people of my age remember the Woodentops singing 'What have we got for dinner today, sawdust and hay, sawdust and hay, that's what we've got for dinner today' – a refrain that was repeated throughout that particular episode, so that all could learn it and join in singing with the Woodentop twins.[1] Other programmes used similar devices. As the toys climbed back into the basket at the end of each episode of *Andy Pandy*, they looked out of the screen as the narrator invited the viewer to join in with 'Time to go home ... time to go home ... ', a tune which was easily embedded in the memory. In *Bill and Ben* the device of involvement also involved a strongly 'tuneful' text; only this time there was also a puzzle for the viewer to solve. In each episode of *Bill and Ben*, an incident occurred, for which one of the Flowerpot Men was solely responsible; only Little Weed knew 'whodunnit', and she wasn't telling! The viewer was invited to guess 'was it Bill or was it Ben . ... which of those two Flowerpot Men, was it Bill or was it Ben?' Through joining in the refrain with the narrator, children were allowed space and time to consider their verdict, before the name of the guilty party was revealed on the back of his large flowerpot body. I can vividly remember trying to guess which was the correct Flowerpot Man, and also being delighted when I got it right. *Bill and Ben* was revived early in 2001; although in the contemporary version, there is much less involvement for the viewer, with no puzzle to guess, and the moral is carefully and explicitly spelled out at the end of the programme.

The textual devices from the older *Watch with Mother* series – invitations for reader involvement, repetitive refrains, the solving of puzzles – mirror those of classic children's literature. Think of the refrains in traditional tales – 'Run, run as fast as you can ... ' – the strongly 'tuneful' texts that Meek[2] and Barrs[3] describe as being key to young children's development as readers. The invitation to the reader to solve a problem also occurs in fictions such as those written by Beatrix Potter. At the end of *Mrs Tiggywinkle*, after little Lucie of Newlands sees a real hedgehog scampering away and you are led to think that it was all a dream, she then finds a clean, freshly laundered handkerchief in her pocket. The reader's imagination is reprieved: perhaps it was all true after all. The same permissions are given in the apparently simplistic constructions of *Watch with Mother*. You and the little house know the secret ... but 'we' know, don't we children? Through the construction of this conspiracy with the reader, valuable reading lessons are learned. However, these lessons are never made explicit: they are the 'private lessons' described by Jean–Paul Sartre in his auto-biography as being crucial to the experience of reading.[4]

In this way, the television programmes gave us regular, pleasurable lessons in the power of story. As a young viewer, my 'imagination was recruited', as Jerome Bruner puts it.[5] In many episodes of these programmes, the characters inhabited the 'possible worlds' so powerfully described by Bruner. The stories were multi-layered, inviting the viewer into an ever-increasing complexity of narrative. One of the most powerful episodes of *Bill and Ben* was one in which they, fictitious characters themselves, passed through a hole in the garden fence into a beautiful, frost-covered magical land. This scene was to reverberate in my memory when, many years later, I read C. S. Lewis's vivid description of Lucy's first steps through the wardrobe into the mystical world of Narnia. The media texts of my early childhood were helping me to interpret and gain admittance into more complex literary texts.

These texts for children were also related to literary texts in a more obvious way. You could buy, or borrow from the library (as I did), *Andy Pandy* books.[6] TV-related merchandising is often talked about as though it were a relatively new phenomenon, although it has a long history, even in the comparatively 'protected' world of public service broadcasting. There were numerous books about Andy Pandy, Looby Loo and Teddy; and while they could hardly be described as classics of children's literature, they did provide a link between the world of television and the world of books. There were at least 34 Andy Pandy books, with titles such as *Andy Pandy and the Green Puppy* and *Andy Pandy in the Country*. (The latter was my personal favourite. The toys travelled on their toy train to a cornfield, and frolicked in the poppies; and to this day I can remember re-playing this book on my own toy train out in the garden – although there were no cornfields in the heart of Liverpool!) Andy Pandy books were in print long after the programmes had ceased to be shown, at least until 1978.

Hearst[7] describes how narrative has leapt successfully from page to screen; but I would argue that the reverse is also true. These narratives devised originally for the televisual medium provided material – the pages of books – from which children could explore the world of their favourite characters more thoroughly. These books gave (and, in their contemporary versions, still give) children a sense of ownership, in the very way that video recordings have also made increasingly possible. The television viewing of the late 1950s and early 1960s was of a more transient nature than it is now. Once watched, the programmes were gone – at least until the repeats were shown. Nevertheless, one must wonder at the power of such narratives, since so much has been remembered by so many people after (comparatively) so few viewings.

A widening range of stories

As the technology of television progressed and developed, further opportunities for modelling a variety of story genres for children emerged. As strings disappeared from puppets, programmes like *Pogles' Wood* appeared,[8] and the talent of Oliver Postgate and Peter Firmin began to have a significant influence. Like their predecessors, these programmes gave powerful messages about the importance and the power of story. In one episode of 'The Pogles', Mrs Pogle takes particular care of 'Plant', a magical botanical specimen, who inhabits the Pogles' garden, existing on copious doses of home-made bilberry wine. She does this when the other Pogles are not being quite so respectful; and so Plant decides to reward her for her care. But rather than choosing three wishes, or untold riches, she chooses instead to have a story told to her. Not only does she choose a story, but she makes it quite clear exactly what sort of story she wants: 'Not a sad story, Plant, but a happy story with a prince and princess and such … ' The stories spun by Plant are magical and/or moral in nature, and clearly depict the significance of the oral tradition. They are also spun from Plant's imagination – by extension, giving status and value to children's own imagination and storytelling.

The work of Postgate and Firmin combined the power of well-written stories with the fascination of carefully crafted puppets and sets. Indeed, the creation of the imaginary worlds seems to have been as important to them as the stories themselves. As Postgate later wrote:

> The house in the tree root that Peter [Firmin] built for the Pogles in my studio was particularly realistic and handsome. It had a stout wooden door with a bell beside it which the hedgehog who called in the morning would ring, and an upstairs window with

shutters. Real ivy was growing up it and the garden was green-grocer's grass ... [9]

In *Noggin the Nog*,[10] another of their classic works, the episodes always began with a scene depicting Norsemen around the fire, telling tales of heroes and villains, and good versus evil, in the specific 'voice' required to tell such tales. They did not begin with 'Once upon a time', but with 'In the Lands of the North, where the black rocks guard against the cold sea ... '. This was the language of epic and saga, quite different from that of folk or fairy tale. As in many of Postgate and Firmin's collaborations, the role of the narrator is paramount. In *Pogles' Wood*, there was a variety of narrators, including the human voice leading you into the world of the Pogles in the opening sequences, and subsequently Plant as narrator, telling the story within the story. Complex time-frames are also dealt with, offering child viewers sophisticated models of reading. In *Noggin the Nog*, the role of narrator is taken by Thor Nogsen, telling stories to fellow Norsemen around the campfire, until we are led into the action, where the story appears before us, as if unfolding before our eyes. In this way, these programmes offered the youngest children the opportunity to 'tune their ear' to many different types of narrative – and hence enabled them to build their confidence as future readers. They also offered children access to genres which they might not otherwise have come across. The narrative voices and language registers to be found in such programmes encompassed a vast range: different dialects, accents, tones of voice and sentence constructions appeared in dialogues, jokes, songs and poems. And, like the authors of literary texts, the creators of these programmes were of course catering for two audiences – the child and the accompanying adult – creating texts that are sophisticated and multi-layered.

Perhaps more than any other children's programme, *Bagpuss* epitomizes the ways in which Postgate and Firmin constructed these different genres of narrative. Recently (1999) voted 'the most popular BBC children's programme ever' in a telephone poll, *Bagpuss* told the story of an old cloth cat, kept in a lost-and-found shop and looked after by a girl called Emily. As with *Andy Pandy* and *Bill and Ben* – and more recently *Toy Story* – the toys inhabited a twilight world, where no human knows that they come alive. These devices draw on what James Britton[11] describes as children's ability to separate the real world from that of fantasy; and they employ plot structures similar to those in works by Hans Christian Andersen (such as *The Tin Soldier*). Bagpuss and his colleagues, consisting of the mice from 'Mouse Organ', Professor Waffle, Gabriel the Toad and Madeleine the Rag Doll, regularly featured in a broad range of stories. In the 13 episodes that were created, which ran from 1974 and were repeated twice a year until 1987, stories began with the finding of a mysterious object in the shop. The rest of the narrative was built around the search to explain the existence and purpose of such objects. This, of course, clearly exploits one of the primary functions of narrative: the need to explain and justify. The stories were narrated in such a wide variety of styles that they were accessible to all; and the balance of characters chosen to relate the stories was similarly inclusive. Viewers might have been extremely irritated by Professor Waffle, yet still enjoyed the twittering of the mice, the singing of Gabriel the Toad, or, of course, wished passionately that they could have owned a cat like Bagpuss.

Bagpuss might be described as the original multi-modal text. The combination of cartoon animation, puppetry and film offered viewers a multiplicity of points of access. Consider one particular episode, where the mice have found a ballet shoe. The viewer is offered (within the breadth of one 18-minute episode) the opportunity to sing along with Gabriel the Toad in the style of the traditional sea shanty or folk song, to join in with the singing of nursery rhymes with the mice and to listen to the doggerel verse of Bagpuss, as a story explaining the appearance of a broken ship in a bottle appears above his head. In an episode entitled 'The Owl of Athens', the viewer is given an opening to explore the world of the Greek myth, a form of story not traditionally seen as accessible to pre-school children. The dominant aim of these programmes seems to have been to exploit the power of story in all its forms, and thereby to transport the viewer to a wide variety of 'possible worlds'.

As with *Andy Pandy* and *Noggin the Nog*, it was possible to buy published books of the *Bagpuss* stories. Although they do build a bridge from the media text to the written one, the books in no way match the sophistication or complexity of the TV series. I own two such titles from my early years in the teaching profession, when I was driven (somewhat misguidedly) to share some of my past with the children whom I taught. *Bagpuss in the Sun* and *Bagpuss in the Rain* tell stories similar to those told in the TV series, and introduce many of the same text genres. Within *Bagpuss in the Rain*[12] you can find narrative, traditional rhymes, parody, explanation, lullaby, traditional and moral tales within the covers of one book. But however accurate the illustrations, the books somehow fail to entice the imagination in the same way that watching the puppets did.

From page to screen

In the examples that I have described so far, it was the televisual texts that came first, with the print texts following close behind. Most of us are also familiar with a different kind of relationship between literary and media text: that which develops when the literary text came first. Of course, times have changed things in this respect. When I was young, it was almost certain that you would have met the literary text before it had been turned into a film, although even in those far-off days there was no guarantee of this. (For instance, I saw Walt Disney's *101 Dalmatians* long before I read Dodie Smith's original.) What was lacking was the possibility of *owning* your favourite films on video; whereas repeated re-viewings are now as common as re-readings. This has, of course, been possible for almost a quarter of a century now; and it has inevitably contributed to the ways in which children (and adults) now interpret the narratives of different media.

As Maire Davies explains in her chapter, filmed versions of classic texts frequently have complex relationships with their published forebears. In the most recent version of *Little Women*, directed by Gillian Armstrong (Columbia Pictures), there is a scene where the girls have their own 'Literacy Club'. They share the reading of their own newspaper, to which they have all contributed with varying degrees of success. The girls' contributions are all equally valued (although Beth gets a certain amount of teasing for submitting a recipe) and the creation of texts is shown as pleasurable, sociable and fun. For Jo, of course, the play holds even more significance. She goes on to become a famous author and, in being part of the Pickwick Club, she is imagining her future. But there is more to this brief interlude than messages about the power of writing, important though they are. From their attic den, the girls spy their new neighbour, Laurie. In trying to figure him out, they ask: 'Could he be like Smike, in *Nicholas Nickleby* . . . .' Just like *Bagpuss*, the scene is showing how we use narrative to explain all sorts of unknowns in our lives.

Those of us who grew up in the age of the BBC's Sunday tea-time serial will remember other versions of *Little Women*, which we may consider compare favourably (or not) with the version described above. The fact that a multiplicity of versions of a wide variety of texts is now available gives the relationship between written and media texts an increasing complexity. Consider the case of Robin Hood, for example. In picturing this character, we may recall the dashing figure of Errol Flynn, from wintry Sunday afternoons watching old Hollywood movies; or we may think of Richard Greene or Michael Praed or Kevin Costner. Children may imagine two further possibilities: Walt Disney's fox in the animated movie (directed by Wolfgang Reitherman), or the hapless Robin from Tony Robinson's TV parody *Maid Marian and Her Merry Men*.

It is interesting to compare how one key incident from the Robin Hood legends, his meeting with Little John at the stream, is dealt with by three of these versions. In the Walt Disney version, it is not part of the main body of the film, but is instead dealt with briefly in the introductory ballad sung by the cockerel. This opening sequence is interesting in itself. Like many other Disney movies (at least until *Aladdin*), the feature-length cartoon begins with the opening of a book. The turning of the pages brings us to the cockerel-turned-strolling-minstrel, playing a lute, who opens the film's dialogue with the words: 'Robin Hood and Little John strolling through the forest . . . ', sung in the style of an 'olde English' ballad. The confrontation at the stream is portrayed as comical, a playful encounter between two animals which leads inevitably to a strong friendship. By contrast, in *Maid Marian* the encounter is treated quite differently. The weak-willed Robin is already fleeing the Sheriff's men when he encounters Little John on the bridge. In this version, Little John is indeed little, being played by a dwarf. Robin has to be exhorted by the much stronger-willed Marian to fight his opponent, and inevitably comes off worse. Finally, in *Robin Hood, Prince of Thieves* (director: Kevin Reynolds), Kevin Costner's Robin Hood approaches the legendary stream accompanied by his Moorish companion, the pair having escaped from Jerusalem. At the time of the film's release there was a certain amount of protest about this 'inaccuracy', although it is no more or less inaccurate than the portrayal of Robin as a cartoon fox, or as a feeble man dominated by the 'in control' Maid Marian. Kevin Costner attempts to cross the stream, to be met by the singing of a ballad (incidentally, in a style not dissimilar to that of Disney's cockerel); and he meets his match in the form of a very large 'Little John'. The fight scene is played out in full, in a way that is probably 'truer' to the original version of Robin Hood than either of the other two versions. (It is also interesting to note that *Robin Hood, Prince of Thieves* opens with views of the Bayeux tapestry, thereby paying homage to another method of storytelling through pictures: however innovative texts might appear, they are necessarily bound by their predecessors, and pay homage to them in a variety of ways.)

That the meeting with Robin Hood and Little John is dealt with in such different ways is interesting if not surprising. Children who have access to all three versions, and may also have had stories told to them or have played Robin Hood with their Play Mobil toys, have the opportunity to build a store of frameworks for comparison that the experience of only one version could not give. What is equally, if not more, interesting is that all three versions chose to keep the episode in at all. What remains constant in this era of diversity is as interesting as what has to change. Is the Robin Hood/Little John incident so central to the story that no film-maker or TV producer felt that they could leave it out? Is it to do with the reading biographies of the creators of these texts? Do they take into account what they themselves know about a story before re-creating it for others? Are there some components of stories that remain central to the narrative, whatever else may change? The creators of these new texts are effectively acting as custodians of the history of narration, releasing certain exhibits for us to see. For those of us for whom the new version 'is' the 'original', these key elements also allow us a way back to the written or spoken versions from which the new texts have been derived.

Jim Henson exemplifies this in his version of Charles Dickens's classic tale, *The Muppets Christmas Carol* (director: Brian Henson). It is a supreme example of how a text never intended for mass consumption by children can be presented to them in such a way that it becomes accessible. Here, Scrooge is played by Michael Caine, whilst Gonzo, the bent-beaked bird from *The*

Muppet Show, plays Dickens himself, acting as the narrator. The relationship between teller and told is further augmented by the introduction of Gonzo's sidekick, Rizzo the Rat, who acts as a sort of 'voices off' for most of the film.[13] Much of the script is true to the original Dickens, and somehow the words do not lose their power even when spoken by a Muppet. Yet the interpolations of Rizzo add comedy and intellectual rigour, inviting the viewer/reader to reflect on the actions of both the storyteller and the characters in the story. As Scrooge approaches his front door, to be met by the ghostly door knocker (in this instance played by the two hecklers from *The Muppet Show*) Dickens/Gonzo gives a running commentary on what is happening, continuing as Scrooge enters the house: 'Scrooge entered the house and went upstairs … '. 'How do you know what he's doing in there?,' demands Rizzo. The reply is significant. 'The storyteller is omniscient' retorts Dickens. Such discussions occur throughout the film, whilst the atmosphere and themes of the original Dickens text are successfully retained. Gonzo and Rizzo even comment on the possible unsuitability of such material for children. Discussing the visits of the ghostly apparitions, Rizzo asks 'Hey, isn't this a bit scary for children?' 'No, it's all right, it's culture,' responds Dickens/Gonzo.

Henson's ability to create a bond between storyteller, listener and viewer is celebrated by Jack Zipes. In this instance, he is writing about Henson's work on a series called *The Storyteller*, although his comments are equally applicable to *The Muppets Christmas Carol*:

> The films are creative experiments with classic tales, puppetry, cinematic techniques, painting and music that reveal the potential of film through television and video to recapture the communal aspects of storytelling. Brought together in front of the small screen, viewers see the storyteller actively engaged with a listener who interrupts, questions, mocks, laughs and sighs when the story is told and enacted. A bond is formed between storyteller, listener and viewer, and the sharing of the story becomes a unique experience that does not call for identification or envelopment of the viewer.[14]

I do not entirely agree that the addition of a narrator prevents the envelopment of the viewer: it is difficult to watch *The Muppets Christmas Carol* without wanting a happy ending for Tiny Tim.

Nevertheless, the addition of the narrator in Henson's work, as in that of Postgate and Firmin (where Professor Yaffle regularly interrupts with comments and asides), clearly offers children alternative views and ways of reflecting on texts. The viewer is shown that although the storyteller may be omniscient s/he is not beyond question. As Zipes implies, we should recognize that new forms of texts can be as effective as those from the oral and written tradition if we are to understand the changing relationship between media texts and reading.

Multiple literacies

Zipes's benevolence towards media-based storytelling does not, however, extend to the Disney Corporation. In his book *Happily Ever After*, Zipes discusses the dilemmas that many people feel about Disney: however difficult adults may find it, children seem irrevocably drawn to the films. Citing the example of *The Lion King*, he describes how his young daughter is mesmerized by the film, whilst he himself is repulsed by it, seeing Nazi imagery and condemning the film's political manipulation of children. Whilst I empathize with many of the difficulties that Zipes has with the works of the Disney Studios, I also feel it is important to recognize some of their strengths. As a consumer of Disney products, first as a child myself and latterly as a parent, I feel that the Disney films have contributed to literacy in my family in ways that maybe Disney did not foresee. For example, the films provided the basis for much of my daughter's imaginative play during her younger years, through re-enactment, dressing up and play writing. I do not feel that these instances were less valuable than when she re-enacted her favourite books. Zipes describes Disney as formulaic, with the comedy sidekick characters and their imitation of the Hollywood musical of the 1930s. He seems to assume that children accept all Disney films blindly, although in my own experience and that of other parents whom I know, this is simply not the case.

Disney has also evolved, not least because of the changing forms of literacy in contemporary society. Considering the openings of Disney films gives some indication of this. As I have noted, until the release of *Aladdin* in the early 1990s, Disney films began with the opening of a book, with the voice of a narrator reading the text. The cartoon was then seen to be literally lifted from the page of the book. The cartoon was recognizing and acknowledging the text from where it came. By contrast, *Aladdin* begins with the narrator talking directly to camera: in fact, he bumps into the 'camera'. No reference is made to books.[15] In *Hercules*, the story begins with singing women stepping down from the side of a Grecian urn, implicitly paying tribute to pictorial forms of storytelling. The beginning of *Toy Story 2* is even more complex, and pays homage to narratives of a completely different nature. The film opens with Buzz Lightyear involved in a battle with the Evil Zorg (some shots will remind 'Star Wars' aficionados of the battle between Luke Skywalker and Darth Vader); and it is only when Buzz appears defeated that the scene is revealed to be that of the cowardly dinosaur playing a computer game, watched by Buzz Lightyear himself. Such an opening has only become possible because of the advent of computer games: here we see a toy effectively making use of its own merchandise. As a viewer, I pondered this opening in the same way that I used to puzzle over copies of the *Beano* comic, where characters were seen to be reading the story of themselves reading the story. The film is not only using intertextuality (with its references to computer games and *Star Wars*) but also 'intra'textuality, with its references to itself. Such textual devices entertain and involve in the same way that you were invited to guess which Flowerpot Man had carried out the 'naughty' deed of the week; but they also demand reflection on the part of the viewer. In discussions of literary texts for children such as the Ahlbergs' *The Jolly Postman* and *Each Peach Pear Plum*, we are often called upon to celebrate such devices. The texts are described as polysemic, or as 'writerly texts' in the style proclaimed by Roland Barthes.[16] Such devices serve similar functions in media texts, and are no less valuable.

Thus, when the genie introduces himself in Walt Disney's *Aladdin*, repeated viewings are necessary in order to catch all the textual references. Some of these are visual (references to well-known TV personalities), while others are contained in the words of the song that he sings: 'Well, Ali Baba had them forty thieves, Scheherazade had a thousand tales, well Master you in luck, 'cos in my book, I gotta brand of magic that never fails.' Watching with an adult, the child has an opportunity to discover who Ali Baba and Scheherazade were. Through film, children can also be introduced to other versions of the story: while the works of

Marcia Williams and her version of Sinbad, heavily reliant on the comic-strip layout, will appeal to one sort of reader, *Stories from the Arabian Nights* retold by Naomi Lewis with sumptuous colour plates will no doubt appeal to another.

It is worth noting that Disney was by no means unique in deriving stories from the Arabian Nights. In discussing his composition of stories for *Noggin the Nog*,[17] some of which were set in 'The Land of Silver Sand', Postgate writes:

> When they arrived [there] the Nogs entered a country that was just as fictional as the Land of Nog but much better known, being recognizable as the setting for The Arabian Nights, and Ali Baba and the Forty Thieves ... it was more or less inevitable that they would become involved with such clichés as genies, magic carpets, impersonations and palace intrigues simply because such things are known to be the stuff of ordinary life in that imaginary country.[18]

Perhaps that is why Disney too used identical 'clichés' in *Aladdin*, right down to impersonations and palace intrigues. It also might go some way to explaining why, whatever the version of Robin Hood, the meeting with Little John is retained – it is the stuff of such stories. Thus, Victor Watson quotes Peter Hollindale's description of some texts as 'richly generative for other, lesser works of derivation, which nonetheless have interest of their own'; and he goes on to describe how, when such texts are closely scrutinized, their 'intertextuality accentuates rather than overrides their originality'.[19]

Not all versions of stories find it necessary to alter the story so dramatically or create innovative techniques to win the viewer's interest. Some film-makers stick faithfully to the book from which they are derived, yet still manage to offer a fresh perspective. One such film is *The Railway Children* (Warner Bros., 1970, directed by Lionel Jeffries), based on the book by E. Nesbit. The book and the film tell the story of a family whose father is wrongfully imprisoned, their adventures in the country and their father's return home. The children are aided by a helpful 'old gentleman', a regular on the nearby railway. I was an avid reader of the book as a child, re-reading it frequently, particularly the last chapter when the father returns home. As a slightly older child, I went to see the film when it was released, having also watched it serialized on the BBC and heard it read (along with many other stories written by E. Nesbit) on the BBC's *Jackanory*. What I could not do in 1970, of course, was to own a copy of the video, so that I could re-watch it as often as I re-read the book. I want to focus here on the way that the book and the film deal with the day of the father's homecoming, and to return to the question of whether one is more 'worthy' than the other.

The book describes Bobbie's (the eldest daughter's) feeling of malaise and her desire to be alone. Released from lessons by her mother, she walks to the station, and as she goes there she passes various characters who are obviously in possession of information that Bobbie is not. Throughout this scene, the narration is in the third person, including that of Bobbie's meeting with the friendly Perks, whose explanations are drowned out by the sound of the oncoming train. Nesbit talks directly to the reader in a way that acknowledges the reader's part in the storytelling: 'Of course you know exactly was going to happen. Bobbie was not so clever. She had the vague, confused, expectant feeling that comes to one's heart in dreams.'[20]

As with Scrooge, Bagpuss and others before them, we have here the omniscient storyteller: although in this instance it is the story reader as well as the story writer. Nesbit's novels are largely about emancipated, clever children;[21] and here she is recognizing and acknowledging the cleverness of her readers, whilst at the same time attempting to maintain their identification with the character. It is a powerful piece of writing, but not quite as powerful as what follows:

> Only three people got out of the 11.54. The first was a country-woman with two baskety boxes full of live chickens who stuck their russet heads out anxiously through the wicker bars; the second was Miss Peckitt the grocer's wife's cousin, with a tin box and three brown paper parcels; and the third – 'Oh! My Daddy, my Daddy!' That scream went like a knife into the heart of everyone in the train.[22]

Despite the forewarning, the relief created in the reader by the father's safe return is very powerful.

How then does the film deal with such emotion? As with *The Muppets Christmas Carol*, many of the words spoken by the characters are identical to those in the book, as are the people that Bobbie encounters on her way to the station. As she arrives, Perks (played by Bernard Cribbins) taps her with the newspaper and leaves her standing, waiting for the passengers to disembark from the train. Here the similarity in the way of storytelling ends, although the power of the scene is not diminished. Tension, created by Nesbit in the listing of the people disembarking from the train and the packages that they carry, is created in the film by simple music and the clearing of the steam on the station plat-form. We might now look back on this film from our technologically jaundiced eyes, as Bobbie runs in slow motion towards her father, and cringe at the freeze-frame shot of their embrace, but we cannot deny the emotional pull of this sequence. The camera pauses on the young girl's booted feet as they are lifted in the air by her father, and we sigh the same sigh of relief as we did when we 'heard' her scream in the book.

What, then, is the relationship between the written and filmed versions of Bobbie's reunion with her father? We might argue that those who have come to the filmed version of the story will buy the book and read it for themselves, and deliberate on which version they preferred. It is also easy to recognize the origins of the film, and the debt that it owes to the book. What is more complicated to analyse is the emotional response that both texts can evoke in the reader; although ultimately this is where the crux of the relationship lies. For me, Jenny Agutter became (and still is) Bobbie, whenever I read the book or a portion of it.[23] In my mind she has become inextricably linked with that girl. The 'possible worlds' created by both the film and the book merge, and new versions of my own are created: the writer in the reader is at work, creating texts of her own. After my father died, when I was training as a teacher in Bath, I frequently used to dream that I was on Bath station, that steam was clearing from the station platform and that he was there – just like the father in the movie. I cannot attribute this meaning either to the book or to the film of *The Railway Children*; rather, it derives from a powerful combination of the two.

Conclusion

In this chapter, I have argued for a view of the relationship between children's literature and the media that is fundamentally to do with narrative, and with the different types of literacy that narratives require. This is more than a matter of analysing the impact of television on book sales, as in the statistical studies outlined by Stephen Hearst.[24] It is also more than an argument about whether book-based or televisual literacy is more desirable. We cannot deny the existence of televisual texts: they are part of all our literacies, whatever our preferred form or definition of reading. There are good and bad books, just as there are good and bad television programmes; and there is no reason why a story should automatically be perceived as more valuable simply because it exists in the form of a book.

Both literary and media texts are kept alive through talk about and around them. In fact, they have a tendency, as I hope I have shown, to maintain this discussion within themselves. Victor Watson talks about the instability of certain texts over time, and discusses how they transform and mutate.[25] This too is achieved through discussion. The origins of all stories lie with the oral tradition, and it is this tradition that supports the production of new and increasingly sophisticated narratives with the passage of time. As well as instability, there is also continuity. Some story ingredients appear to be absolutely necessary, even within the most innovative of texts. Oliver Postgate writes:

> When it was looking for stories, my mind would go trawling through a mud of memory, a morass of experience, life and literature to see what it could find ... I have always had to respect the fact that *novelty* is not in itself either interesting or valuable. Its interest and value lies in the degree to which it is able to give a particular view of the condition that we, as human beings, find interesting and valuable, i.e. being alive.[26]

The notion that we read to find ourselves is not new; but it must be recognized that we can find ourselves not only in literary texts but also in those produced by other more technological means. The potential for this increases almost on a daily basis. My daughter's current enthusiasm for inhabiting the world of Spyro the Dragon on her Playstation is no less valuable than if she chose to read *Jason and The Argonauts* or *The Labours of Hercules*, or any other tale of triumph over adversity – for that is what Spyro the Dragon is, albeit a story told in a different medium and with a different voice. We need to pay heed to these voices. We need to listen to them and the way they manipulate narrative, in the same way that we listen to each other manipulate the stories in our lives and of our lives. We need to find words analogous with 'literature' to describe televisual and computer texts of quality, so that we can sufficiently recognize their contribution to the intellectual and emotional growth, both of ourselves and of our children.

Notes

1. This episode was first broadcast in September 1955, before I was born – which indicates the use of repeats even in those far-off days.
2. Margaret Meek, *How Texts Teach What Readers Learn* (Stroud, Glos.: Thimble Press, 1986).
3. Myra Barrs, 'The tune on the page', in K. Kimberley, M. Meek and J. Miller, (eds), *New Readings: Contributions to Understandings of Literacy* (London: A. & C. Black, 1992).
4. Jean–Paul Sartre, *Words* (Harmonsdsworth, Penguin, 1967).
5. J. Bruner, *Actual Minds, Possible Worlds* (Cambridge, MA: Harvard University Press, 1986).
6. These books were written by Maria Bird, who was also responsible for writing all the early *Watch with Mother* programmes with the exception of *Rag, Tag and Bobtail.*
7. S. Hearst, 'Television and its influence on reading', in B. Cox (ed.), *Literacy is Not Enough* (Manchester: Manchester University Press, 1998).
8. First shown in the 1960s, *The Pogles* came in the second wave of *Watch with Mother* programmes, along with *Mary, Mungo and Midge* and *Tales of The Riverbank.*
9. Oliver Postgate, describing *Pogles Wood* in his autobiography *Seeing Things* (London: Sidgwick and Jackson, 2000).
10. Although not shown in the *Watch With Mother* slot, *Noggin the Nog* was shown as a serial in ten-minute chunks during afternoon children's television. This same slot was later occupied by such favourites as *Captain Pugwash* and, later, *The Magic Roundabout.*
11. J. Britton, 'A note on make believe and mummery', *Language Matters: Early Years* 1, 1993–4 (Centre for Language in Primary Education).
12. *Bagpuss on a Rainy Day.* Story by Oliver Postgate, pictures by Peter Firmin, published by Picture Lions in 1974.
13. These techniques are similar to those used in the children's comic *The Beano.*
14. From *Happily Ever After: Fairy Tales, Children, and The Culture Industry* (London: Routledge, 1997).
15. Victor Watson discusses this issue in 'Innocent children and unstable literature', in M. Styles, E. Bearne and V. Watson (eds), *Voices Off* (London: Cassell, 1996).

Helen Bromley

16. Meek Margaret, *How Texts Teach What Readers Learn*.
17. The characters from 'Noggin the Nog' were inspired by a Viking chess set in the British Museum.
18. Postgate, *Seeing Things*, p. 243.
19. Peter Hollindale in Watson, 'Innocent children and unstable literature'. This extract is from Hollindale's 'Peter Pan, Captain Hook and the book of the video', *Signal* 72, 1993.
20. E. Nesbit, *The Railway Children* (London: Wells Gardner, Darton and Co., 1906), p. 264.
21. Including *Five Children and It, The Phoenix and The Carpet* and *The Story of The Amulet*.
22. Nesbit, p. 265.
23. A version of *The Railway Children* has recently been released in which Jenny Agutter plays the mother.
24. Stephen Hearst, 'Television and its influence on reading'.
25. Watson, 'Innocent children and unstable literaure'.
26. Postgate, *Seeing Things*.

INDEX

227

Index